MW01193610

This is in accordance with a principle once formulated by poet Bertolt Brecht: political change is only possible for those who fear bad life more than death."

"I am a possibilist and optimist by heart and intellectual conviction, and I recognize the wonderfulness of the human being, their achievements, and their conquests, but the future of humanity is not predetermined. The current course or trajectory we have taken apparently puts us in grave danger. John Mills tells us, through a rich array of historical, philosophical, and psychoanalytic sources, of the genealogy of causes (from instant gratification at the individual level to the economic organization of our societies) of the existential risks and threats of global catastrophe that humanity faces. It is in our hands, or perhaps in the hands of our children, grandchildren, or great-grandchildren, to act wisely and correct this course. This book can help us do that."

END OF THE WORLD

Civilization and Its Fate

JON MILLS

ROWMAN & LITTLEFIELD
Lanham • Boulder • New York • London

Published by Rowman & Littlefield
An imprint of The Rowman & Littlefield Publishing Group, Inc.
4501 Forbes Boulevard, Suite 200, Lanham, Maryland 20706
www.rowman.com

86-90 Paul Street, London EC2A 4NE

British Library Cataloguing in Publication Information Available

Library of Congress Cataloging-in-Publication Data

Names: Mills, Jon, 1964- author.
Title: End of the world : civilization and its fate / Jon Mills.
Description: Lanham : Rowman & Littlefield, [2024] | Includes
   bibliographical references and index.
Identifiers: LCCN 2023041434 (print) | LCCN 2023041435 (ebook) | ISBN
   9781538189009 (cloth) | ISBN 9781538189016 (epub)
Subjects: LCSH: Civilization, Modern—21st century—Psychological aspects.
   | Civilization, Modern—21st century—Forecasting. |
   Crises—History—21st century. | End of the world. | End of the
   world—Forecasting. | Social psychology—Philosophy. | Social
   change—Philosophy.
Classification: LCC CB430 .M557 2024 (print) | LCC CB430 (ebook) | DDC
   301—dc23/eng/20231228
LC record available at https://lccn.loc.gov/2023041434
LC ebook record available at https://lccn.loc.gov/2023041435

For my daughters, McKensi, Chloe, and Ivy
—with the hope that their children will inherit a better world.

Contents

Preface ix

Prolegomenon: On the Brink of Extinction xi

1: Here on Earth 1

    A Promise of Hope 2

    Global Bystanders in the Face of Ecological Crisis 3

    The Revenge of Gaia 10

    Too Big to Fix 16

2: Ten Billion 19

    What Can We Learn from Rats? 19

    Overpopulation and Food Supply 23

    Withering Water 27

    The Worst Is Yet to Come: Pandemics, Economic Paralysis,
    and Societal Collapse 30

3: The Evil That Men Do 37

    The Need to Kill 41

    The Ontology of Prejudice 53

    On the Universality of Evil .60

    The Ethics of Killing 62

    Institutionalized Evil 65

4: The Doomsday Clock Is Ticking 71

    Dropping the Bomb 72

    The Doomsday Argument 83

    Existential Risks 88

    Should We Take the Doomsday Argument Seriously? 91

    Our Final Century? 93

5: Apocalypse Now. 97

On Sin. 99
Apocalypse, Millennialism, and *Eschaton*. 102
The (un)Holy Land 106
Apocalyptic Discourse in Postmillennial Culture 110
Futuristic Fantasies 112
Disparities 114
The New After. 116

6: Global Catastrophic Risks. 119

Defining Risk 120
Big-Picture Hazards. 123
Economic Disintegration 132
Techno Nihilism. 138
Superintelligences 142

7: A World without Recognition 149

The Need to Be Acknowledged 151
Dysrecognition as Social Pathology 158
Unconscious Politics and the Other 161
A Failure of Empathy 163
Transgenerational Transmission of Trauma 166

8: Living in the End Times 171

From the Plague to a Plastic Island 172
The Doomsday Vault. 173
It Took a Child 175
Predicting the Future 180
Democracy Incorporated 187
From Catastrophe to Renewal. 191
Environmental Conflict and Peacebuilding 195
The Last Resistance 199

References 209

Index 221

About the Author 235

PREFACE

We live in increasingly precarious and polarized times. How did we get here? As if COVID were not enough, then the travel bans, mandatory lockdowns, school and day-care closures, businesses folding, pandemic panic, health-care and infrastructure failure, and the frantic race to discover a cure were just the beginning. Geopolitical tensions started breaking out all over the world, followed by increasingly large segments of societies unable to keep the lights on or put food on the table; then supply chain shortages disrupted every conceivable way of life, the brouhaha over mandatory vaccinations, restrictions on freedom, the explosion in mental health crises, and millions of people dropping like flies pretty much sum up the past few years. Add to this global scenario that the planet started burning, economies tanked, and people had to stay cooped up like chickens if they were lucky enough to retain their jobs or could work from home. Then came the immoral invasion of Ukraine, tension over nuclear engagement or a Third World War, East versus West, soaring gas prices, energy and commodity sticker shock, crippling global food markets including famine in developing countries, followed by inflation, and now recession. With Hamas's surprise barbaric massacre of Israeli citizens, the looming Taiwan question, and a potential unholy alliance between Russia, China, Iran, and North Korea, could it get any worse?

Throughout this book, I explore the main key existential risks and global catastrophic threats to human existence that currently command our world attention. The conclusion is not pretty. We are in dire straits. We are witnessing our planet slowly disintegrate as devastated economies, social implosions, and anarchy during the pandemic have brought us to our knees. Why are we passive global bystanders to our ecological crisis? Why do we allow obscene disparities in wealth and social divisions to proliferate, remain silent about the prevalence of psychopathy in politics and globalized capitalism, and bow to the imbalances of power that could ultimately bring about our own extinction? It is only on the condition that we are under the unconscious spell of a compulsion to destroy ourselves.

The exploitation from unbridled capitalism only benefits the rich while much of the world population suffers. As politicians think about their reelection campaigns, governments are preoccupied with their military optics and gross national products rather than the environment. As we watch the desolation of Being alongside our geopolitical tensions, the nuclear bombast, terror, and racial, gender, education, and health-care inequity, overpopulation and infectious diseases of the future will only bring about more economic collapse, mental illness, culture wars, and crippled societies left to scrounge in the dirt. The range of global threats invites calls to action that seem impossible to ignore. But we can and do ignore them, for the world *remains unconscious* of our global predicament. Inertia and idleness in the service of dissociation and disavowal become an unconscious strategy to protect us from the very thing we are bringing about. Humanity is guilty of such inaction, for turning a blind eye, hence unwilling to see, and for sticking its head in the sand.

We need to awaken a new ethic of responsibility to the planet, where empathy, solidarity, and becoming better global citizens in the service of the common good will lead to a better demos and polis. For this reason, the time has come to critically examine those elements of the human psyche that defeat efforts to mitigate our looming catastrophe. While we continue sleepwalking through our anesthetized states of moral torpor, denial and self-delusion impair our capacity to collectively rise to the occasion. The question becomes, will our collective unconscious death wish bring about our demise?

Prolegomenon

On the Brink of Extinction

ARE WE ON THE BRINK OF HUMAN EXTINCTION? IS CIVILIZATION DES-
tined toward self-annihilation? We must not underestimate the risk of
the possibility that we may become extinct fairly soon. Let us examine
some cold sober facts: We are facing a planetary ecological crisis due
to global warming, despoliation of our natural resources, mass scale
industrial pollution, desertification, deforestation, widespread collapse
of ecosystems, and extreme climate change. World overpopulation is
nearing a record tipping point, where food and water scarcity will bring
about more famine, drought, pestilence, and death. Human violence and
aggression in concentrated pockets are on the rise worldwide, with every
inhabitable continent in turmoil, civil uprising, military conflict, or war.
Unbridled capitalistic exploitation of consumer masses by corporate
conglomerates, financial institutions, Big Pharma, and insurance sectors
are unprecedented, with obscene disparities in wealth and poverty to the
point of social implosion. Global catastrophic hazards have escalated due
to the environmental crisis, encroachment by man, destabilized markets,
hegemonic national politics, collective ideologies, corrupt governmental
policies, deranged despots, nuclear threats, terrorism, religious fundamentalism, internet espionage, cyber hijacking, space wars, threats to
public health, bioterror, pandemic infectious diseases, and psychological
self-interest driving everything from vain desire to the local economy
and international relations, not to mention the anathema of evil, abuse,
trauma, criminality, greed, and the psychopathology of everyday life.

Regardless of the degree of threat we assign to these calculated risks, we cannot ignore the ominous dread hovering over a wishing humanity.

Our recalcitrant dependency on fossil fuel is slowly digging humanity a shallow grave. The burning of coal, whether in industrial manufacturing or to heat a home, is gradually suffocating the planet. The problem is so bad in India and China that you can hardly breathe in Delhi and Beijing. Soot from woodstoves covers the roads of Kraków to the point that it feels like walking on a floor of oil. From hazards due to refining oil, fracking, tar sands extraction, natural gas leakage, pipeline distribution, transport accidents, off-line rig explosions, to runaway greenhouse effects, our ecosystems are deteriorating rapidly, hence threatening the sustainability of our natural resources and life on this planet. Glaciers and polar icecaps are melting, sea levels are rising, heat waves, droughts, bitter cold, wildfires, severe storms, torrential rains, floods, mud slides, rising ocean temperatures, hurricanes, tsunamis, freshwater scarcity, and unpredictable weather phenomena so varied throughout the world signal our changing global climate.

All these issues leave us in a profound and compounded predicament of future survival. And with the projected statistical prediction of adding another billion people to the world population every decade, our lot in life hangs by a hair. As our world economies are in flux and tumult, hence threatening the availability, price, and affordability of basic human requirements for sustenance, such as water, food, shelter, and medicine, as well as education and valued commodities that nourish the physical, emotional, and spiritual lives of the masses, we are likely headed for calamity. But we dissociate these realities, because they are not happening to everyone at the same time and in the same place. We can no longer afford to bury our heads in the sand.

The world population is now eight billion people, which has proliferated by two billion in less than two decades. Following this unprecedented, hurried growth, it is estimated there will be more than ten billion inhabitants by 2050. Most scientists believe that the Earth will not be able to sustain that many people, and if possible, not without grave consequences. The mass consumption of resources will likely be too taxing to support the plenitude of food required, which takes most of our water supplies and fertile earth surface to grow. Given that mass industrial and environmental pollution has severely tainted global water availability, compounded by unforgiving climate change, the paucity of clean drinking water is an urgent ecological and humanitarian crisis. The bottom line is that now, within current times, we do not have enough water or food to go around. Imagine what it will be like with billions more people crowding the planet all vying for the basic necessities of life?

No longer is the threat of world destruction simply due to the forces of nature itself; rather, it is from man. We continuously poison our seas, land, and air; plunder our natural resources with callous disregard for future consequences; and disrupt Earth's regulatory mechanisms, hence insuring the slow but steady deracination of our planet. Our ecosystems are deteriorating rapidly, and with the rampant marauding of our environments, such as with the industrial excavation and burning of fossil fuels, cattle and sheep farming, mass mining, agribusiness, and the artificial manufacturing of biofuels, this systemically harms biodiversity and the atmosphere by accelerating greenhouse gas emissions, which further contributes to the global climate crisis that threatens our sustainability.

As if the despoilment of our globe is not enough to worry about, we must continuously face the prevalence of human aggression. All occupied continents are engaged in military battle, with no foreseeable end in sight. World superpowers, rogue nations, dictators, tyrants, revolutionists, insurgents, and international politics fuel existing warfare, hence leading to repetitive cycles of death, despair, transgenerational trauma, and systemic ruin. Global economies have been shattered, social infrastructures effaced, and daily ways of life destroyed, where entire communities have perished. Whole societies have been displaced, historical traditions broken, established customs nullified, and cultural identities lost. Diasporas, mass-scale refugees, asylum seekers, and the walking wounded scurry to neighboring territories, often herded at their borders. Chaos, uprisings, and revolt over impoverishment, maltreatment, and retaliatory aggression lead to further warfare, civil disorder, violence, and crime.

Within our warming world, as the size of the global population balloons, and as we become even more overcrowded, there will be more scarcity, competition for resources, ruthlessness, and qualitative abjection.

Dearth and human angst will likely motivate mass panic and brutality under the so-called influence of social Darwinism, which will predictably lead to more human tensions, exploitation, war, and suffering. Here the danger is of internal disintegration. Rather than mimic an empathic civilization, we will likely devolve into primitive desperation where the ability to consider the lives of others will be eclipsed by the need for immediate benefit and tribal survival, even if that means we abandon a moral stance toward the inalienable Other. This is as predictable as rain.

As our world economies are in flux and tumult, hence threatening the availability, price, and affordability of basic human requirements for sustenance, such as water, food, shelter, and energy (e.g., electricity and heat), the world is becoming less stable, predictable, and safe. No longer can we pretend that everything is fine as long as "We," in our sheltered, privileged Western lives, remain unscathed or untouched by the events that transpire around us. Here universal security becomes an illusion. As we experience greater economic and social disparities worldwide, leading to concentrated pockets of civil protest, disobedience, and mayhem, such as what we currently witness in Eastern Europe, the Middle East, Africa, Central and South America, East Asia, and the United States, every nation feels a trickle-down effect that not only threatens universal well-being but also safety at home.

And when enemies are no longer foreign, conflict is generated from within a society where economic and class discrepancy, racial division, religious intolerance, political injustices, and governmental mistreatment of collectives lead to societal dissent, uprisings, riots, coups, and rampages, for we all have the need to find enemies. We owe this tendency— sometimes paranoiac, sometimes justified by real circumstances—to the psychodynamics of human emotion, much of which is unconsciously motivated, hence outside of our conscious reflection and social awareness. Because we are primarily driven by unconscious affects and prejudice, not by rational analysis and constraint, we are guided by our primordial desires, conflicts, and complexes. This is equally true of nations, states, and superpowers, where politics serves to manipulate multiple psychological variables and vulnerabilities in the masses that further oppose different cultures or peoples while promoting the self-interests of those sailing the ship. This is human nature, for man is a political animal. However, politics is inherently corrupt without a watchtower ensuring that human exploitation is curbed.

Even within well-meaning democracies, inverted totalitarian principles based on self-interest operate unconsciously within societies that are complicit with national policies, self-instituted laws, and actions that mistreat and harm opposing nations and groups without provocation. Here the silent collectives implicitly condone the deeds of their nation's leaders. And when other societies are affected negatively by a superpower, the backlash is violence. This occurs both from within the citizenry affected by the decisions of a nation-state and from external protest and reaction. These vectors create a two-way relation of dialectical strains, namely, pressure from within and without. Political injustice and social exploitation predictably lead to civil disobedience, bloodshed, insurrections, and rebellions. When an individual, community, or nation is done wrong, even if it is only perceived, the toll is resentment and the need for revenge.

In today's world where every form of transgression enjoys a psychological motive, rational justification, legal defense, and/or pastoral forgiveness, the limits of evil seem to be standing on a crumbling precipice. Once deemed the unequivocal antithesis to moral absolutes, evil has acquired a new form of acceptability. From commonplace cheating on university entrance exams, income tax evasion, fraud, and economic bleeding of consumer society, to partisan lobby manipulation, bribery, corruption, breach of trust, political illegalities, and military campaigns that couldn't care less about collateral damage, we have entered into a techno age of anonymity, facelessness, digital zombification, and disposable objects where dehumanized alterity becomes the projection, displacement, and denial of our own interiority: in other words, the evil within.

When people feel abused and experience no sense of justice, it violates a universal ethical principle, one that is shattered with the realization that there are no universal ethics, that is, no metaphysical dispensary of the "good and right" watching over them. From anarchy and ochlocracy to nihilism, the human animal becomes a machine of violence.

Aggression begets aggression, a simple iteration as repetition compulsion. Tempestuous human relations lead to further social discord, animosity, and bellicosity with no hope in sight of reversing this discernible pattern.

Developmental traumas and attachment pathology besiege the plight of the human being, hence hampering the ability to have healthy relationships, to feel genuine love and intimacy, and to have empathy and compassion for others, where normativity is colored by pathos. Child abuse in all its odious forms is a primordial scab on humanity: it becomes the bedrock of suffering in every society where children are held hostage in emotional concentration camps by their parents or culture, victims who themselves have been abused, oppressed, subjugated, and demoralized. Here the enemy lies within our families and community cryptically threatening our sense of refuge, well-being, and safety at home.

Disease, migrant prejudice, refugee influx, child slavery, ground ghetto fighting, mass execution—barbarian style—and the drop or rise in black gold sustain our attention every night while watching the daily news. The world has become a very dangerous place. Whether we admit it or not, we all live in fear of being assaulted, mugged, or raped. Road rage, purse snatching, abduction, and home invasion are common occurrences. Anyone could be targeted or murdered for the change in their pockets, where safety is sought in gated communities, rural isolation, or in owning firearms for self-protection. From random crime to gangs, the mafia, drug cartels, the sex trade industry, child soldiers, and human trafficking, no one is immune from danger even if they own a Glock.

When nuclear armament, bioterror, world overpopulation, major climate change disasters, global warming, mass-scale industrial pollution, water scarcity, food shortage, nanotechnology used for ill, and extreme economic disparities threaten universal security, what shall we expect next?

The internet has become a prominent global weapon: cyber spies and computer hacking can derail technical operations anywhere, which can endanger the safety of nations and kill people at whim. With the manipulation of a computer mouse, one can readily steal, obstruct, and infect information programs with viruses that cripple corporations, banking systems, communication networks, and world economies, not to mention dupe the ignorant masses with false information. Rapid advances in technology, persistent distortion of facts by news outlets and through social media, and generative artificial intelligence (GAI) compound our existential risks.

When the transnational price of oil plummeted, the fickle economic fluidity in the Eurozone, Middle East, India, Brazil, Africa, the United States and Canada, China, and Russia all felt the pinch of recession; and with the spread of the Taliban, Jihadist extremism, Boko Haram, and Islamic State militants such as ISIS and ISIL, including Hezbollah and Hamas, the destabilization of global security adds another layer of panic to a foundering world economy already worried about public safety.

The tribal warfare in Middle Eastern Islamdom is perhaps one of the greatest threats to global stability, where Armageddon and messianic holy wars are manufactured by psychopathic leaders in the name of God, affecting everything from air travel and tourism to border crossings, national security, counterintelligence, and unbridled global surveillance. Racial uprising and social volatility in the United States, United Kingdom, South Africa, and Europe, among other nations, only remind us that skin color means something to a hating Other. And with religious chauvinism among Muslims, Hindus, Christians, and Jews alike, radical fascism, tyranny, totalitarianism, and more beheadings are just around the corner. Christendom in America is interfering with civil liberty rights and conditioning how government should view education, morality, health care, and private affairs, while autocrats in North Korea and Iran flex their muscles with nuclear testing, only adding to more alarm in global security and instability in foreign affairs.

Deregulation of industry and the push for privatization of business under the auspices of free democracy, open markets, neoliberalism, and global capitalism only leads to systemic corruption, for without regulation, checks and balances, and central oversight, every modality of dishonesty, venality, exploitation, and vice will enjoy its swindling moment or else pay a parasitic lawyer to find a legal loophole. Banksters and the mega-financial sectors have become too big to jail.

Human nature is replete with psychopathology. We are not warm, loving, gentle creatures by disposition; rather, those qualities are developmental achievements due to domestic socialization practices inherent to a civilization process. We can easily regress to animality when hard times hit, the underside of evolution. The way we aggress, abuse, oppress, and use others as throwaway objects speaks to the dark shadow side of the psyche: family cruelty, sexual molestation, physical abuse and intimidation, crime, sadism, murder, human trafficking, sex trade, baby buying, children sold into slavery, and so on, become the new abnormal. Although I claim no call to Armageddon, unlike the cult crazies, conspiracy theorists, doomsayers, and religious fanatics, we may be hard-pressed to ignore an obvious question: Are we living in the end times?

Once the four horsemen of the apocalypse, namely, flood, famine, fire, and war, including pestilence and death, have now been replaced with global pollution and climate change, rapid proliferation in the world population, shrinkage in natural resources such as water and food, terrorism and sects of death, technological hubris and risk (e.g., biogenetics, nanotechnology), economic corruption and squandering, and the prevalence of psychopathology in politics, governance, and national leaders. The problem of evil makes these global prophecies of fate all the more expeditious. Will humanity avail itself to subvert its selfish and aggressive propensities toward self-annihilation? Knowing that the world is going down the pea patch in a hurry, how ought we to live?

Before jumping to conclusions, we would do better to study the situation soberly. If we get caught up in reactionary polemics or emotional hyperbole, it becomes way too easy to lose rational perspective. It is not incumbent upon a philosopher or psychoanalyst to solve the world's problems, yet perhaps it is sufficient to point them out. Although I do not profess to resolve this planetary crisis, I would consider myself modestly lucky to be able to reframe the issues in such a way as to offer a foreboding warning to humanity. What sets my analysis apart from others is simply this: our *unconscious* remains the primal threat to our collective existence. Until we become aware and reverse our trajectory toward self-annihilation, humanity will teeter on the edge of extinction.

Through our continued maltreatment and sullying of the Earth, we are slowing committing global suicide. Like a sadomasochist or a drug addict, we know that we are hurting ourselves, yet it just doesn't move us to action. Is this due to apathy, an eclipse of empathy, and/or a failure to take responsibility for our self-destructive deeds? Or is this a crass defense, the momentary dismissal of reality for the more immediate desire to consume and gratify our pleasures and whims? Our pursuit of immediate satisfaction overrides the rational necessity to delay gratification and secure more healthy parameters for future enjoyment. We may also posit a collective interpellation that lies at the heart of global psychology: humanity is so immersed in its own immediate presence that it cannot fathom a future absence, hence the cessation of human life due to our emotional geocentrism. I suggest that this is largely attributed to an omnipotent grandiose denial fueled by unconscious social fantasies that condition the worldview of the masses. Collective humanity simply will not entertain the sobering truth of such foreseeable catastrophic risks to our continued survival. Unconscious wish fulfillment is so strong that the need to believe in a futurity that for all practical purposes will go on forever is delusional: it is only on the condition that we suspend empirical evidence for the politics of unconscious ideology that we can go on living in denial. These fantasies fly in the face of the reality principle, for we cannot negate the fact that we are incrementally killing ourselves. But despite all the evidence, deep down we really can't allow ourselves to believe it is so.

These observations lead us to the conclusion that our immediate concerns and desires we fulfill in the present are more important than the future, and that of our own children's and grandchildren's future, a rather myopic form of selfishness indeed. Here we have failed to contemplate the ethical and have not held sacred the covenant we have pledged toward respecting and preserving our earthly alma mater, the nurturing ground of our existence, without which we will no longer sustain life. In our technological and planetary devastation of Being, we may observe the omega principle at its zenith, working silently yet ever so conspicuously, half hidden. As the world cataclysmic decay of civilization through ecocide and self-annihilation is looming in the shadows of the abyss, the failure of collective rationality, guilt, shame, and ethical rectitude to act has devolved into its own pathos, the ignorance and inertia of self-consciousness, our moral day of reckoning—social Armageddon. In the wake of all knowledge, we continue to conquer, consume, exploit, and kill. This is humanity's death drive.

In our age of ecological devastation, we have abandoned Being to a wasteland of its own desertification where nothing grows but a vast sprawling desolate vacancy of beings, a devastation that spreads. Such dereliction emerges from the root of its own self-destruction and creepily expands like a rhizome. But can there be an overcoming and reversal of such corrosive processes, to devastate the devastation we have caused? Can we create a clearing that opens a prospect to heal our abject colonization of Being? Can we recover and repair such world alienation and undo our ontological crisis by reshaping the culture that has given rise to it?

We can expect no real security, only a split or fracturing of the ontological—human nature divided by itself. What semblance of security remains is only a *sense*, a chimera, a figment out of the fundamental fissures of human existence. We live in a schizophrenic dream torn asunder by reality that masquerades as consensually validated social ideologies. When such unconscious illusions ingress in the most fundamental fabric of our beings, which is part of our cultural ontology and material thrownness, interpellation becomes the backdrop of how our fantasies are fashioned to cover the unseen reality that is always operative, hidden yet always present.

We must not delude ourselves in our dissociative denial or global disavowal of the present hazards looming before us yet disconnected from our consciousness, as if we can crudely discount the real through a form of infantile omnipotent narcissism. The destruction of our planet at our own hands reflects the death drive at its apex where a psychotic negation of reality has taken hold of world masses. Here we may observe an undercurrent of the Shadow—a primordial force drawing us back into darkness, into the chthonic austerity of nothingness, the netherworld of death. The collective unconscious shadow of humanity is bellowing through its own self-destructive manifestations, what we must engage and abate before it's too late.

The end of civilization is not a preordained fatalism but will, rather, be an imprudent consequence of our cavalier dismissive hubris of our own unconscious tendencies toward self-eradication, that is, humanity's death wish that will cause our extinction if we don't wake up from our dream world and stop it from becoming real.

Here on Earth

WE BEGIN OUR STORY WITH WITNESSING A CRIME. WE SEE IT HAPPEN-
ing, but nobody intervenes. It just happens and keeps on happening as
some indifferent occurrence where everyone says, "It's not my problem."
We find ourselves as bystanders hoping that others will intercede, but no
one wants to get their hands dirty. Citizens are frozen. Police walk by.
Not even government officials care that a murder is being committed.
World collectives become onlookers who accept no responsibility, let
alone an obligation to act. We are passersby to ecocide.

Throughout this chapter I argue that we are hypnotized by a global
bystander effect as we aloofly watch the Earth slowly being destroyed.
Like a cigarette addict, we know that smoking is bad for us, but we
don't want to kick the habit even as our lungs are filled with smoke and
tar. I explore some possible reasons for this apathetic phenomenon and
why we continue to allow ourselves to be idle bystanders to our climate
emergency.

One issue to consider is our lack of consideration for anything non-
human. Why would we assume that man is the normative measure of all
things when this epistemological arrogance and sovereign entitlement
deny the prehuman status of existence and the impersonal Earth forces
a life of their own, let alone a right to exist by virtue of their ontological
preexistence to human affairs? This perpetual reoccurrence of alienating
the Earth as a postmodern consequence of diffuse global technologies
and geopolitical operations of late capitalism that dominate the current
scene cannot fathom the inhuman; while the materiality and naturalized

kinetic fabric of nonhuman entities is an irrefutable factor that conditions all of humanity, which we coexist with and depend upon to survive. If we do not have a sustainable planet, then *existence will expire*, and we will enter a posthuman ecology—that is, a future without humans and all its estranged arrangements. For this to be subverted, we must entertain a change in ethical sensibility, affection for the environment, creative social solutions, and enhanced agentic potentiality that contemplate heterogeneous political space and conservation justice that situates humans within a system of nature requiring an ecological conception of collective political action. It is my hope that reenvisioning moral futures will lead to collective global change that resuscitates Gaia from her deathbed. But is this possible?

A PROMISE OF HOPE

At the United Nations Climate Change Conference held in Paris in 2015, nearly 200 countries agreed under the COP21 accord to limit the *increase* in global warming by 2020 to an ambitious, if not miraculous, 1.5 degrees Celsius above preindustrial levels.[1] They didn't make it. Most scientists agreed that this was not possible given our current rate of human population growth and entrenched reliance on fossil fuels. This goal would require a complete cessation of any new exploration of gas, oil, and thermal coal, including new coal mines, oil and gas wells, fracking initiatives, and pipeline expansions, as well as a complete global shift away from dependence upon carbon-based resources to clean or renewable energies and alternative technologies.[2] Given that the fuel sector is a $1 trillion industry, it is unimaginable that the world would stop manufacturing automobiles, concrete buildings, power plants, and disposable

---

1. The international trade agreement was reached on December 12, 2015, involving 196 countries committed to reducing carbon emissions as a global priority with an eventual intermediary goal of not breaching the 1.5 degrees Celsius mark, .5 degrees less than the 2 degrees Celsius limit set at the 2009 Copenhagen climate talks (Orlando, 2015; United Nations Framework Convention on Climate Change, 2009; Weaver, 2015). Refer to Article 2: "to pursue efforts to limit the temperature increase to 1.5 degrees C above preindustrial levels" (United Nations Framework Convention on Climate Change, 2015). See Schaefer (2015) for criticism of the accord and Anderson, Broderick, and Stoddard (2020) for their analysis of how climate progressive nations have fallen far short of the Paris-compliant policy.
2. Cf. Leahy (2015).

goods that require carbon fuels simply out of financial self-interest and practical need. Put concisely, it would be tantamount to economic suicide. More unfathomably, it would require relinquishing our immediate comforts and overall quality of life as we know it.

Regardless of pedestrian social indifference to green movements and stubborn resistance to change, the renunciation of carbon energies would wither and devolve the global standard of living to that of primitive times. In fact, the Paris resolution is not an international enforceable treaty nor is it legally binding; it is merely a *promise* to try. In other words, a hollow platitude: as long as fossil fuels are the cheapest and most readily available forms of energy consumption, they will continue to be burned out of ease and necessity.[3] Without enforceability, accountability, liability, or compensation, such assurances reveal the caricature of political cackle. Impractical commitments, dubious governmental policies, and duplicitous politicians were scarcely able to live up to such pledges when superpowers and capitalist incentives condition the infrastructures of our world societies, ensuring that the lights and furnaces will remain on. The need for economic security, social stability, predictability, habit, and ready-at-hand resources will hardly disappear, let alone change overnight. Further, human nature guarantees that desire, avarice, consumerism, and the quest for materialism will do their best to preserve the existing situation, even as every international climate accord since then has sounded the alarm bell. Now we are at the tipping point.

GLOBAL BYSTANDERS IN THE FACE OF ECOLOGICAL CRISIS

Here on Earth, we are destroying our planet. This is an irrefutable empirical fact. Greenhouse warming, climate catastrophes, and aberrant weather phenomena occur every day throughout the globe and yet we do very little to prevent them, let alone reverse their course. Moreover, we have caused them. Even though we see the ruin with our own eyes and do practically nothing to mitigate the ecological crisis, world masses have adopted a *global bystander syndrome*,[4] where denial and abnegation

---

3. Cf. Orlando (2015).
4. In a series of now famous social science experiments, social psychologists John Darley and Bibb Latané (Latané & Darley, 1968) discovered how average citizens would fail to act to intervene with

of social responsibility lie at its very core. In fact, we may even go so far as to claim that our shared inaction constitutes a global psychological *disorder*—a collective psychopathology where the order, homeostasis, and conservation of nature are negated, ignored, and neglected through delusional grandeur from world masses unwilling to acknowledge and preempt our looming fate. Given that such denial contradicts and thwarts all instincts toward self-preservation, what possible reasons could be behind such lunacy?

We may argue that much of humanity is under an unconscious trance fueled by anxiety and psychological defense against suffering and despair, so we naturally wish to avoid recognizing unpleasant truths, let alone confront them head-on because they are too overwhelming to bear. But when we defy the reality principle, all defenses come crashing down by the weight of actuality. Our failure to be conscious of the objective reality of the external world and our impending peril is patently detrimental to our survival, if not lethal. Not only is such myopia disastrous for our planetary future, but our failure to act is an illogical outpouring of stupidity. Such suspension of rational and practical judgment may be partially explained by an unconscious paralysis of intelligence headed down a predictable path of self-obliteration. We see the train wreck coming but can't believe that it really will happen. Such torpor suggests that humanity is seized

---

individuals in distress or during emergency situations when collectively witnessed by a group of strangers or small crowd. Throughout various staged scenarios, those who were alone during a mishap or crisis were more likely to act to help a person in need than in a group of people randomly experiencing the same situation. Bystanders were often observed to exhibit a diffusion of responsibility, even apathy, when in the presence of others who could just as readily respond to visible emergencies or requests for help. For example, in a series of smoke experiments in a public setting, individuals would collectively fail to report the incident even in the presence of fire. Given the degree of perceived threat, felt responsibility, the social monitoring of others' reactions to the situation, and required need for assistance, bystanders would often defer to others, feign ignorance, watch what others do, fade into anonymity, and/or walk away.

The degree of ambiguity, the severity of the situation, the perceived judgment and competence of the bystander to assist, the familiarity of the environment where the emergency occurs, and the level of personal safety felt will influence the degree of action taken. The more ambiguous the situation, lack of knowledge on the part of the bystander, the significance of the consequences involved, the forms of action required, the cohesiveness of group membership, and the implementation of choice of assistance contemplated or taken all inform the level of bystander effects and moral lassitude manifested. In general, the more people around a scene, the less likely one feels personally responsible to assist or intervene in times of need or crisis, instead believing, "It's somebody else's problem."

by a collective dream state ensconced in a macroscale ecological complex hoping to wake up unscathed. In other words, we are slowly committing suicide on the course toward eventually bringing about our own death.

The global bystander effect not only reflects a collective social disorder potentially leading to societal collapse; it reveals an eclipse of conscience. Such lethargy, placidness, and unwillingness to act on a global scale are tantamount to moral transgression. Although many conscientious, concerned bystanders are wielding protests against rampant ecological despoliation and organizing civil disobedience campaigns such as the youth climate change and Extinction Rebellion (XR) movements, many global citizens—particularly in the developed world—are simply watching or idly strolling by as our planet is sluggishly being destroyed from collective inactivity to prevent, subvert, and rehabilitate our dying mother Earth.[5] Such bystander apathy, pluralistic ignorance, and diffusion of responsibility are psychological phenomena that are recalcitrant to reason. As with the homeless and vagabonds on the streets, we have largely become spectators passively observing the deterioration of the Earth's biosphere without so much as lifting a finger to help. We just watch, waiting for someone else to jump in and fix things. What explains such lassitude? Whether in passivity or pushback, the collective bystander syndrome serves as an existential threat to humanity.

This disturbing global phenomenon is evident from the fact that much of world citizenship, including all national governing leaders in every civil country, has sound scientific knowledge of our planetary plight; the severity of our ecological emergency and the dangerous consequences that befall us are unambiguous. The world watches and looks on, whether helplessly, indifferently, or interpassively as the impending

---

5. This analogy or metaphor obviously does not apply to developing and disenfranchised countries where large portions of the world's population live in poverty, many in war zones and under inhumane conditions, where they are at best food insecure and at worst starving. If they are indeed concerned about climate change, it seems likely that this will be in the context of their ability to feed and house their families or cope with austere climate realities they did not foresee as part of their daily existence. Those in developed and democratic nations, however, take such privileges for granted; there, the failure is of political leadership in addressing our ecological crisis. The United Nations may have given Greta Thunberg a big round of applause, but it's pretty meaningless without effective action from individual governments and given the often-insidious role of those with vested interests in perpetuating the status quo.

death of Gaia is slowly succumbing to preventable inaction. Although many claim to be ignorant of climatology and the Earth sciences, even adopting skeptical and dismissive attitudes toward the validity claims made by natural scientists who study such matters for a living every day, we cannot deny empirical facts without succumbing to delusion.

What we know about the Earth's climate system—namely, how our atmosphere, lands, and seas are affected by heat absorbed from the sun and displaced onto weather phenomena such as storms, heat waves, rising ocean levels, droughts, and so on—is that human beings have altered it from the way it would have developed organically if no humans were inhabiting the Earth.[6] What is certain is that carbon dioxide (CO_2) in the Earth's atmosphere traps the sun's heat, and that burning fossil fuels, such as natural gas, oil, coal, peat, and tars, produces more CO_2 beyond what would exist or is already there in nature. Since the industrial revolution, we have systematically cultivated and are dependent upon carbon fuels, which have increased CO_2 levels by at least one-third than they would have occurred naturally. As a result, the planet has become hotter; ergo, human beings are the cause of global warming and the Anthropocene.

Satellite and ground-based measures have shown that warming ocean levels are on average eight inches higher than before 1900, and the Earth's temperature is 1.3°F hotter. Periodic reports issued by the Intergovernmental Panel on Climate Change (IPCC) generally agree that by 2100 the Earth's likely temperature will be between 3.2°F and 7.2°F above what it was in 2000, depending upon how much fossil fuel consumption continues during the next century.[7] As warming sea waters

---

6. Although I rely on many authorities and sources (see Diamond, 2005; Emmott, 2013; Flannery, 2010; Lovelock, 2006; Rees, 2003), Climate Central (2012) is a highly respected independent, nonpartisan, nonprofit science and journalism organization composed of scientists specializing in all climate-related matters such as ecosystems and adaptation, chemistry, energy systems, and climate statistics. The following empirical facts and statistics are largely culled from this organization's findings, the Intergovernmental Panel on Climate Change (2015, 2021, 2022a and b, 2023), and more recently, the World Weather Attribution (2023).

7. See the IPCC's (2015) Climate Change 2014 Synthesis Report: Fifth Assessment Report, and the 3 Working Groups reports (2021–2022) that comprise the more recent Sixth Assessment Report. The IPCC was formed in 1988 by the United Nations Environment Programme and the World Meteorological Organization due to the increasing awareness of the effects of human-generated greenhouse gas emissions on the rise in the Earth's temperature and its relation to climate change. Its mandate is to "provide the world with a clear scientific view on the current state of

expand and hotter air melts polar ice caps and glaciers, a trickle-down effect on the Earth's atmospheric systems has produced complex interaction effects and redistributions of climate phenomena. Because the Earth does not respond passively to changes in temperature, it may produce various unpredictable and variegated climate-related responses to the effects of human intervention that supervene on climate systems on a global scale. Melting ice and glaciers increase water levels and flooding,[8] while increasing cloud cover reflects light back into space, affects vegetation, and holds in greenhouse gases. Opposing phenomena and exchange effects are inevitable and are different throughout the world. With thawing conditions in the Arctic, permafrost could release extra carbon dioxide and methane frozen for thousands of years into the atmosphere, while rising tides, changes in ice sheets and ocean currents,

---

knowledge in climate change and its potential environmental and socio-economic impacts." The Panel is comprised of several different working groups dealing with specific aspects of climate change, including observations from the past in comparison to the present and future prediction models, the tangible effects humans have made on the world's ecosystems and the Earth's biosphere, the potential impact of alternative and renewable energies, and so on. The main task of the IPCC is to collect, analyze, weigh, and distill the work of all the major scientific discoveries and published research findings that bear on all aspects of climate systems and the Earth sciences and provide written assessments and summaries on technical applications and the results for both professional audiences and policy makers. Each assessment report is examined and critiqued by hundreds of independent scientists from different disciplines and subdisciplines, who often disagree with each other, before final reports and recommendations are presented in an objective, nonpartisan manner before governments and external experts who rereview the findings; while review editors make sure that all research and professional opinions are considered, are accurate, inclusive, and valid. The IPCC assessment reports, therefore, are the most scientifically objective and authoritative sources of knowledge we have on climate change in the world today. Anyone refuting this authority, comprised of hundreds of independent sources, would have to be prepared to defend alternative empirical findings that would challenge this body of knowledge. To date, I know of no other credible authority or databasee that can support alternative claims to the contemporary state of affairs we face.

8. Greenland's ice caps are melting at three times the rate since 1997 due to rising ocean temperatures, which account for one-third of the world's sea-level rise; and Antarctica's melting ice sheets make the Eastern coastline of the United States particularly vulnerable to extreme weather events, including flooding due to rising tides and high sea levels as ocean currents sweep the melting waters northward (*Scientific American*, 2017, pp. 18, 21). The forecast is so bleak that researchers at Ohio State University have recently concluded that the Greenland ice sheet has melted past the point of no return and would continue to shrink even if global warming miraculously stopped today (*The Economist*, 2020). Also recently, at least one-third of the huge ice fields in the Himalayan Mountain chain are fated to melt, affecting almost two billion people throughout Asia (Carrington, 2019). And with the so-called doomsday glacier melting at an accelerated rate in Antarctica, we can reasonably predict that if the melting continues, it will reconfigure the majority of the world's coastlines.

and La Niña's and El Niño's Southern Oscillation climate patterns could bring on severe storms, floods, tornadoes, hammering winds, hurricanes, tsunamis, and the like, followed by deadly heat waves, droughts, compromised agricultural production, and depleted water supplies in other parts of the globe.

Climate in the past cannot be compared to climate today, which is a category mistake, because this assumes that all the conditions in the past apply equally today and that the Earth's ecosystems can withstand anything regardless of what is being dumped into the atmosphere. But we must seriously consider how the Earth's climate systems have been impacted by human activity and how the increase in greenhouse emissions over the past 200 years has profound implications for the future of civilization. Our anthropogenic infestation, including increased toxins and pollutants, is what any substantial talk about global warming or climate change is really about. Due to the proliferation in the human population since the industrial revolution, accompanied by vast consumption and waste across all civilizations, today's climate emergency becomes a whole other ball game. When mountain glaciers melt, they feed and alter the course of rivers differently, which leads to flooding in some places and drought in others. When ocean currents are affected, this alters weather and atmospheric climate patterns, while differing evaporation levels on both sea and land may lead to rain or snow or increased temperature. These complex interaction effects are varied throughout the world, hence happening at different rates and in different places.

Because differences in temperature affect wind force and weather patterns, they can lead to a whole host of varying local and regional climates, which may affect ecosystems, plant life, and animal migration looking to adapt to harsher environments or face the specter of extinction. A warmer world will also force extra carbon dioxide to be absorbed into the oceans leading to increased acidification, hence permeating all living creatures and underwater ecosystems such as coral reefs. Plonking more human CO_2 emissions into the atmosphere, along with methane, nitrous oxide, and other industrial chemicals, increases the amount of water vapor due to evaporation, which traps in even more heat and augments the warming process.

Burning noxious coal churns out most greenhouse gases, supplying the world with about 25% of its energy demands and about half of the electricity used in the United States alone. China, the United States, and India are the biggest producers of coal, mainly because it is cheap and plentiful, and accounts for nearly 40% of the world's energy-related CO_2 emissions. As the world population increases, so will its energy demand, and coal use is likely to be our number one source of warming over any other fossil fuel. But even if we stopped burning fuel, driving gas-guzzlers, and turned off our air conditioners, we would still emit greenhouse gases due to agriculture, food production, concrete manufacturing, pollution, aerosols, and deforestation, just to name a few. Clearing forests and tilling land for farming releases large amounts of carbons stored in the soil, such as methane and nitrogen oxides, as well as when plant matter decays and wood is burned, not to mention the unmonitored flaring and venting of natural gas that take place in the fossil fuel industry, such as in the Southwestern United States where a methane cloud besets indigenous cultures. And with eight billion human inhabitants today, more than six times more people since 1800, we produce so much waste containing saturated stores of methane that we now have landfills so large they can be seen from space.

No natural source can explain our current global warming predicament. Deluded politicians, conservative reactionaries, and misguided researchers or academics who play on people's emotional prejudices and spoon-feed the ignorant masses propaganda or pseudoscience as natural justification for the recent warming are merely incompetent charlatans or speculative fools brazenly spouting nonsense without a proper appraisal of the facts. And political, capitalist, corporate, and personal self-interests likely are the main culprits motivating climate skeptics, criticism, and denial of the planetary crisis that is altering the Earth's energy balance. This is particularly the case when big business, such as the oil and gas sector, has invested capital in extracting oil from ground wells and tar sands, or in probing natural gas sources even though hydraulic fracturing (fracking) has triggered earthquakes during its exploratory operations, such as in Canada.

Mining, drilling, and transport accidents also have had disastrous consequences for the environment; they have polluted our lands, ecosystems, and waters, such as sour gas destroying lakes, drinking water, and aquatic resources used for irrigation; as well as petroleum spills and leaks on coastal drilling rigs and offshore platforms that have decimated animal and marine life while sullying our oceans. And government has an invested interest in excavating these resources because it is good for the overall welfare of the state. The fossil fuel industry is deeply tied to a nation's economy because jobs, prosperity, and personal well-being depend upon carbon energies for production and commerce, which in turn supports a whole host of vital industrial, trade, and factory occupations including steel, cement, plastics, appliance and automobile manufacturing, engineering, construction, and small business. And when political policies threaten to interfere with established social expectations and financial profits, everything from the gross domestic product to social class, material wealth, public health, and personal happiness are affected. And here lies our paradox and fundamental ambivalence: to save the planet, including ourselves, we must give up the primary means we depend upon to enjoy life.

THE REVENGE OF GAIA

Scientist James Lovelock posits that the Earth or Gaia, named after the Greek goddess, is like a supra-living organism that regulates our planet. Composed of all its features, such as the atmosphere, biosphere, upper layers of rock, mountains and oceans, and minerals and chemical compounds deep in its core, Gaia functions to regulate its internal environment like an evolving superorganic system. An assumption governing contemporary Earth System Science, Gaia theory is defined by Lovelock as:

> A view of the Earth that sees it as a self-regulating system made up from the totality of organisms, the surface rocks, the ocean and the atmosphere tightly coupled as an evolving system . . . having a

goal—the regulation of surface conditions so as always to be as favourable as possible for contemporary life.[9]

Although Gaia does not have agency, choice, or a command-and-control system, it does involve what Tim Flannery calls an "unconscious cooperation of all life that has given form to our living Earth" through evolutionary forces.[10] Because both living and nonliving aspects of the Earth are indissolubly interwoven, it becomes logical to posit that the Earth as a complex, evolving self-regulatory macrosystem is akin to an organism that would do what it could to control, adjust, and synchronize its surface temperatures in sea and on land to favor life. Regardless of whether we view this hypothesis concretely or metaphorically, the continuous interaction and commerce between complex ecological systems is beyond any doubt. Now, Lovelock insists, Gaia is "sick," infected by a disease called man.

The Earth system no longer operates effectively within its set of bounds and constraints because its conditions have been strained and pushed to the limits governing the principles of homeostasis that maintain order, optimal temperature, and climate stability. In fact, Gaia's future looks grim: although she's "a tough bitch,"[11] Lovelock predicts that "she will die from overheating."[12] Since circa 1970, the world's mountain glaciers have shrunk at an alarmingly accelerated rate. The poles and ice caps are melting, and sea levels have risen by 8 inches on average worldwide. Greenland's ice sheets are breaking up or disappearing, and warmer air and ocean temperatures rapidly contribute to sea-level rise. As polar ice sheets continue to shrink, islands will begin to sink. Arctic animal life will decrease, migrate, or die off, and loss of habitat will make it difficult for polar bears as a species to survive. And below the Arctic, a mountain pine beetle epidemic has ravaged indigenous forests of pines and spruce

---

9. Lovelock (2006), p. 162.
10. See Flannery (2010), p. 36, 57. Cf. Lovelock (2006): "I call Gaia a physiological system because it appears to have the unconscious goal of regulating the climate and the chemistry at a comfortable state for life" (p. 15).
11. This quote is attributed to Lynn Margulis by Crispin Tickell in the foreword to Lovelock's *The Revenge of Gaia* (2006, p. xvi).
12. Lovelock (2006), p. 45.

in western Canada and the northwestern United States due to increased warming. Millions of bees are dying throughout North America and Europe due to the so-called colony collapse disorder that affects pollination; hence, the loss of agricultural crops, and we still don't know why, although the use of pesticides, insecticides, infections, pathogens, loss of habitat, and so forth are the usual suspects.

The Earth's temperature is approximately 1.3°F higher than it was 100 years ago, with some places warming more while others less, and the continental United States has had more than twice as many record highs as record lows in the first decade of the 21st century. Milder winters and early spring thaws alter the naturally occurring temperature cycles of the seasons, hence hastening seed sprouting, blooming of plants and flowers, migration, disrupting hibernation, feeding and breeding patterns, nesting timing of birds, insects, and mammals, and the spawning of fish, amphibians, crustaceans, mollusks, and other aquatic animal life such as corals, fungi, algae, and the like—all affecting ecosystems on a mass scale.

Changing geologies, altitudes, and climates trigger changes in ecosystems all over the world, affecting everything from vegetation growth to desertification, shifts in insect and animal populations, drastic alterations in terrains, ocean and land habitats, and food and water supplies. As some ecosystems dissolve, new ones will form, just as climate feedback loops account for irregularities in temperature, cloud formations, wind, reflection of light and heat, and other weather phenomena. Our greenhouse planetary sweat suit has led some scientists to predict that due to Arctic amplification (viz., increased melting leads to less reflection, leads to increased warming, leads to more melting, and so on), the Arctic Ocean could potentially be ice free (in the summer) by 2100 if not by 2050 or before, depending upon our rate of warming. And the global sea level could rise anywhere between 2 and 6 feet by 2100. We may also expect to see more weather extremes such as excess heat waves, droughts, forest fires, severe storms, and floods all over the globe like we have already witnessed. The hotter it is, the more water evaporates from soil and water bodies, which leaves the land dry and brittle, affecting crops, bush, and topography ripe for wildfires; and because water vapor is stored in the atmosphere, when it rains it pours, leading to rising water levels, erosion, flooding, storm surges, monsoons, hurricanes, and so forth that will become increasingly more destructive in scope and severity.

As sea levels become more elevated, land will be subsumed under the ocean tides, from Miami to coastal Bangladesh, potentially displacing millions of people who are forced to move, while low-lying island nations such as the Maldives in the Indian Ocean could simply disappear. Climate change conceivably could make matters even worse in disenfranchised countries where political instability, violence, poverty, military conflict, and civil wars are historically correlated with warmer temperatures and drought, such as in Sudan and other parts of Africa. We only need to be reminded of the recent mass diaspora of Syrian refugees flooding Europe to imagine millions of displaced, panicked, and desperate souls invading foreign lands due to climate migration. Think of the breadth of pandemonium, injuries, illnesses, social trauma, civil disorder, looting, death, and escalating police and military violence that would occur within nations and between borders. Entire continents could be affected, shaking the foundations of modern societies; even major superpowers likely will lack the infrastructure to deal with mass migration due to insufficient resources, processing facilities, housing, food and water supplies, public-health systems, medical intervention, civilian unrest, state opposition, threats of criminality and terrorism, and concerns about national security.

We are likely to see an exponential increase in heat-related deaths, such as in the summer of 2015 due to anomalous heat waves that roasted Iraq, Egypt, India, Pakistan, and Europe, among other countries; and health and public institutions will be overwhelmed by the chaos. Climate-related health risks such as ground-level ozone and other forms of air pollution can burn the eyes, bring on asthma attacks or allergic reactions, and inflame the lungs, especially in those who have respiratory difficulties such as the old and very young. Infectious diseases could become airborne or carried by insects such as mosquitos transmitting malaria, dengue, Chikungunya, or the Zika virus, and public health systems would be scrambling to prevent or stop their spread. Changing patterns of rainfall, including droughts and floods, will affect farming and food crops, where malnutrition and death are to be expected, especially in developing countries such as India and Africa where half the deaths of all children are attributed to hunger, malnutrition, sickness, and starvation. And when food and water supplies become contaminated, especially in countries with poor sanitation and feeble public-health systems, outbreaks of diarrheal disease, cholera, typhoid fever, pestilence, and the like are inevitable. We don't need to be reminded of the recent horrific COVID-19 pandemic that changed the world, and other epidemics before that, such as SARS, swine flu, and Ebola: magnify that by millions, if not more.

We have no crystal ball to foretell the future, but regardless of the fallibility of climate (simulation) models, statistical calculations, and the uncertainty of future predictions, it doesn't take a rocket scientist to see that we are in deep trouble. The question becomes, can we sustain our planet under these conditions? Or is it too late? If things continue this way, as the world continues to heat up but carries on with business as usual, it only becomes a logical matter of time until it will be impossible to reverse the damage. Likely, we will accelerate our own demise. With the continued sprawl in overpopulation competing for water, food, and basic material resources necessary for survival, only to have more babies under the blazing sun adding to already unbearable social conditions among the existing privation and economic impoverishment, not to mention national, cultural, and religious factions teeming with envy, hate, and malice fueling further division, criminality, and war, we may anticipate a future full of destitution, anguish, despondency, and gloom. Regardless of our inability to predict futurity, we may only reasonably conclude one thing: the number one threat to human annihilation is actions produced by man.

James Lovelock and many other noted climate scientists are painting an ominous picture of the fate of humanity: as the planet continues to warm, most living things eventually will die. Once we pass a threshold state, a proverbial point of no return, the damage is irreversible. This is not simply hysterics or paranoia, as climate skeptics and denialists will attempt to persuade us to believe, but cold sober facts based on all the available objective evidence we have. In Lovelock's estimate, "before this century is over, billions of us will die and the few breeding pairs of people that survive will be in the arctic region where the climate remains tolerable . . . Not only will wildlife and whole ecosystems go extinct, but the planet will lose a precious resource: human civilization."[13] With the thought of an exodus to the North Pole as our sole chance of survival, it becomes fitting that Lovelock's conclusion is rather biblical: "Gaia now threatens us with the ultimate punishment of extinction."[14] Will she take her revenge? Sir Crispin Tickell nicely summarizes the penumbra of this menace when reflecting on our current predicament:

> Looking at the global ecosystem as a whole, human population increase, degradation of land, depletion of resources, accumulation of wastes, pollution of all kinds, climate change, abuses of technology, and destruction to biodiversity in all its forms together constitute a unique threat to human welfare unknown to previous generations . . . When applied to the problems of present society, the concept of Gaia can be extended to current thinking about values: the way we look at and judge the world around us, and above all how we behave. This has particular application in the field of economics, where fashionable delusions about the supremacy of market forces are so deeply entrenched, and the responsibility of government to protect the public interest is so often ignored. Rarely do we measure costs correctly: thus the mess of current energy and transport policy, and the failure to assess the likely impacts of climate change . . . We are dangerously ignorant of our own ignorance, and rarely try to see things as a whole.[15]

If the Earth is unable to continue to regulate itself due to runaway greenhouse effects, destruction of tropical rainforests, suffocation of the oceans, and diminution in planetary biodiversity, the whole house will collapse. With increased desertification and deforestation, as well as the disintegration of oceanic ecosystems deprived of precious nutrients such as algae and phytoplankton, which food chains depend upon, little woodlands and ocean life will be left to absorb the various gases out of the atmosphere. And with increased heat coming from the sun through

---

13. Lovelock (2006), p. xiv.
14. Lovelock (2006), p. 147.
15. Foreword to Lovelock (2006), pp. xvi–xvii.

the ozone and with decreased surface and cloud reflection, cooling systems operative within these vital regulatory ecosystems on land and sea, the Earth will become largely uninhabitable. As plant and algal life die and decompose, and when ice glaciers melt and permafrost thaws, they release carbons and methane into the air, amplifying the warming. And as increased temperatures bake forests, scrubland, timber, peat, and crops, the continents become one giant tinderbox. Here Lovelock warns of a massive expansion of tropic deserts and oceans so hot you can soft boil eggs.

Too Big to Fix

When large numbers of people are less likely to react to emergencies to help victims and people in distress, eschewing any personal responsibility, how do we understand the global bystander phenomenon when it involves billions of people? It would be fallacious and disingenuous to deny knowledge or assume pluralistic ignorance of our ecological emergency when the leading scientific authorities, research and academic institutions, private industry, policy analysts, economists, world governmental agencies, and international climate and Earth science advocacy groups all plead with the world masses to curb our carbon emissions and turn to more environmentally friendly forms of renewable energy to subvert our portentous catastrophe. The ecological apocalypse is looming before our very eyes, yet we are unable to overcome the diffusion.

How do we make sense of our global bystander effect? Why do world collectives turn a blind eye to the commonsense reality that lies before them? Is this simply due to denial, cognitive dissonance, participation mystique, or the unconscious illusion of constancy? Despite the fact that we need to take very seriously the possibility that we may be on the verge of human extinction if we do not take immediate collective global action, individuals in solitude and in social masses simply are not contemplating our perilous future with any foresight. There may be many reasons for this: cognitive or information overload, collective self-deception or bad faith (*mauvaise foi*), optimistic overconfidence or blind faith in the future, failure to consider futurity in terms of its possibilities and probabilities, underestimation of the stakes involved, overestimation of the predictability of the past while underestimating the unknowns of the future, ignoring the need for future preparation without the benefit of hindsight, or simply looking to others to provide evidence for *why* we should act while trying to appear poised and unflustered to save face, cover shame of ignorance, and/or project the tacit conviction that others are enveloped in a naive, reactionary defense.[16] Perhaps a simple economy of dissociation, splitting, compartmentalization, and/or emotional detachment is at play, or some grandiose hubris governing egotistical narcissism that opines, "We are the center of all things," hardly giving a passing thought to a world greater than us? May I further suggest it is because the problem is simply too big to fully understand, let alone fix. And even when we have sufficient understanding of the problem, individual action alone can do nothing to ameliorate it. Solutions require collective actions on a mass scale. Until this happens, we will remain bystanders witnessing our own gradual deterioration due to powerlessness and ennui.

When collective societies are under the influence or dominion of state power, it becomes cognitively reflexive, hence natural, to turn over responsibility and accountability to society or one's nation to remedy, as citizens have come to expect from government, leaders, or political patriarchy conditioned by parental transference. It is also an issue that is too complex for any one person or group to fully mend, let alone reverse a worldwide phenomenon. All of humanity's psychological defenses are mobilized—from disavowal ("Yes, I know, but"), dissociation, rationalization, intellectualization, and so on when confronting such a massive conundrum. How do we just shut off the lights, stop driving to work, and stop using fuel when the world revolves around every form of energy we rely on for our livelihoods and survival? By definition, this makes it a systemic structural issue that involves the agreement and cooperation of greater social collectives willing to be valuationally unified and committed to concrete change through resolute and deliberate action. But given human nature and the competing array of desires, emotions, ideology, and psychological complexes that constitute the political animal, can we

---

16. Cf. Cialdini (2001) and Yudkowsky (2008a).

really expect a global meeting of minds that will end in consensus and united action? Or will want, greed, politics, capital, and military strategy ensure that such collective valuation practices remain only a fantasy?

Individuals, communities, and even whole nations that adopt environmentally conscientious practices, such as limiting the consumption of fossil fuels, having fewer children, adopting green practices using renewable energies such as wind and solar power, and using alternative technologies such as electric automobiles and geothermal sources of heat and cooling systems to reduce their carbon footprints, will make virtually no difference in the grander scheme of the Earth's biosphere. Although such efforts are noble, it will take a union of nations committed to concrete change on a worldwide scale. And how would this be accomplished without state intervention? Moreover, how could it be enforceable given that national self-interest governs all policy in every nation-state willing to go to war to protect its sovereignty? And even if this were for our own good and were enforceable, would this not violate the very principles of liberty, democracy, and distributive justice? And what will happen when the Earth becomes too overpopulated, as the projected growth and scientific evidence suggests? With billions more people to feed burning more and more fossil fuels, our planetary sweat suit is bound to become one big unbearable sauna. More people, more warming, less food, less water, less land, less money: here we have a perfect formula for death.

2

Ten Billion

What Can We Learn from Rats?

In the 1940s, ethologist John Calhoun began to study the effects of population density on rats.[1] He confined wild Norway rats to a quarter-acre enclosure where they had a bounty of food, plenty of space to mill about, no source of predation or conditions for disease, and he watched. Soon a colony formed, and the population boomed. But by the end of 27 months, the population stabilized at only 150 adults, despite the fact that reproduction rates were predicted to be 5,000 by that time. One reason for the low population was due to an extremely high infant mortality rate. Despite an adequate amount of space, stress from social interaction led to disruptions in maternal functions, so very few young survived.

This observation in the wild led to a series of more controlled experiments using domesticated rats indoors. As the population density increased, the most salient degree of behavioral pathology immerged among females. They were largely unable to carry their pregnancy to full term, died after delivery if they did, or neglected their litters if they survived. Males became more frenzied, aggressive, resorted to sexual deviation, even cannibalism, followed by morbid withdrawal, where they would only come out to feed or roam about when others in the community were asleep. Social disintegration soon occurred: factions of

---

1. Summary findings of his initial studies are outlined in "Population Density and Social Pathology" (Calhoun, 1962).

rats divided into different groups with modified sex ratios, congregated in certain pens while leaving other areas sparse, rarely ate or only in the company of other members, and eventually crowded together in a pen as one big mob. This aberrant social phenomenon, a "pathological togetherness," disrupted courting practices, building of nests, and nursing and caring for the young. Infant mortality rates ran as high as 96% for the most disordered groups in the colony.

With this background in mind, Calhoun set out to create the perfect world, this time with mice.[2] He constructed Utopia: Universe 1. The basic design was used to construct a number of experiments and consisted of a closed physical universe that was approximately 9 feet square and 4.5 feet high with 1.5 feet galvanized metal walls at the top that the mice could not climb over. Within this world there were several tunnels and layers comprised of segmented units and segregated cells with separate story apartments, retreat nesting boxes, food hoppers, water dispensers, and an open congregation floor area covered with ground corncob to allow for communal feeding, social interaction, and access to each tunnel. The mice had everything they could ever dream of compared to life in the wild: unlimited food and water; shelter to keep them from the elements, disease, predation, and invasion from other species; and an ambient temperature. The initial four pairs of mice set loose in their new world doubled rapidly until reaching a population of approximately 620 before the exponential growth started to slow when a new social organization arose.

All was good in paradise until males began to compete for dominance and hierarchy in this closed social system, the most successful of which were associated with brood groups that produced the most litters. But as the population expanded, the youth grew into adult male counterparts competing for roles in an already established social order. With no place to emigrate, those who failed withdrew "physically and psychologically," became despondent and inactive, and pooled on the floor near the center of the universe. Neither seeking out affiliation with their former associates nor eliciting attacks from territorial males, they turned on each other, exchanging many wounds and scar tissue from fellow reserved

---

2. See "Death Squared: The Explosive Growth and Demise of a Mouse Population" (Calhoun, 1973).

males. Sudden shifts in activity or increase in excitation would precipitate attacks from resting males on other inhibited ones who, too passive to flee or defend themselves, would become immobile and endure vicious assaults in a state of learned helplessness, later attacking other weaker members, likely in reaction to being traumatized or through some animal equivalent of mimesis or identification with the aggressor.

As the senior territorial males became more fatigued in fending off their maturing associates, they were also less successful in defending their territories, which left nursing females more exposed to invasion of their nests. As their nest sites became more vulnerable, females adopted the aggressive role of territorial males, which included attacks on their own young, who were maimed and forced to leave the nests before normal weaning. Soon inception declined, pregnancies were aborted, offspring were wounded during delivery, and mothers carried their young outside the nest to abandon them. The social matrix began to collapse when females neglected their nurturing roles, rejected their progeny, and pushed them out into the dense and dangerous jungle before the development of attachment or affectional bonds was achieved. The deleterious effects induced by such interactional stress led to increased infant mortality and a steady decrease in population growth to the point of complete organizational disintegration.

With failure in social bonding, mechanical interference from hostile rivals, increased competition for role occupancy, and aggressivity, successive generations were increasingly unable to engage in reproductive and species normative behaviors including courtship, procreation, maternal care, territorial defense, and hierarchical intra- and intergroup organizational complexities to the eventual point of extinction. The last surviving births were on day 600 after colonization. Conclusion: when the spirit dies, the species dies.

What we may garner from Calhoun's experiments with rodents is remarkably analogous to the human animal. When children are neglected and forsaken by their mothers, abandoned on the streets, abused by their elders and society, and subjected to insecurity and ferocity, they become traumatized, feel unsafe and persecuted, cease to function adaptively, experience ongoing stress and deterioration in health, wellness, and social adjustment, aggress on others, become hopeless and depressed, and/or withdraw to an autistic state of simple instinctual behaviors aimed at physiological survival until death. Calhoun sees no reason why the lessons learned from mice cannot apply to humanity:

> For an animal so complex as man, there is no logical reason why a comparable sequence of events should not also lead to species extinction. If opportunities for role fulfillment fall far short of the demand by those capable of fulfilling roles, and having expectations to do so, only violence and disruption of social organization can follow. Individuals born under these circumstances will be so out of touch with reality as to be incapable even of alienation. Their most complex behaviours will become fragmented. Acquisition, creation and utilization of ideas appropriate for life in a post-industrial cultural-conceptual-technological society will have been blocked. Just as biological generativity in the mouse involves this species' most complex behaviours, so does ideational generativity for man. Loss of these respective complex behaviours means death of the species.[3]

In other words, if people do not have the opportunities to fulfill their aspirations, ideals, and shared communal needs, where enjoyment, purpose, creativity, and mutuality give meaning and provide a social link to life, pathology and mayhem will ensue. Calhoun called this the "behavioral sink," the tendency of disenfranchised groups to become fragmented in their behaviors to the point of societal decay due to the accumulation of negative interactions with others, absence of defined roles, and overpopulation.

Even though it is illegitimate and reductive to equate the superior intelligence and complexity of human life to that of a mouse, it nevertheless remains a chilling reminder of what overcrowded conditions can potentially lead to in a controlled society where plenty of food and water remain available. Just imagine what it would be like without obtainable food and water in an environment with limited space, not unlike many parts of the Holy Land and the developing world where large

---

3. "Death Squared" (Calhoun, 1973), p. 86.

populations and scant resources lead to desperation, starvation, pestilence, death, subjugation, violence, domination of subordinate members, anarchy, and a complete breakdown of social infrastructure. Our current total world population is eight billion,[4] and the United Nations estimates it will likely be more than ten billion by 2050.[5] What will life on this planet be like with billions more rats?

Overpopulation and Food Supply

Since the agricultural, scientific, industrial, technological, and public-health revolutions, we as a species have evolved from austere and ignorant beings relying on subsistence living to enjoying a rather comfortable life with all the amenities from cheap and available food, sanitized water, textiles, transport, public education, medicine, televisions, and computers to a cell phone. Even in the most impoverished regions of the world, our advances in human civilization have influenced everyone on the planet to some degree and scope. Since the dawn of organized agriculture and the mechanization of food production in the 20th century, famine was largely a plight of the past. When it occurs today, it is mainly due to a failure at technology, distribution, or societal disarray, such as during times of political instability, acts of military violence, or humanitarian crises, such as the recent mass starvation in Madaya, Syria; South Sudan; and Tigray, Ethiopia, seen by most as war crimes. But with our ecological planetary emergency, including greenhouse warming and

---

4. For the most updated account of the world population growth, see The World Counts and Worldometers, www.worldometers.info/world-population. On June 12, 2023, the world population was estimated to be 8 billion, 38 million people. It was 8 billion, 12 million on January 20, 2023. As of April 13, 2020, the world population was estimated to be 7.816 billion people (The World Counts, 2021). As of June 26, 2021, it was 7.866 billion (Worldometers, 2021). According to Worldometers, on January 8, 2016, the total world population was 7.393 billion. As of April 13, 2020, the world population grew to 7.777 billion. As of June 26, 2021, it was 7.875 billion.

5. According to the medium fertility estimate by the United Nations Department of Economic and Social Affairs (2015, 2019), Population Division, it is anticipated that the world population will be more than 11.2 billion by 2100. Although there are valid disputes over the projections of future population growth, claiming that the number could be closer to 8.9 billion by 2100 (Roser, 2020), given that the poorest breed faster, this will largely depend upon Africa if it continues its current trajectory of improved health and education, both of which are closely associated with reduced fertility. According to the United Nations (2023), India has now surpassed China as the most populated nation on Earth.

climate volatility, disruption in the manufacturing, supply, and allocation of food is predictable. We were alerted to this potential problem in the 1980s when Ethiopia experienced an unparalleled famine due to extreme drought. It is no coincidence that this malady corresponds to major changes in the Earth's climate cycle due to global warming. What makes this more worrisome is when we will have billions more people around to feed in our lifetime. Where will all the food come from, and how will it be distributed? And even if it is possible to produce sustenance for ten billion +, will it be available and affordable in magnitude? Or will capitalist kingpins, such as the banking and financial sectors, oil and gas corporations, insurance companies, and the medico-pharmaceutical industry control the price, rate of production, and delivery of such basic commodities that only certain privileged individuals, groups, classes, and nations be granted accessibility? Here it does not take much imagination to anticipate a future apocalypse and collapse of civilization as we know it.

We use massive amounts of land to grow food, farm, raise, graze, and warehouse animals, as well as more space and combustible energy to manufacture food that is digestible, publicly safe, nutritious, and transportable on a large industrial scale. Animals also rely on copious amounts of food (e.g., grain) and chemicals (e.g., antibiotics and hormones) to grow and thrive until they are ready for slaughter and human consumption. We largely owe the capacity to feed the masses to the Green Revolution, which developed mechanical and chemical technologies to grow food rapidly, inventing new breeding techniques and strains of grain, wheat, maize, and plants that are hardier, healthier, and more abundant; as well as the modernization of harvesting, raising animals for nutriment, battery cage and fish farming (pisciculture), genetic engineering, and the wholesale industrialization of nourishing the planet. But with these advances also came agricultural and industrial contamination through chemical fertilizers, pesticides, herbicides, biochemical waste products, and so forth that are sprayed in the air, seep into the soil, flushed into water supplies, and dumped into surrounding ecologies to the point that we have generated an intractable mess. The cost has been enormous in terms of pollution runoff, loss of habitat, overfishing, poaching, and the compounded erosion of ecosystems.

The recent Blue Revolution, which once broadly referred to water management systems to ensure adequate drinking water and crop irrigation security, is transforming industrial aquaculture or aquafarming (i.e., commercial fishing and shrimping) in tropical south nations, thereby changing agrarian landscapes in the global South that is purported to be far more ecologically damaging than many earlier Green Revolution technologies, including increased water pollution, destruction of coastal wetlands, salinization and depletion of aquifers, new invasive species, and loss of communal resources due to environmental politics and the highly exploitive nature of globalized capitalist culture.[6]

When humans began to proliferate and consume more and more, they wanted more and more, not only in terms of food but also in terms of objects of desire and manipulatives, to such a degree that mass production of goods required mass expansion of lands, sprawling highway infrastructure, hence tearing up more of the earth and using more and more combustible energies in the process of forging roads, digging soil, constructing factories, running equipment to manufacture goods, and transporting goods via air, sea, and land all over the world to account for what we have to date. And who do we have to thank? Although humanity has elevated itself in sophistication and quality of living in most industrialized parts of the world, we now must pay the piper due to the rapid proliferation of waste, pollution, crud, corrosion, vanishing biomes and deteriorating ecologies, and the loss of sustainable resources we have come to depend upon for our sustenance, enjoyment, and survival.

Stephen Emmott warns us about the dangers of world overpopulation.[7] In anticipating the bunny explosion of more than ten billion people, he points out the weighty fact that we will require far more resources—far more food, water, land, manufacturing, transport, and energy—to accommodate a crowded planet scrounging for the basic necessities of life, especially when you consider the enormous disparities

---

6. See Islam (2014), p. 71.
7. See Emmott (2013), who was head of computational science at Microsoft Research and runs an interdisciplinary team of scientists that draws on findings from molecular and plant biology, climatology, immunology, biogeochemistry, terrestrial and marine ecology, conservation, neuroscience, and artificial technologies.

in demand that different populations make on the planet's resources. In a pithy observation, he nicely summarizes the prevailing issues:

> An increasing population accelerates the demand for more water and more food. Demand for more food increases the need for more land, which accelerates deforestation. Increasing demand for food also increases food production and transportation. All of these accelerate the demand for more energy. This then accelerates greenhouse gas emissions, principally CO_2 and methane, which further accelerates climate change. And as climate change accelerates, it increases stress on water, food and land. And at the same time, an increasing population also accelerates stress on water, food and land. In short, as production increases, and as economies grow, stress on the entire system accelerates sharply.[8]

This all amounts to the fact that the demand for food and agricultural land will double by 2050. The magnitude of more land necessary for food production will also require more manufacturing and transport, increased air traffic, shipping, and distribution centers, which will lead to increased CO_2 emissions, black carbon, air pollution, industrial waste, and more global warming.

Another obvious question is, where will everyone live? Major world cities are rapidly proliferating, many having doubled in population in the past decade, such as in the Amazon. It is no coincidence that the demand for and procurement of land and water rights has spawned astonishingly high rates of competition (and real estate prices) in securing for our future requirements, goading the privatization movement and corporate business to buy up anything they can lay their hands on through brokerage manipulations, political kickbacks, massaging governmental land deals, and consequently, driving up costs. Whoever owns the land, whether private individuals, business conglomerates, or nation-states, has political and capital advantages over the rest of the world, and there is only so much to go around. With more land use comes more environmental degradation and loss of biodiversity, habitats, biotas, and

---

8. Emmott (2013), pp. 39–40.

species populations headed for demise. This leads us to predict with some margin of certainty that we will produce the next wave of mass disappearances of life on Earth, including the sixth mass extinction since the dinosaurs, namely, the termination of man.[9] With climate collapse and the loss of our ecosystems—the planet's water, glaciers and ice sheets, plants and animals, and the air we breathe—how can we survive?

The demand for food has intensified at a far greater rate than population growth due to the fact that we want, rapaciously acquire, and consume more, are eating more meat, organize our social and recreational activities around dining, and have disposable incomes in economically developed nations, all requiring more crops to feed livestock, such as soy and alfalfa production, not to mention space to warehouse them. With more crop production comes more deforestation, and with more food production comes an increase in climate change. Given that food production is entirely dependent upon stable climate patterns, with fairly predictable conditions for planting and harvesting, and with the increase in fertilizers, herbicides, and pesticide use that enables more food growth, the rates of deterioration in soil and water will only increase. More food production means more greenhouse gas emissions; more assaults on the atmosphere, the cryosphere, the biosphere, and the hydrosphere; more extreme weather events, such as drought and subsequent loss of food bounties. In turn, they will inflate existing prices for food basics, drive up the futures market, and impose austerity on access to basic commodities, not to mention luxuries, that the poor already cannot afford. And when the poor have nothing to eat, we can expect mass revolt including looting, rioting, and mayhem due to dearth and exorbitant increases in the price of grain and rice, such as the reminiscent events in the Middle East that triggered the Arab Spring pandemonium.

WITHERING WATER

What about water, the lifeblood of existence? More than a billion people already suffer from water shortage, and most of the freshwater currently available is used for irrigation. As most of the Middle East burrows down

---

9. See Emmott (2013), Kolbert (2014), and Weisman (2013) for their unique takes on the matter.

into the Earth to find underground wellsprings or aquifers to quench thirst, a region where drip hydration is key to agricultural survival, we should embrace ourselves for a future where water supplies are scarce, heavily exhausted, and in increased demand for irrigation to produce food for animal and human consumption as well as sundry consumer products—including meat, textiles, plastics, computer chips, and so forth—on a mass scale. In short, at the rate we are going, our continued ravenous appetite for both food and water is completely unmanageable.

Water shortages and droughts are salient in the great plains of the western United States, where the Ogallala Aquifer has dropped by more than 200 feet in parts of Kansas and Texas, while the Colorado River, the Yellow River in China, and the Ganges in India go dry during certain parts of the year due to overuse. As monsoons transform the landscape from desert and scrub to lush green land, disruptions in power, blackouts, and infrastructure collapse follow; next come altering summer weather systems and blazing heat waves that decimate the electrical grid, deform geography, and supplant people and species throughout all South Asia. With accelerated climate change and warming, glaciers and snow cover are decreasing, which affects precipitation rates and about one billion people who depend upon snowmelt for water. With less snow thaws that feed rivers and streams in the spring, by the time summer rolls around, water sources are all but bone dry, and at a time when water is needed the most. And when the glaciers melt even more, perhaps even to the point of being virtually nonexistent, those freshwater stocks will be gone.

As temperatures go up, so do speeds of evaporation in all water bodies and from the soil, which leads to increased cloud cover that, in turn, generates more precipitation, and so on. But as the water cycle races ahead rather than spreading itself proportionally throughout the seasons, this produces higher rates of flooding followed by droughts. Akin to rapid snowmelt problems, sudden spill offs and gushes occur at once and then run off before the land can absorb the water, and as with cycles of evaporation, are prevented from trickling down into underground water reserves. The water stress that pervades the southwestern United States is at a historical crisis point, including California where reservoirs and aqueducts are dwindling due to drought, irrigation overuse, illegal siphoning, state sale of water rights to nurture agribusiness and the almond industry, and piping out water for hundreds of miles to quench the millions of masses in the greater Los Angeles area alone, while the rest of the state goes dry. Raging wildfires have only added to an already stressed system.

The water footprint it takes to produce our global food supply takes up more than two-thirds of our water stores, while 80% of all available freshwater (at least in the United States) goes to agriculture. The hidden nature of water consumption to raise livestock is astonishing. It takes more than 2,000 gallons of water to produce one pound of beef. How's that for a steak dinner! As population growth increases, the level of water stress will spike, watersheds will be depleted, and aquifers will not be replenished. Accelerated evaporation, decreased precipitation, and poor soil moisture coupled with higher temperatures will predictably lead to more droughts reminiscent of the U.S. dustbowl in the 1930s. With intensified soil degradation largely due to pollution, fertilizer over-use, water runoff, overgrazing, and salination from irrigation, as well as encroaching desertification in certain regions of the world and vast defor-estation in others to grow more crops to feed the hungry, we should pre-pare for times of privation. With the threat of limited phosphate-based fertilizers, which we are literally dependent upon to feed the globe, as well as the introduction of fungal pathogens infiltrating crops and live-stock, we could face famine-like starvation scenarios of epic proportion.[10]

Human activity spurring climate change has already set into motion irreversible changes in the Earth's hydrological cycle, and water contam-ination due to wholesale dumping of chemicals, pesticides, metals, fuels, waste products, industrial agents, and the like make water quality poison-ous and unusable, adversely affecting the environment and human health. With such dim predictions, food costs will soar, and so will revolts, crim-inality, and violence, such as those observed in the 2011 Algerian food riots. We can even imagine a future in which water will cost as much as beef. We should be prepared for such occurrences, for I can foresee worldwide chaos, uprisings, looting, murder, and social disorder that are

---

10. See Emmott (2013), pp. 130–131.

bound to result due to paucity of food and water. We may very soon live in an unpredictable crime-ridden world with some societies and nations in total disarray. We can already see an inkling of this happening with the migrant fiasco taxing the Mediterranean, Baltics, Europe, and Central America.

Given that the world population is slated to double since 1980 in just a few more decades, climate change will destabilize the world food supply. Regardless of the number of people the Earth can hold—its so-called carrying capacity, food and water abundance will shrink, prices will rise, diets will involuntarily change, and people will be forced to manage with much less than in today's hedonistic Western world of gluttony and "all-you-can-eat" buffets. Increased heat and lack of water will badly damage (if not destroy) produce and crops, disturb rainfall, leading to shorter growing seasons, especially in the tropics, and will hasten the rate at which crops optimally mature, thereby affecting their quality and value with real economic consequences to industry and consumers alike, all of which are essential to the integrity and security of food production. Here the relationship between water and food is indissoluble. It should surprise no one that those from more impoverished countries will simply starve to death.

THE WORST IS YET TO COME: PANDEMICS, ECONOMIC PARALYSIS, AND SOCIETAL COLLAPSE

All of this is to say, if we don't do something now, it will only get worse. And with ten billion people come other kinds of compounded risks. With more people come congested cities where everyone is crowded into quarters like rats, sanitation and hygiene problems, economic inequalities, social disparities, threats to personal security, increased crime, human health problems, and higher prevalence rates of aggression, robbery and assaults, home invasion, domestic violence, rape, child abuse, murder, and psychological disorders leading to more violence, addictions, mental breakdowns, hospitalizations, and incarcerations. Increased air travel heightens the risk of the spread of viruses, sicknesses, contagion, catastrophic diseases, and epidemics, such as the Spanish flu pandemic, which was estimated to have killed between fifty million and one hundred million people worldwide according to some speculations. We only need to be reminded of the potential for alarming global pandemics based on the recent outbreaks of COVID-19, SARS, swine flu, and Ebola taking place within the past 15 years.

World politics and daily affairs will likely become more mistrustful, vigilant, strained, unpredictable, and paranoiac. Runaway climate change will change global security; developed countries will become more like militarized police states with heavily defended borders against climate migrants seeking food, water, shelter, and medical attention due to decimated economies and lack of basic necessities. It is predictable that there will be an escalation in violence, civil turmoil, terror, war, and international military conflict over real or perceived threats to national self-interest and domineering grabs for capital, land, and resources where asylum seekers will be denied access to other countries due to limited reserves of food and water, fears of poaching, bringing disease, and attracting the criminal, immoral "evil" Other who will harm citizens, steal, rape, pillage, and kill. If organized terrorism and religious fundamentalism continue to create havoc over the world, more vulnerable nations will simply atrophy or implode. With lawless religious fanaticism come new holy wars backed by military invasion, wholesale slaughter of innocents, infrastructure collapse, complete destitution, spread of pestilence, and mass starvation where humanitarian aid would simply grind to a halt. Yemen is a good example. Citizens would be confined within the circumference of their communities and nation-states, left to the peril of whatever crises, victimization, or oppression that besiege them at any given moment. Mayhem and mass hysteria are just around the corner, perhaps even a third world war, which I predict. It is bound to happen sometime given the increasing geopolitical tensions among national superpowers and ethnocentric warfare that destabilizes world accord, peace relations, and regional stability.

I see no viable way of technologizing our way out of such a menacing mess: no amount of spin or salesmanship can take away the real danger to our future existence. We should be very leery of quick-fix remedies, platitudes, silver-tongued politicians, beguiling entrepreneurs, and technocrats who claim to offer concrete solutions, even if they are complex and time consuming, for any pitch at fixes belies a financial motive disguised as social altruism concealing a desire for profit behind propaganda reliefs. We need radical behavioral change on a supraordinate scale, and no one is willing to do that. Despite shifts in social consciousness and enthusiasm for green energies such as solar and wind, nuclear power, geoengineering, desalination, and renewables, this is not a planetary solution, for almost all these technologies require ongoing exploitation of our natural environments based on altering ecosystems and extracting metals through extensive mining. And even if we are forced to choose the lesser of two evils, humanity is not on board for a global synchronized effort to give up what we currently rely on for a futurized state of affairs based on speculative theory, even if it is scientifically sound or plausible.

Human nature doesn't work that way: very few people like radical change simply because it upsets the applecart. No one likes disruption in stability. This is why social collectives are so susceptible to the lure of ideology: as long as certain social fantasies are nurtured by an authoritarian force beyond their control, they are willing to believe it is the best thing for them. The unconscious mantra of humanity becomes, "Don't worry, we will take care of everything. We are too clever and intelligent. We will invent our way out of this mess!" This is not a sobering truth but, rather, an imaginary wish, and we must face it. What we wish to be the case and what truly are the facts can be an annoying inconvenient actuality. This is also why social collectives have fickle temperaments: when various fantasies are not fulfilled or sustained, dissent and insurgencies occur.

Let's face it: most people are stupid sheep in the meadow. The feeble lassitude that infiltrates uninquisitive society contributes to the problem. So do the politicians who become unpopular if they call to arms a change in the status quo, as they know they won't get reelected but, rather, deposed. Of course, any call to sacrifice the immediate for the future is met with a dismissive groan, because human beings want instant gratification without delay or nuisance. People vote for the here and now and want their needs met immediately, not in an abstract future. In Emmott's words, "the way governments justify this level of inaction is by exploiting public opinion and scientific uncertainty."[11] What this means is that personal gain, emotional prejudice, partisanship, and the desire to please others' desires are more important than what is right or beneficial to us all. The superficiality and narcissism of politicians is more than transparent when they freely select to ignore our ecological crisis under the rubric of dubiousness and epistemological fallibility, or even more egregiously, think they can pull the wool over our eyes by feigning sincerity or lying to the public.

Manipulating public opinion and uncertainty to justify self-interest is easy, despite the fact that living in denial is ultimately self-destructive. Who will give up economic advantage and political self-interest when one is profiting? It makes no logical sense financially to give up our dependence on fossil fuels, metallurgy, and the raw materials industry when we need these resources to drive economies and continue to prosper. The solar industry is a case in point: without mining for precious minerals, we would not have alternative renewables. And stakeholders and corporate executives with their million-dollar salaries and golden parachutes are hardly likely to change their worldviews, let alone their own livelihoods. Why would government and big business leave that money in the ground?

Jared Diamond calculates that there will be a continued collapse of societies based upon the historical observation of ecological decay, economic disparities, cultural clashes, and political hegemonies precipitating vast social declines that will eventually lead to a drastic decrease in the human population over a considerable expanse of our world civilizations for an extended period of time.[12] In his anthropological analysis of the degeneration and ruin of many ancient cultures, a clear pattern emerges: societies collapse due to their own negligence and failure at choosing viable, hence rational, alternatives. We are fascinated by the rise and decline of humanity in its historical contexts to the point that we romanticize the real and symbolic achievements of earlier civilizations. And we are unconsciously drawn to this for many psychological reasons, one of which is that we learn valuable lessons from not repeating the past.

---

11. Emmott (2013), p. 175.
12. See Diamond (2005), p. 3.

But we obviously have not paid attention. Previous societies have simply destroyed themselves because they did not attend to the environmental problems they created. Diamond refers to this unintended "ecocide" as neglect over respecting the environment and the natural resources upon which they depend.

> The processes through which past societies have undermined themselves by damaging their environments fall into eight categories, whose relative importance differs from case to case: deforestation and habitat destruction, soil problems (erosion, salinization, and soil fertility losses), water management problems, overhunting, overfishing, effects of introduced species on native species, human population growth, and increased per capita impact of people.[13]

What is relevant about Diamond's analyses is that many great ancient civilizations, such as the Greenland Norse, Polynesian (Easter, Pitcairn, and Henderson) Islanders, the Anasazi, Maya, and Vikings, as well as recent contemporary societies including Rwanda and Haiti collapsed due to unanticipated growth in population, need for increased food supply, and water required for farming and irrigation. Those circumstances, in turn, led to environmental destabilization, abandonment of lands, and unsustainable practices, not to mention societies fraught with famine, disease, wars, civil unrest, fighting among neighbors, internal corruption, ethnic hatred, and overthrows of elites by disgruntled masses. Diamond continues to admonish us:

> The environmental problems facing us today include the same eight that undermined past societies, plus four new ones: human-caused climate change, buildup of toxic chemicals in the environment, energy shortages, and full human utilization of the Earth's photosynthetic capacity . . . Much more likely than a doomsday scenario involving human extinction or an apocalyptic collapse of industrial civilization would be "just" a future of significantly lower living standards, chronically higher risks, and the undermining of what we now consider some

---

13. Diamond (2005), p. 6.

of our key values. Such a collapse could assume various forms, such as the worldwide spread of diseases or else of wars, triggered ultimately by scarcity of environmental resources. If this reasoning is correct, then our efforts today will determine the state of the world in which the current generation of children and young adults live out their middle and late years.[14]

Here, at the very least, we would be plummeted into a lower quality of life in terms of material standards, economic and social security, safety from physical threat, health risks and shorter life spans, and the deterioration of modernization as we know it—including loss of subjective happiness, value, and meaning, the very ingredients that make life worth living.

I am more pessimistic. I fear that we are broaching a point of no return in our pathognomonic tendencies to self-destruct. Although we all live a finite life, and the abstract future transcends our immediate existence, this seems to be precisely the point: humanity's psychological defense is to postpone futurity for the present. The future simply does not matter to the masses who consume and want more. The distant non-experiential future becomes a hypothetical thought experiment contrived by our imagination that has little to do with our current concerns and needs, especially from those who cannot afford to focus on anything else but the pressures of the here and now, let alone adopt an ethical stance toward the future of humanity as an altruistic ideal to live up to despite the fact that our current attitudes and behaviors substantially impact what the future will conceivably be like. Notwithstanding the threat of ecological disaster due to human cause, many more existential risks up the ante and accelerate the compounded crises we are currently facing as a human race. In addition to the looming environmental demise, including extreme weather events, natural catastrophes, biodiversity loss, ecosystem collapse, failure at climate change mitigation and adaptation, food and water shortage, pandemic outbreaks, chronic diseases, and mismanaged urbanization unprepared for the human population explosion, many more variables multiply, hence substantiate, our cause for alarm. Among these global dangers are systemic risks amplified by economic,

---

14. Diamond (2005), p. 7.

geopolitical, societal, technological, and existential factors that threaten to intensify our global crisis, which coalesce around many possible troubling scenarios including the following:

- Problems of evil, aggression, illegality, corruption, fraud, illicit trade, organized crime, terrorism, religious extremism, public health and safety ineptitude, profound social instability, migrant invasions, mass diasporas, deployment of weapons of mass destruction, and war;

- Global governance failures, governmental collapses of geopolitical importance including interstate conflict leading to regional consequences, international diplomacy failures, and escalation in conflicts among international superpowers;

- Fiscal and liquidity crises in key economies; major financial institution breakdown, mismanagement, and lack of oversight by central banks; failure of critical infrastructure; fossil fuel shocks to the global economy; chronically high unemployment; stock market flux and panic; housing inflation; financial lending irresponsibility; decline of the U.S. dollar as the world's leading currency; severe income disparity; and financial exploitation by elites and wealthy capitalist corporations;

- Breakdown in critical information infrastructure, communication networks, cyber hacking, technological data theft, internet espionage, and generative AI; and last but not least,

- Economic hardship on families; unemployment; increased health-related illnesses; thereby more loss of jobs and income; disruptions in maternal-infant attachment; systemic familial pathology; transgenerational transmission of trauma, addictions, domestic abuse, and resultant psychological disorders and mental illness that maim the masses.

Here we have a very grave problem indeed.

3

The Evil That Men Do

EINSTEIN APPROACHED FREUD ON BEHALF OF THE LEAGUE OF NATIONS
and asked the question, "Is there any way of delivering mankind from the
curse of war?"[1] Freud responded with reservation, suggesting that perhaps
it may only be mitigated. This is the general tenor of his anthropological
treatment of humanity: until base instinct (*Trieb*) is sufficiently harnessed and transformed in the service of reason, our world communities
will continue to be plagued by the dark marauders of our own insidious
nature. Why war?—because hate and violence are "a piece of unconquer-
able nature . . . a piece of our own psychical constitution."[2] With this
dismal portrait of human relations, we may never come to throw our
hatred down.

People are slaughtering one another all over the world in the name
of religion, ethnic purity, and nationalism under the guise of freedom,
justice, ethical duty, and social reform. Within the past few decades
alone, contemporary ethnopolitical warfare has raged throughout the
strife-torn territories of the Middle East, Africa, Eastern Europe, South
and East Asia, Central and South America, Russia, and the Ukraine
where civilian populations are the primary targets of terror—marked by
sadism and butchery, while women and children comprise a large percentage of the incurred human rights atrocities. Those close to the front
lines of ethnic and religious conflicts are oppressed by political violence,

---

1. Letter to Freud, July 30, 1932, "Why War?" [see Einstein–Freud Correspondence], *Standard
Edition*, p. 199.
2. Freud (1930), p. 86.

from refugees who have lost their families in ethnic cleansing campaigns or terrorist persecutions, to civilians who must dodge sniper fire every day to run to the market to fetch a loaf of bread. When the constancy of violence, horror, and war continues to saturate our daily consciousness, we can only anticipate where it will emerge next.

To what degree will our disparate cultures be able to rise above this mode of existence, where violence becomes the right of a community, either chosen or impugned? This is further compounded by the historical fact that brutality was the driving force behind the emergence of law, which still requires the use of violence to be enforced. Can actual force be replaced by the force of ideas, or are we condemned to the perversions of pathos? Given Freud's ontological treatise on the structure of the psyche, "there is no use in trying to get rid of men's aggressive inclinations,"[3] they are as natural as breathing; for we can never escape from the fact that our minds are primitive. *Homo homini lupus est*—"Man is a wolf to man."[4]

The history of the human race is forged on traumatization, resentment, and the need for revenge, which preoccupies collective human consciousness and fuels pathological enactments. Aggression and violence directed toward others is part of human nature, an insidious derivative of our pathos. For the Greeks, to be human is to suffer, to be susceptible to pain (*pathētos*), to endure illness, in short, our accruing pathology. Our pathos may even become fused with desire, as in "antipathy," a passion (*patheia*) against (*anti*) another. Mental illness stems from this basic constituency of mind. This is why Freud observed that we are all "neurotic"[5]—that is, ill, whereby the human aspect is saturated with anxiety, suffering, and despair. It's just a matter degree. We are all deeply affected by our pathos to the point that what truly differentiates individuals and societies from one another is our level of functionality and adaptation to psychic pain. In other words, human pathology is normative throughout

---

3. Freud's reply to Einstein (1932), p. 211.
4. Derived from Plautus, *Asinaria* II, pp. iv, 88; see Freud (1930), p. 111.
5. Freud (1916–1917), p. 358.

all cultures and all times. Being "normal" is merely another word for pathos.[6]

Psychopathology (πάθος) is the essence of man,[7] and it is from this standpoint that all else shall be measured. Desire precedes and supersedes reason, for primitive forces govern the psyche; they are arguably responsible as well for the exalted achievements of reason itself. Irrationality—pathos—is our primordial being, and it is from this ontological ground

---

6. I realize that the antipode between normativity and pathology poses numerous definitional and epistemological problems, as does my attempt to obviate the issue by collapsing their differences into a universal category that would apply to all human beings. This is equally difficult when speculating on a collective psychopathology because we lack a clear referent or criteria on what exactly constitutes health and illness to begin with, which is likely to shift based on different cultural norms and social practices. I do not wish here to engage this complex issue, which deserves serious attention in another forum. I only ask the reader to entertain the notion that although we may not agree about the hermeneutics, scope, and breadth of the phenomenology of pathology inherent in individual and collective social life, let alone the issue of the type or form and the degree of their instantiations, I wish to stay focused on the psychoanalytic premise that internal conflict is intrinsic to the human psyche and social relations, which manifests itself in both individuals and groups. A return to the ancient notion of pathos helps us locate a common shared, lived experience where anxiety, despair, and emotional anguish are acknowledged as a universal ontological dimension to the development of civilization and humanity. It is within the confines of this context that I wish to situate my arguments. Here the question does not become whether there is a core of health in our subjective or collective strivings that stands in relation to our pathologies, only that any discussion of such pockets of health or flourishing is to be situated within the psychological predicament of our throwness as being in relation to pathos.

7. Within this context, I specifically use the masculine gender to emphasize the notion that men are usually deemed to be the chief instruments of power, aggression, and institutional violence; they have historically and primarily inflicted suffering on others more than women have. Here I do not wish to assign principal responsibility for collective prejudice and aggression to only one sex or gender, only to highlight the particularly identified phenomena of male dominance. However, an equally plausible case can be made for how women, the first and original love objects for both sexes (see Freud, 1940, p. 188), and usually the crucial attachment figure that dominates the early child-rearing scene, can easily foist their personalities and will on their children, sometimes quite insidiously, to the degree that either gendered child is equally and potentially exposed to such power differentials. The cycle of relatedness from parents of both genders, further fortified within various familial and cultural practices, ensures that pathological accommodations and manifestations, which arise within everyone, have overdetermined sources. Just as females who are born within an oppressive patriarchy inevitably suffer in various ways, whether directly or indirectly, so do males who receive an austere maternal factor during their upbringing due to cyclical patterns of real or perceived modes of relatedness from parental authority. These patterns may, of course, become entrenched within personality structure and form the basis for a transgenerational transmission of developmental trauma that have cultural specificity leading to further repetitions and pathological enactments. What is essential, hence necessary, and non-accidental, is that the human species has an intimate relation to pathos that inevitably saturates our being.

that all else materializes and makes itself known through various forms of human enactments. Reason always remains a tool, if not a slave, of desire.

Throughout this chapter, I will endeavor to introduce a speculative account of the future of humanity based on a discernible pattern of violence and exploitation of the Other that characterizes human motivation and deed. I must confess that I can hardly do justice to this topic in the limited scope of this project, which would take volumes to address. At best I hope to frame the issue and the inherent problematics it poses, and certainly not pretend to offer any viable solutions, for I am unable to resolve the dilemma. Instead, I shall be concerned with a narrow scope of questions that investigate whether our pathological propensities as a human race will likely bring about our extinction, or whether we can transmogrify our destructive impulses through the relational negotiation of collective valuation practices that transcend our more primal constitutions. I hope the reader will forgive me for raising more conundrums rather than furnishing practical answers. Will the fate of civilization succumb to sordid desire inspiring our demise, or will human accord triumph in the end? The real issue involves to what degree will the will toward violence be sublimated into the higher tiers of self-conscious ethical reflection that reason can afford?[8] We are a world divided by race, religion, ethnicity, economics, politics, and culture, where strong emotional bonds fuel and sustain separation and difference among our communities. I do not wish to express platitudes, illusory ideals, or provide false hope—the evidence, the brute facticity of impoverishment, suffering, cruelty, and murder points to the most archaic configurations of psychic development that permeate our valuation practices.

Within today's multicultural world community, differences and prejudices continue to divide and polarize human relations into firm

---

8. Here I agree with Hegel's (1807) architectonic dialectical trajectory that reason is a developmental achievement borne of conflict and negation, the poignant striving for self-consciousness. Ethical reflection becomes a necessary part of the sublation (*Aufhebung*) of reason even though it resonates within the feeling soul (*Seele*) and comprises our most basal desires and strivings, which Hegel (1830) nicely enumerates in the Anthropology section of his *Philosophie des Geistes*, part 3 of the *Encyclopaedia of the Philosophical Sciences*. In other words, we do not have a clean bifurcation between desire, reason, and ethical self-consciousness, for they are subsumed within the synthetic strands of the dialectic as a complex holism.

oppositions that become fortified within rigid group identifications that inform collectively shared value systems. What I mean by "prejudice" is that human beings are inclined toward the preferential self-expression of valuation based on self-interest and self-valuation, whether explicit, implicit, or based in unconscious bias. Ethnic, religious, cultural, and national identities are forged through prejudicial valuation practices, in some cases even legitimate heinous forms of injustice such as genocide, terrorism, human enslavement, and child trafficking, just to name a few. When collective identity is so firmly established in bipolar relation to the Other, is it possible for such valuation practices to abate under the rubric of peace? Prejudice, hate, and violence are no more likely to disappear than the reality of the external world; therefore, the question becomes one of amelioration.

THE NEED TO KILL

Freud tells us of two competing forces in human nature: the will toward life and the will toward death manifested as Eros or libido (*Lust*), the sexual force responsible for erotic life, and its antithetical companion conceived under the drive toward destruction.[9] This dual class of innate psychic energies comprise those that seek to preserve and unite and those that seek to kill and destroy, both giving rise to what may be equiprimordially characterized as our caring and aggressive propensities. "Neither of these drives are any less essential than the other; the phenomena of life arise from the concurrent or mutually opposing action of both."[10] Further, they scarcely operate in isolation, both borrowing from the resources of

---

9. See Freud (1923), ch. 4, for an introduction to his mature theory, yet Freud's (1915) pivotal work on the drives (*Triebe*) continues to be a source of misunderstanding among English-speaking audiences more than a century after it appeared in print. Customarily translated as "instinct," this is not only a mistranslation, but it also inaccurately implies a set of propositions that Freud neither intended to convey nor espoused—namely, that the human psyche, which Freud referred to as the soul (*Seele*), was composed of behaviorally hard-wired, physiologically determined instincts that formed the edifice for human motivation and action. *Instinkt* was a word Freud rarely used in the context of the human subject; rather, he reserved it for animal species, loathing it for its simple equation to material reduction. This is precisely why he deliberately chose the word *Trieb*—more appropriately translated as drive, pulsion, impulse, impetus, or urge—to characterize human motivation. See my book *Underworlds* (Mills, 2014) for a thorough discussion of Freud's unconscious ontology.
10. Freud's (1932) letter to Einstein, "Why War?," p. 209.

the other as an accompanied or alloyed counterpart, drawing a certain quota from the other side, which in turn modifies its aim or is even used to achieve its aim.

This union between life and death is the ontological fabric of the human condition to which all other dialectical polarities arise, including the universality of Love and Hate. Self-preservation is clearly an erotic (evolutionary) impulse, but it must have aggression at its disposal to accomplish its task; just as in love, the aggressive drive is used to gain mastery and possession over an object which the attachment to it brings about. Although self-preservative currents stand in stark opposition to destructive ones, the two are dialectical complementarities that reflect their confluence.[11]

The primary significance of destruction is never so forceful as in Freud's postulation of the death drive (*Todestrieb*),[12] the foundation that

---

11. Here we have a similar structural dynamic of the Hegelian dialectic with negativity begetting progression in the service of achieving higher aims. Just as Being is in opposition to Nothing, so is life and death, two sides of a symmetrical relation, their necessary complementarity within a structural unity.

12. Freud's technical use of *Trieb* (drive, not instinct) is distinguished from the ordinary usage, which describes a craving, itch, or yearning, such as a whim or a caprice. For Freud, *Trieb* is the *driving force* behind the mind compelled and fueled by unconscious desire. Here the principle of destruction plays a central role in the psyche and society. Death-work for Freud (1933) was ultimately in the service of restoring or reinstating a previous state of undifferentiated internal being, a drive "which sought to do away with life once more and to re-establish [an] inorganic state" (p. 107). Freud did not argue that death was the only aim of life, only that it maintained a dialectical tension in juxtaposition to a life principle under the ancient command of Eros, yet the two forces of the mind remained ontologically inseparable. The force of the negative is so prevalent in human affairs that it is perplexing why the death drive would remain a questionable tenet today. From a phenomenological standpoint, it is impossible to negate the force and salience of the negative. The evening newscasts are about nothing but death, destruction, chaos, conflict, tragedy, and human agony. Even advocates who champion a pure trauma model of self-destruction or externalized negativity in the service of explaining human aggressivity must contend with inherently destructive organizing elements that imperil the organism from within. Even medical science is perplexed by the internally derived forces (e.g., cancer, AIDS, ALS) that drain the healthy organism of life due to attacks perpetrated by its own immune system or endogenous constitution. Consider the paradoxical processes that result in sleep being both regressive and restorative and, particularly, how going to sleep is associated with wanting to return to a previously aborted state of peace, tranquility, or oceanic "quiescence"—perhaps a wish for a tensionless state, perhaps a return to the womb. Excessive sleep is also one of the most salient symptoms of clinical depression and the will toward death. Further, it would be inconceivable to argue that humankind's externalized aggression is not inherently self-destructive for the simple fact that it generates more retaliatory hate, aggression, and mayhem, which threaten world accord and the progression of civil societies. Given the global ubiquity of war, genocide, geopolitical atrocities,

governs psychic development in which "*the aim of all life is death.*"[13] The death drive is responsible for the will toward murder: it becomes the projection of our inner need to destroy. Freud is clear in telling us that death and its derivatives or representatives, such as aggression and destruction, as well as Eros and its manifestations of libido or the life-enhancing processes that promote self-preservation and social advance, are "struggling with each other from the very first."[14] Harnessing and diverting the internal powers of death, the destructive principle must be deflected outward, which serves the libidinal progression or life-enhancing prowess of the psyche in its ascendance toward self-development.[15] The energetic or libidinal impulses thus become defined and refined in opposition to competing forces that seek to bring about their demise or premature decay. Here the life force is at odds with its destructive antithesis, both conjoined in conflict, yet punctuated by oscillating moments of self-manifestation. Freud could not bifurcate Eros from Thanatos, despite their dual forms of appearance, because he observed that each always interpenetrates the other; hence they are not ontologically separated. As for Hegel, death becomes the foundation of life.

Negation and lack are always the base agitation of any organism—a primal disturbance that stimulates life—the purpose of which is to return

---

and the despoliation of our planet, in all likelihood we as a human race will die by actions brought about by our own hands rather than by the impersonal forces of nature.

13. Freud (1920), p. 38.

14. Freud (1920), p. 61, 2n1.

15. But what is to become of death if life supersedes it? What Freud concludes particularly highlights his genius, for death is ultimately in the service of the pleasure principle. This is a very delicate theoretical move and is only successful when you observe the logic of the dialectic as the confluence of mutually implicative oppositions that share a common unity. Following the laws of psychic economy, the pleasure principle is a tendency to free the psyche of excitation, or at least to minimize stimulation levels so that there is a tolerable degree of constancy. The ultimate condition of pleasure would, therefore, be a state that is free of tension: through this end, cessation of tension would represent its fulfillment, hence its completion. From this impersonal account of unconscious teleology, what could be more pleasurable than death, than nonbeing? Death is a tensionless state, unadulterated peace. But Freud's teleology is not strictly Aristotelian: although the unconscious mind aims toward death, it has the capacity to choose its own path toward self-destruction. It is only under this condition of determinate freedom that the psyche can bring about its own end, which makes death-work inherent in the life-enhancing processes that repudiate the will toward self-destruction while embracing it. Here we may observe two opposing forces operative within the single purpose of the pleasure principle: death and life are ontologically conjoined yet differentiated from one another. It is here that Freud's dual classification of the drives is solidified.

to the original lost unity of its symbiotic state,[16] a state that is tensionless, what we heuristically call peace, but only achieved through circuitous paths.[17] It is precisely through this "tarrying with the negative"[18] that leads to constructive advances in human relations and culture. Through progressive dialectical mediation and sublation (*Aufhebung*),[19] mind achieves higher levels of unification as rational and ethical agency until it arrives at a fuller integration of itself as a complex species, incorporating and transmuting more archaic dispositions within its mature process of self-reflection and becoming.[20] This equally extends to society and world-hood as a whole. The need for social order, unification, and harmony are motivational factors that inform the ideal of global tranquility, which human violence, hate, evil, terrorism, and war threaten to deteriorate, an ideal imbued with the residue of early symbiotic conditions.

----

16. The notion of original unity may be instructive for our understanding of a principle of world harmony devoid of the more pathological instantiations of human aggression because, for both Freud
and Hegel, ethical consciousness emerges from an undifferentiated unconscious unity within its
primordial beginnings that become more differentiated and sophisticated throughout its psychosocial development. Just as Freud (1920, pp. 36–39) speculates on how the organic arises from the
inorganic, as the general object of anthropology, Hegel (1830, §§ 388–403) traces the dialectical
emergence of the feeling soul from the abyss of its indeterminations; at first unseparated from its
immediate universal simplicity, it then divides and rouses itself from its mere inward implicitness
to explicit determinate being-for-self. This process is also the logical model Hegel (1812) follows
from his *Logic* in his anthropological description of the soul, where a universal determines itself into
particulars, showing how each mediation forms a new immediate, which is the general thrust of the
dialectic. In other words, the odyssey of human freedom is conditioned on earlier unconscious events
it must transcend by becoming self-consciously aware of its own nature.
17. Freud (1920), p. 39.
18. Hegel (1807), § 32.
19. The unrest of *Aufhebung* is a progressive unfolding of canceling, preserving, transmuting, and
elevating opposition within its internal structure. Here opposition is raised to a higher unity. As I
have shown elsewhere (see Mills, 2002, pp. 11–13, 194–196), sublation has a threefold meaning: (1)
to suspend or cancel, (2) to surpass or transcend, and (3) to preserve. In *The Encyclopaedia Logic*, Hegel
(1817) makes this clear: "On the one hand, we understand it to mean 'clear away' or 'cancel,' and in
that sense we say that a law or regulation is canceled (*aufgehoben*). But the word also means 'to preserve'" (§ 96, *Zusatz*). Hegel's designation introduces a threefold activity by which mental operations
at once cancel or annul opposition, preserve or retain it, and surpass or elevate its previous shape to
a higher structure. This process of the dialectic underlies all operations of the mind and is seen as
the thrust behind world history and culture. The dialectic is the essence of psychic life and objective
social reality, for if it were to be removed, consciousness and unconscious processes would disappear.
20. For Hegel, mind begins, like ego development for Freud, as an original undifferentiated unity
that emerges from its immediate self-enclosed unconscious universality to its mediated determinate
singularity as a subject. This is initiated through a dialectical process of internal division, self-ex-
ternalization, and introjection as the reincorporation of its projected qualities back into its interior.

The emerging self, ego (*Ich*), or subjectivity ensnared in the stage of primary narcissism,[21] like spirit or mind (*Geist*) asleep in the undifferentiated abyss of its self-absorption,[22] constitutes the psychological and ontological precursors for differentiation and development.[23] To what degree do these conditions play in our wish for higher degrees of unity, concord, and moral self-realization? Are we to understand a collective world psyche as "the universal brotherhood of man"[24] that seeks general unity and harmony, or is this merely a wish to return to the "oceanic feeling"[25] of symbiosis like a fetus in the peaceful sea of its mother's womb? To what degree is this an illusion that preoccupies so many minds, like the parallel wish for union with God, the exalted father who shall make our home safe and free from our helplessness and pain?[26] But whether or not these are fantasies, they represent moral ideals: "Thou shalt not take the name of the Lord thy God in vain!"[27]—don't you dare assault my desire!

One would be hard-pressed to find someone who would not value the ideal of peace, with communal solidarity, accord, and moral cooperation marshaled in the service of social progression. But the very nature of the

---

21. Freud (1914), p. 100.

22. Hegel (1978) § 408, *Zusätz*, 2.

23. For both Hegel and Freud, the inchoate ego is originally encased in a unity and is, therefore, modally undifferentiated from external forces—the inner and outer are fused in a symbiotic organization. Freud (1930) informs us that "originally the ego includes everything, later it separates off an external world from itself. Our present ego-feeling is, therefore, only a shrunken residue of a much more inclusive—indeed, an all embracing—feeling which corresponded to a more intimate bond between the ego and the world about it" (p. 68). For Hegel (1978), the natural soul moves from an undifferentiated unity to a differentiated determinate being; so, too, for Freud, ego boundaries gradually become more contrasted, constructed, and consolidated throughout their burgeoning activity. Freud notes that originally an infant is unable to distinguish between its own ego and the external world as the source of stimulation and sensation. But eventually the organism comes to discern its own internal sources of excitation, such as its bodily organs or somatic processes, from external sources of sensation, (e.g., mother's touch, breast, etc.), that become set apart and integrated within ego organization. It is not until this stage in ego formation that an object is set over against the ego as an existent entity that is outside of itself. Once the ego moves from primary to secondary narcissism, attachment to external cathected (love) objects form the initial dynamics of object-relations and character development.

24. H. S. Harris (1983), p. 411.

25. See Freud (1930) on the "oceanic feeling" in relation to religious sentiment and early ego development, pp. 64–68.

26. See Freud (1927); cf. Mills (2017).

27. See Freud's (1930) discussion, p. 74.

need for progressive unification through value inquiry is also dialectically opposed to destructive and regressive inclinations that derive from earlier primitive aspects of our psychic constitution we seek to act out or recover during conflict precipitated by opposition. If the desire for integration and unison are derived from our original psychic ontology, then both progressive and regressive desires may be said to emanate from the same mental (symbiotic) configurations, which may further possibly serve the same aim. Both seek unity or peace of a different kind and in a different form: one through the attainment of higher incorporated complexities, the other a wish to return to the warm blanket of its initial undifferentiated beginning—unity is nevertheless their goal. Here *unity* should be understood within the symbolic context of psychological integration, where strong affective bonds for concord, union, and amalgamation are achieved and experienced internally as a transcendental ideal. Following Hegel, this would require some integrative, synthetic function that would attempt to bind or resolve opposition; or for Freud, serve the pleasure principle through sublimation. But if the drive toward destruction is responsible for both progress and regress, growth and decay, then how are we to determine which one will advance and which one will succumb to the tyranny of the other? This brings into question how the nature of negativity and destruction influences the self-preservative forces in their quest for integration and mastery.

Collective identity is based on the strength and intensity of emotional ties among its members and the mutual identification with shared valuation practices, thus giving rise to diversity, opposition, and prejudicial division among individuals, cohorts, cultures, societies, and nations.[28] The greater discrepancies such as race, religion, ethnicity, lan-

---

28. It may be argued that identity is largely the result of the identification process itself, which is influenced by myriad causal and overdetermined factors that are encountered throughout our life experiences and internalized within personality formation. Along with drives, affects, and their transformations, the nature of identification accounts for much of the intrapsychic motivations, intentions, desires, and conflicts that comprise psychical and social reality. Identity, whether personal or collective, is ultimately in the service of narcissism or self-interest, thereby affecting the ideals we espouse and the valuation practices we choose to identify with over others. Despite the overdetermination of identification, the values and mores individuals and societies adopt are fundamentally the result of the complexities of narcissistic object choice—that is, the idiosyncratic objects of desire, the psychosocial functions they serve, and the evolutionary demands of the self-preservative drives.

guage, culture, nationality, and political affiliation that bring about more pronounced forms of prejudice and contempt are not surprising. The increased enthusiasm in nationalism, populism, religious identity, inter-group identification, and separatism among our diverse peoples points toward the need to define ourselves in opposition to difference, rallying greater collective fellowship among its identified members and thereby strengthening the cultural narcissism that holds societies together—all in the service of the self-preservative forces that align with similarity and social identification.[29] In *Group Psychology and the Analysis of the Ego*, Freud underscores the universality of prejudice:

> Every time two families become connected by marriage, each of them thinks itself superior to or of better birth than the other. Of two neigh-bouring towns each is the other's most jealous rival; every little canton looks down upon the others with contempt. Closely related races keep one another at arm's length; the South German cannot endure the North German, the Englishman casts every kind of aspersion upon the Scot, the Spaniard despises the Portuguese. We are no longer astonished that greater differences should lead to an almost insuperable repugnance, such as the gallic people for the German, the Aryan for the Semite, and the white races for the coloured.[30]

This is a profound observation that equally applies today: regardless of our era of diversity, multiculturalism, tolerance for difference, interethnic, interfaith, interracial, and social pluralism, a suprasignifier of judgment is always unconsciously operative based on the identification of similarity and difference that infiltrates every form of prejudice and ideology. There is such a narcissism of even minor differences between individuals and cultures that the very sound of rap music blaring from an open car win-dow could lead one so judgmentally inclined to conclude that the true meaning of "culture" is to be found growing in the bottom of a petri dish.

---

29. This is not intended to be an ontologically reductive claim, only that consciousness and the complexifications of identity and culture are predicated on embodied biological forces that condition or influence the way in which identity, personality formation, and collective thought and behavior are expressed.
30. Freud (1921), p. 101.

We are further informed by scientists that we now have the empirical means by which to measure the degree and intensity of our disgust for minor differences by observing the pupil size of an individual. It is a universal biological fact that regardless of light differences, our pupils dilate when we like something and become pinpricks when we perceive something to be a repellent.[31] It is comforting to know that when uncertain about whether someone is friend or foe, all you have to do is look at the center of their iris to determine if it is the size of a pinhead.

The nature of identification has its origins in early self-development and socialization whereby the child takes its parents as ambivalent *and* ideal objects who, along with their value systems, become internalized within personality formation and effect the germination of moral conscience as well as the capacities for love and hate.[32] Whether personal or collective, identity is defined in opposition to difference and identification with similarity. But we also realize that identification is overdetermined, multiply instantiated, and based on a plurality of forces and indecisive attitudes that inform how the objects, content, form, valence, qualia, and intensity of identifications are constituted. This structural dynamic alone may be said to account for the need for division, uniqueness, and prejudicial self-preferences as opposed to others who stand in marked difference, but it also potentially explains the dialectical complementarities at play on other unconscious levels. Nevertheless, the confluence of destructive and self-preservative forces compounds the nature of identifications and social relations where desire justifies murder and reason is manipulated to assuage primal instinctual urges in the service of narcissistic pursuits.

Such countless examples of the polarization of values and ideals stand in opposition to others that you could spend the rest of your life trying to catalog them all. In many cases of group prejudice, valuation practices assume a form of collective identification based on a simple rigid economy. Intolerance to difference that precipitates extreme forms of violence may be said to represent a regression to our most primitive constitutions when bad (self)objects are regurgitated from the mouth as

---

31. See Morris (1998).
32. See Freud (1921), ch. 7.

poisonous projections of evil and hatred that must be annihilated.[33] In many cases, extreme prejudice is the product of pathological narcissism. Patriarchal value placed on male children over female children has historically led to infanticide that is still practiced today in parts of China, India, Africa, and the Middle East. Since the Taliban took power of the government of Afghanistan, women have had to wear burqas; and have been beaten and stoned to death in public for not having the proper attire or wearing a hijab, even if this simply means not having their mesh cover the front of their eyes. The murder of Mahsa Amini in Iran while in custody of the so-called morality police, which sparked riots and uprising against the government, is a recent example of how women are treated like meat. After James Byrd Jr. was dragged from his feet down a rural road by a chain secured to the back of a pickup truck until his right arm and head were literally torn from his torso just because he was black, the devastated town of Jaspers, Texas, was greeted three weeks later by a Ku Klux Klan rally. Genocide continues to rip through our world claiming innocent lives, from the Hutus' massacre of the Tutsis in Rwanda to the Serbs mass extermination of Bosnian Muslims, to the systematic slaughter in Kosovo, not to mention the recent plethora of killings initiated by the Arab Spring culminating in the Syrian tragedy, which are still reigning in psychopathic Islamdom. Although these are extreme cases, one need not look further than one's own country to confirm the ethnic, populist, and patriotic narcissism that envelops us all.

Both Hegel and Freud stress the importance that civilization is a process. But the aforementioned events hardly resemble the mores of a civilized culture as irrational fanaticism justifies barbarity approaching the brink of insanity. The primitive economy of rigid identification that justifies these extreme forms of savagery has at its disposal all the unbridled resources of the death drive turned outward. The drive toward death is transformed into a destructive channel when it is projected onto external objects. In this way, self-preservation is maintained by destroying extraneous threats as objects of hate are rendered impotent. "Hate, as a relation to objects, is older than love. It derives from the narcissistic

---

33. This is what Klein refers to as the paranoid-schizoid position (see Klein, 1946, pp. 99–110).

ego's primordial repudiation of the external world with its outpouring of stimuli. As an expression of the reaction of unpleasure evoked by objects, it always remains in an intimate relation with the self-preservative drives."[34] Yet self-preservation versus pleasure induced in killing are two different inflections of narcissism. Sadism, the derivative of hate, is nowhere so evident as with the deranged techniques conceived and used to torture, maim, and murder millions of victims in the Holocaust, and in the killing fields under the Khmer Rouge government, as well as in the death camps that Bosnian Serbs manufactured in the name of ethnic cleansing.

The Bosnian concentration camps were one of the most horrific human slaughterhouses, because the means of extermination were laborious and perverted, the aim of which was to produce the most excruciating amount of pain, mental anguish, and suffering possible.[35] Although it is illegitimate to make comparisons, the killing at Auschwitz-Birkenau was largely mechanized and bureaucratic, whereas the genocide at Omarska was emotional and personal, mainly depending upon the simple and intimate act of beating. These techniques were inefficient, time-consuming, and physically exhausting, yet they were habitually and systematically employed to intentionally demoralize and demolish, bringing warped pleasure to the guards and paramilitary units who, through their innovative means at devising methods of torture, could greatly bolster their prestige. The use of rape warfare on women—especially adolescents and children—is another such example of the chilling psychological and sociological rationale for the deliberate and systematic means of deteriorating the opposition from within their own support systems by depleting their morale, ego defenses, and will.[36] Here we can see how reason is distorted under the dictatorship of psychopathic narcissism. It is in moments such as these that one can hear the voice of Luther—*die*

---

34. Freud (1915), p. 139.
35. See Danner (1997), pp. 55–56.
36. Cf. Allen (1996).

Hure Vernunft—"reason is the whore of humanity."[37] We can rationalize away anything, even our morality.

Is the death drive so intent on persecuting humankind that it will eventually bring us to ruin? The bleak forecast of the continual historical reign of terror by sick minds in positions of power and privilege may lead us rightly to conclude that "men are not gentle creatures who want to be loved";[38] rather they want to exploit, con, use, conquer, humiliate, torture, and kill. In *Civilization and Its Discontents*, Freud writes:

> The fateful question for the human species seems to me to be whether and to what extent their cultural development will succeed in mastering the disturbance of their communal life by the human drive of aggression and self-destruction . . . Men have gained control over the forces of nature to such an extent that with their help they would have no difficulty in exterminating one another to the last man. They know this, and hence comes a large part of their current unrest, their unhappiness and their mood of anxiety.[39]

It may be argued that religion and ethnicity—including race—are the main reasons for divided group identifications, although this mulishly includes language as a culturally infused variable, and these factors are inseparable from certain belief systems and valuation practices. Together, ethnicity, religion, and linguistic practices form the social value structures that become the macrocosm of any culture, which further acquire personal and collective meaning that validates nations and keeps them together even when they are heterogeneous. Ethnic and religious identification is so strong that even between closely related ethnic and religious groups, rigid group identifications, one-sidedness, and polarization keep

---

37. This quotation is attributed to Martin Luther by E. M. Cioran (1998) in *The Temptation to Exist*. Also see "The Last Sermon in Wittenberg, 1546" (Luther, 1546): "And what I say about the sin of lust, which everybody understands, applies also to reason; for the reason mocks and affronts God in spiritual things and has in it more hideous harlotry than any harlot. Here we have an idolater running after an idol, as the prophets say, under every green tree [cf. Jer. 2:20; I Kings 14:23], as a whorechaser runs after a harlot. That's why the Scriptures call idolatry whoredom, while reason calls it wisdom and holiness . . . Such wisdom of reason the prophets call whoredom" (pp. 374–375).
38. Freud (1930), p. 111.
39. Freud (1930), p. 145.

societies from embracing shared qualities simply because of minute differences that threaten cultural narcissism. When dispute over land continues to flare throughout Eastern Europe, the Middle East, and North Africa, ethnicity, religion, and nationalism become more demarcated with group identifications more virulently opposed.

The stronger the intensity of emotional bonds between people develop, the stronger identifications become. Group identity fosters unity and progression, but it may also lead to discord and regression—the dynamic that fuels both peace and war. In my opinion, group identifications are responsible for the process and advance of civilization as collective value systems govern the ideals of a community. As a rule, any movement that encourages greater emotional attachment to others strongly militates against the loom of destruction, for empathy, compassion, and love are engendered ideals and the heart of conscience. When people are governed by empathy and conscience, reason is marshaled in service of justice and the pursuit of the ethical. This, too, requires an inversion of aggression that becomes the internal judge of conscience, where shame and guilt equally inform our moral choices, as does reason.

Take, for example, two different cultural responses to involvement in World War II. Germany experiences a great deal of universal shame for its infamous role in history that fractured world order, yet Germans still acknowledge and remember their history, teach it in the classroom, and maintain public museums, camps, and monuments to memorialize their deeds, whereas the Japanese still live in collective denial of their involvement in the war. The official government policy does not recognize its historical atrocities or past war crimes, which are omitted from textbooks and prohibited from being taught in public schools. Here we have two responses to collective shame: acknowledgment with the educational concern that history should not repeat itself, and denial in the name of "saving face." We shall not deviate far in saying that one is a healthy response of remorse to guilt and shame, whereas the other is an infantile attempt to maintain a cultural narcissism based in state ideology where the superiority of the Japanese race is inculcated in schoolchildren every day and institutionally solidified by national identity.

I use these previous examples arbitrarily as merely illustrative of specific instantiations of collective identification, yet they occur everywhere. Regardless of which examples we focus on, which always runs the danger of introducing ancillary distractions, whether they be distantly historical or more contemporary in world attention, the phenomena of collective identification equally apply to any culture or society throughout time. Although particularity is culturally relative and contingent upon the interaction between group relations and the social environs that inform collective identity, it also transpires within a greater universal process governing object relations or, in ordinary language, our relatedness to others. Here it is important to stay focused on the universal rather than the specific, for the more crucial locus of our inquiry concerns human nature itself, namely, that which is common to us all.

THE ONTOLOGY OF PREJUDICE

The polarity of human desire, the nature of personal and collective identifications, and the combative forces of social and cultural oppositions all operate within anthropologically systemic, socio-symbolic ontological structures that give rise to civilization and the historical manifestations of pathology. For the sake of parsimony, let us simply refer to this as a dialectical process of mutual opposition that is simultaneously operative and implicative at any given moment within civilization. Civilization, even more so than nature itself, is responsible for most of our malaise; but it is also responsible for our remarkable advances in education, technology, science, medicine, human rights, aesthetics, and moral conscientiousness that enhance the quality of human life, social progress that has, for the most part, occurred in our lifetime. But along with these advances have also come the technology to extinguish the entire human race, either by intentional design, human errors, computer malfunctioning, superintelligence AI, or by accident. This is especially disturbing when fanatical and paranoid minds have means and access to weapons of mass destruction. This places us in the precarious position of attempting to anticipate the possible fate of humanity, for the predictive validity of the progression of civilization hinges on whether aggression and violence will be restricted, displaced, inverted, and/or sublimated for higher rational, ethical, and aesthetic-spiritual pursuits.

Although Steven Pinker has made a valid point (despite virulent criticism) that violence has declined on a mass scale from earlier times in human history,[40] he seems to gloss over the fact that this does not mitigate the existential risks of probable future aggressive actions by religious fanatics, despots, nation-states, group collectives, fringe extremists, lone wolves, or machines that could be more catastrophic in scope and ratio than previous periods in the trek of human civilization due to advances in technology, ideological clashes, economic disparities, international threats to enterprise and peace, inter- and intragroup political and ethnic tensions within nations, and fundamentalist religious zealots and terrorists hell-bent on wreaking unprecedented havoc throughout the world. Regarding the question of the possibility of global amelioration of pathological enactments, the issue becomes one of degree. Since prehistory, culture has undergone an evolutionary process of becoming, which is responsible for what we have come to call civilization, namely, our evolved contemporary valuation practices. However, as Freud observed, "uncultivated races [*sic*] and backward strata of the population are already multiplying more rapidly than highly cultivated ones."[41] What this means in contemporary parlance is that the poor, uneducated, disenfranchised, oppressed, economically challenged, and displaced factions of society are having more children born into the same socially impoverished conditions that lead to future repetitions of deprivation, oppression, and austerity, which informs each new successive generation, who, of course, will go on to have their own children in a perpetual transgenerational transmission of hardship and suffering. Although there are many socioeconomic, political, and psychological reasons for this, they nevertheless obstruct the optimal transformation of our pathos.

Prejudice forms a basic constituency in our psychic constitutions, for we all pass judgments on others based on our preferential appraisal of what we value and are accustomed to find familiar and/or pleasing. The dialectical tension between difference and similarity carries a certain

---

40. See Pinker (2011).
41. Freud's (1932) letter to Einstein, p. 214.

psychological hold over people, for our earliest familial identifications are based in shared experiences and values, and we gravitate toward those to whom we feel attracted due to communal affiliation and shared meaning. But the double edge of the dialectic (as negativity resulting in higher unity) exposes us to a dilemma, for the dialectic is the ontological dynamic underlying prejudice itself. Here we may be reminded of Adorno: the dark side of the negative is always emphasized in any act of judgment.[42] In fact, it is the structural edifice for judgment to exist. Most societies *need* to have enemies—that is, they need to have an emotional whipping boy or designated scapegoat to beat and project all their inner conflicts, frustrations, rage, hate, and homicidal fantasies onto. Otherwise, we would never have invented poetics, theater, drama, the arts, music, religion, politics, and so on, for the human psyche requires forms of displacement and sublimation to transform internal discord, affect, and ambivalent experience into palatable outlets so we may psychologically function and adapt to real, perceived, or felt adversity. If we didn't have these psychological capacities and unconscious tendencies, we'd all be nutjobs.

The reality of racism, ethnic discrimination, interethnic rivalries and hostilities, micro-competitions and devaluations within subcultures and fringe subgroups, and prejudicial feelings cast onto objects of alterity are all too human universal propensities: to deny them would be an incredulous attempt at posturing political correctness in favor of truth. The mass contempt in many nations for immigrants, refugees, migrant workers, and asylum seekers of different ethnic and national persuasions, even if only a minority view, speaks to the underground psychic reality of human prejudice worried that the Other will steal their chickens, jobs, sexual partners, and enjoyment. A recent example of this was a mob of more than 1,000 South Africans that raided a Somali neighborhood in Pretoria, killing foreign African settlers based on a hate campaign against foreigners, immigrants, and refugees who are accused of creating unemployment and increasing crime.[43] Here the "foreigner" is transferentially

---

42. Cf. Adorno (1966).

43. South Africa has seen many anti-foreigner attacks in recent years, targeting migrants and refugees, including mobs killing foreign African immigrants in 2008 and 2015. Violence has largely been

constructed as the elected evil Other who will mooch, plunder, and soak up the citizenry's pleasures and deprive them of their national birthrights and liberties, and who, moreover, are left flipping the bill for the outsider to enjoy a free lunch. "Keep that piece of shit out of my country!" This is a common visceral opinion among many American, British, and European communities, to such a degree that the immigrant, migrant worker, or refugee should be deprived of subsidy, welfare, food stamps, unemployment insurance, access to health care, education, day care, and other privileges just because of their foreign status or so-called lack of entitlement to "free" services on the government's dime.[44]

This exclusionary phenomenon speaks to both the individual and collective rupture of feelings of security and safety that are perceived to be imperiled when political changes occur in social strata and potential emergent threats manifest. A paranoid, schizoid, and/or panicky-hysterical process lies at the very heart of human psychological motivations, as it would be illogical not to fear what is unknown and unfamiliar for what is domestic, customary, and familiar. Here the Other is categorically, oppositionally constituted, even if there is no discernible threat. Difference signifies its own meaning based on dissimilarity, fear, and potential personal loss and sacrifice of a country's members or their own kind. Here the personal idiosyncrasy of selective identification with a certain element of one's culture, language, nationalism, or social complex can wreak political consequences. And even when altruistic and humanistic movements prevail, a spoiler is always introduced based on human frailty, desperation, and the inevitability of pathological enactments.

When German citizens protested over the Syrian and North African migrants who allegedly robbed, looted, and sexually assaulted their women after being graciously accepted into their country during the 2015 refugee crisis (which, of course, happens every day everywhere, regardless of where you come from), not to mention several U.S. governors refusing

directed toward Nigerians, Zimbabweans, and Congolese, which has escalated tensions between South Africa and other African countries (see York, 2017).

44. Just as a side note, we would not want to live in a world where everyone has a PhD. We need people to work, to do certain jobs that others are not willing to do, not able to do, or could not do to keep the economy functioning and healthy, and to buy real estate and take care of a nation's aging population. Here is a perfect example of our mutual dependency on each other.

to allow refugees to settle in their home states once it was discovered that ISIS connections were part of the Paris attacks based on refugee involvement, it is no surprise that panic would set in and the floodgates would be closed based on mass protest. These events even sparked President Donald Trump to ban Muslims (as everyone knows) from entering the United States and to build a wall on the border of Mexico to keep out the "illegal freeloaders," only to later separate migrant children from their mothers and callously throw them into detention cages (alone and estranged from any familial and emotional comfort). Here it becomes obvious that the foreign unknown Alien Other, who have their own needs, desires, adversity, and trauma, will likely have their own "psychological baggage" and material losses that other nation-states will have to pay for, and this is likely how a large percentage of the populace thinks. Why else would people get so emotionally bent out of shape by an influx of new people into their country? The fear of so-called hard-working citizens supporting and taking care of foreigners on their sweat and taxes, where food, shelter, transport, economic subsidies, and entertainment (such as access to TVs, cell phones, computers, and the internet) are given away without merit (even in the spirit of humanitarian aid), spurs bad feelings among the working class and rich alike. Who wants a dependent child when you never wanted to get pregnant to begin with?

Part of the problem facing us is that prejudice is ontologically constituted in the most rudimentary aspects of human consciousness as psychological disposition. Like the nature of the dialectic, prejudice has both negative and positive valences. While violence and destruction are the instruments of prejudice, so, too, are caring and love. Prejudice is not merely a negative construct; prejudice defines our valuation practices, which are the Mecca of individual and communal life. Rather than conceive of prejudice as simply a pathological anomaly, prejudice is also responsible for our most revered ideals. As we have said previously,[45] prejudice in its essence is the preferential self-expression of valuation, as corrupt as that may be.

---

45. Mills & Polanowski (1997), pp. 11–13.

All prejudicial disclosures express value preferences. Preferences are prejudicial because they signify discriminatory value judgments that are self-referential. Preference presupposes prejudice, for preference typifies the priority of determinate valuation. To prefer is to value, and to value is to judge: judgments by nature are evaluative. All judgments are imbued with value, which presuppose self-valuation and self-interest, because valuation is a particular form of subjective self-expression. Thus, valuation is prejudicial, for it involves a relation between difference and similarity that is necessarily self-referential. Every human being by nature is prejudiced; it is simply a matter of degree, directed toward specific objects of one's displacement, desire, and animus.

Prejudice is a neutral psychological predisposition that informs the ontology of human subjectivity. Prejudice is an elementary aspect of conscious and unconscious life that gives rise to the nature of personal identification, individual and collective identity, culture, and shared value practices. Prejudice as valuation is, therefore, responsible for our shared ideals as well as the deviations of abnormality and perversion. In its ideal condition, prejudicial valuation informs our social mores and ethical practices. In its larger scope, ethics is the harvest of subjective universality. As such, selfhood and culture give rise to morality that is individualistic and interpersonally bound within a psychosocial matrix of negotiation and intersubjective validation. Value determinations, I suggest, are the result of interpersonal mediations and identifications with collective ideals and are, therefore, intersubjectively constructed and verified through the dialectical process of our social and cultural prejudices. In applying Hegel, the succession toward greater unity, cooperation, and peace among nations is progressively forged by the movement of the dialectic as prejudice constantly gives rise to new and higher-order forms of novelty and creative complexity. These existential complications ontologically stand over and above individual practices, for they are mediated in the face of social and cultural interpersonal forces that negotiate and intersubjectively affirm collectively shared value systems and practices over others. As with the epigenesis of the self, the process of this negotiation rests on the nature of identification.

Ideals do not exist in a moral vacuum: they are created by the larger sociocultural milieu that becomes individually and idiosyncratically internalized throughout development; yet they are always open to change and transmutation. These early internalized ideals become the formative basis of a cohesive self and social structure, which remain in flux and unrest due to the dialectical unfolding of the nature of subjectivity and social relations. The parallel process of valuation in individual and collective development is constituted a priori within the larger ontological structures that make worldhood possible. Such preestablished ontological conditions (as thrownness) provide the ideal objects of identification that are necessary for selfhood and for the emergence of values—yet they are always up for renegotiation. This emerging process of valuation gives rise to greater *aporias* in selfhood, communal forces, sociopolitical drift, and international relations. However, the dialectical nature of prejudice that gives rise to civilization leads to an internal ambivalence, a dilemma it fights within itself. In this sense, values can never be fixed truths or universal essences. Instead, they necessarily materialize out of prejudice, negation, and conflict. Acquiring new life in the wake of destruction, the death of specific values is preserved in the ashes of history, nostalgia, and desire. As humanity elevates itself to higher degrees of complexity, so do its ideals.

From this account we may say that valuation inherently yearns for greater levels of unification and complexity. This would seem to suggest that the structurally constituted dynamic progression of the dialectic ensures that civilization will remain psychologically predisposed to seek and maintain order, accord, and social progression while allowing for a vast variance of novelty, freedom, and complexity to emerge. But with complexity and freedom comes the inherent risk of individual and collective psychopathy and social regression that threatens the progressive unification and self-preservative acclivity toward harmony and holism. To what degree will progression win out over regression in the face of our contemporary international, economic, ethnic, and religious conflicts? To provide a more systematic and rigorously justified account of the constructive forces of civilization within the destructive shapes of worldhood, we need to closely examine whether the positive significance of the negative will, in the end, vitiate the barbarous propensities that compel human relations toward destructive acts. But what is apparent from all cursory accounts is that evil is everywhere.

ON THE UNIVERSALITY OF EVIL

On January 10, 2015, Nigeria's militant Jihadist group Boko Haram (which literally means "Western education is forbidden"), after going on a mass killing spree in Baga on Lake Chad, strapped explosives to a 10-year-old girl and sent her off into a market in Maiduguri as a human detonator.[46] This atrocity comes after the April 14, 2014, kidnapping of nearly 300 schoolgirls from the Chibok Government Secondary School by the terrorist group, of which the girl is believed to be one of the abductees. Although reported accounts vary, many of the original 276 children were missing until recently;[47] all are believed to be used as sex objects and domestic servants. Despite some escaping or being freed, approximately 100 girls remain in captivity or have refused to leave Boko Haram in governmental negotiations due to becoming radicalized or for fear of stigma, ostracism, and shame over being forced to marry and/or have babies by their abductors.[48]

On December 16, 2014, seven members of a Pakistani Taliban extremist group entered the backdoor of an army public school in the dustbowl border city of Peshawar and indiscriminately opened fire with machine guns and explosives strapped to their vests, killing 132 school-children. The Taliban proclaimed that the attack was a vendetta for an army offensive in North Waziristan in June that beset militant insurgents. Pakistan's Taliban spokesman, Mohammed Umar Khorasanin, plainly stated their motive: "We targeted the school because the army targets our families . . . We want them to feel our pain."[49] Among the copious voices of world outcry, Canadian Prime Minster Stephen Harper said in a news conference:

---

46. See Nadeau (2015).
47. Mbah (2019) reports that 112 are still missing.
48. See Faul & Olalekan (2016); Amnesty International (2023, April 14), https://www.amnesty.org /en/latest/news/2023/04/nine-years-after-chibok-girls-abducted/
49. See Inayat, Qazi, & Bacon's (2014) journalist report.

> I think it's hard for any of us as rational and compassionate people to understand terrorism, to understand why people would want, in the name of some political cause, to simply terrorize, hurt, kill innocent people, whole sections of society, but I think it is just beyond, it is beyond our comprehension why somebody would target children.[50]

These words read alone do not convey the felt emotionality of his speech. This psychological perplexity of disbelief nicely encapsulates the unfathomability of bearing witness to a universal horror. What is beyond comprehension is that helpless innocent children would be brutally murdered by deliberate, malicious, and calculated actions of men. It is as if the response of the collective psyche were to say, "How could human beings do this? Only animals prey, for they are instinctual evolutionary organisms that have no self-reflective function or moral conscience by natural design. Humans are supposed to be different." But whether or not we accept the inherent animality to humanity, the line has been crossed.

It is only on the condition that slaughtering innocent children in cold blood would be permissible in any possible world that one would even question its moral significance. In other words, it would never occur to most civilized people to ask whether it is moral or immoral to kill innocent children who have done nothing to others, for the Kantian categorical imperative already speaks a universal language of prohibition. In such instances, where the masses identify with the purity and holiness of childhood, whether as a cultural symbolic or through the direct empathic identification with their own families and personal lives—namely, their own relatives and the child within—the immediate dissociation of understanding any rational means behind such atrocities is emotionally unfathomable for the simple fact that it disrupts our psychic need for a moral order in the universe. Such an imposed confrontation with universal horror forces us to question the presupposed universality of a moral universe to begin with, for it eclipses all value as we know it. Here our rational "unfathomability" that is "beyond comprehension" is none other than our own emotive dissociation from the realization (that must be disavowed) of the *dissociation of ethics*—hence the renunciation

---

50. Canadian Press Video (2014).

of "right"—perpetrated by the Other. In other words, we would have to suspend or abandon a universal concept of what is right and wrong, not to mention entertain a mentalized stance that others would not share our own sense of values. Here lies the pathological breach, an incipient a priori knowledge, that human nature is at base a primitive, feral process that fractures all illusory notions of a civilized, just, and loving world, for it only takes one act of barbarism to remind us that evil is no illusion.

THE ETHICS OF KILLING

We live in a sick society, one chosen yet unconsciously determined. Here evil is the natural consequence of the cost of freedom. We kill people for this cost, for the privilege, politics, and principle of freedom, itself a lamentable and ethically dubious dilemma. Military intelligence has studied and strategized about the best way to kill people, to deracinate, to dismember their spirits, to rob them of soul, to crush entire peoples of their dignity to the degree that warfare and state murder have become both a technological and mechanized industry. A weapon is an instrument designed to kill—from the steel and bronze age to a drone. The atomic bomb was invented for one thing: human extermination.

The technology of evil is witnessed every day on our television sets, from Wall Street to mass-scale corporate corruption, to internet fraud, and cyber bullying, all abetted by advances in computer science. The use of global information exchange, digital communication, social media, robotics, nanotechnology, and the engineering of terror has become its own science. From WikiLeaks, Edward Snowden, and the Panama Papers to the Arab Spring and *Charlie Hebdo*, no nation is immune from its own homegrown transgressions. Sometimes the craft or art of *techne* enlists a certain psychological intelligence condoned through state torture, such as inducing learned helplessness through waterboarding and "rectal rehydration" at Guantanamo, to rape-murder warfare used in the ethnic cleansing campaigns perpetrated in Bosnia, Croatia, Kosovo, and Rwanda.

The ethics of evil is the distortion of an inverse relation, namely, the justification of self-righteousness while perpetrating evil under the guise of moral superiority. When ethical arguments are employed to justify evil acts, we reason in a hegemonic circle of self-interest that betrays a philosophy of right, even if such actions are deemed necessary to combat an identifiable threat. Ethical rationale can be exercised by any individual, group, or nation-state to legitimate its activities and foreign policies affecting other lives regardless of the legitimacy of one's belief system, veracity of events, or the flimsiness of moral reasoning employed. Under the rubric of national security and the crusade against terror, people simply "disappeared" into CIA custody, were detained against their wills without criminal charges laid, and systemically subjected to the use of "enhanced interrogation techniques," a euphemism for torture, in the hopes that reliable intelligence could be procured despite the legal and ethical prohibitions against torture instituted since the Geneva Conventions' forbiddance of it even during times of war. Not only is this a good example of moral hypocrisy under the justification of state ethics, as are drone attacks, military commissions, and mass electronic surveillance by a superpower that bases its global political platform on democracy, freedom, and human rights, but further, it underscores the universality of national self-interest at the expense of democracy itself.

When nation is against nation, narcissistic national identity forms a firm antithesis against the Other that becomes legalized within state foreign policy or totalitarian rule, even if duped or deluded. Under the Bush administration following 9/11, the United States manufactured a war on terror because it needed to have enemies to pillory as revenge for its castrated ego. Here the Other becomes alien, a xenophobic object prone to hurt us. And after they found Saddam Hussein tucked away down a spider hole, there were no weapons of mass destruction to be found. But he served a utilitarian public purpose: he was the symbolic Bad Man who was put to death under state execution, itself a practice deemed "primitive" and "evil" despite enjoying a cathartic welcome by the West.

We may readily observe the paranoid position at work on a global scale: otherness is the enemy. This primal fear is even further spread within our own nations and communities, where private lives are under state surveillance, neighbors spy upon neighbors, race riots are on the rise, and home invasions are becoming the norm. Under Big Brother, anyone could disappear. And with global economic unrest due to the fuel crisis before the pandemic, Russia's earlier infringement (before the invasion) on the Ukraine to seemingly attempt to recover its lost Soviet Union has generated a new paranoia where citizens can't speak freely due to fear of police arrest or public assassination. Paradoxically, after the country had lost almost half its value and people couldn't afford a mortgage payment, the nation's approval ratings for Vladimir Putin skyrocketed. Whereas in the United States, the disgruntled public craves a swing of the pendulum toward any politician selling hope for a recovering economy, Russia can't get enough of its leader while blaming the greedy West for its own financial malaise.

When the class genocide in Rwanda occurred, initiated by rival ethnic tensions between the Hutus and Tutsis, where mass mayhem was organized by Hutu paramilitary personnel and locals having much to gain from the systematic extermination of the Tutsis, the world remained curiously passive and silent. Even after reports of entire villages and individual family members killing their own kind with machetes and the crudest of utensils were known to be factual, the West looked on as a detached spectator unwilling to do anything until it was too late. Lethargic in its enthusiasm to intervene, after nearly a million dead, world superpowers finally felt motivated to lift a finger to stop the genocide at the UN's beckoning. The Dark Continent, I suggest, held little value to democratic and developed countries, which had little to gain and many economic costs to bear for intervening in a country that is (symbolically) associated with poverty, famine, AIDS, overpopulation, and disease, hence the alien Other. But when SARS, swine flu (H1N1), Ebola, Zika, and COVID-19 can conjure up the paranoid position and threaten another global pandemic, the world has become more gracious and attuned to social realities that affect us all. The cold, hard facts are that some peoples and countries are valued over others based on their discernible worth, others on their discernible threat. Even humanitarian aid is never devoid of political self-interest, especially if it means thwarting global anxiety.

Is it evil *not* to think of alterity or other peoples, cultures, and continents, to not consider their needs and social challenges? This would not only imply an admonition as failure to acquire self-consciousness and empathic attunement for the other but, rather, incites an intransigent condemnation for not caring to do so in the first place. Yet Levinasian ethics barely occur to the masses engrossed in their everyday lives, let alone being handed down a moral sentence for not thinking about the plight of the disenfranchised abstract sufferer residing somewhere in an arbitrary land. It is too much for the individual psyche to bear; that's why it is turned over to the collective social psyche to contemplate and do something about. Even in the most well-intentioned and conscientious soul who envisions a better humanity and wishes to serve altruistic causes, in the end we do what we can, because that's all we can do. Is it evil that we don't do more, that we cease to try because we value our own needs over others? Or do we merely accept our beleaguered humanism that we cannot live up to the demands of the ideals we place on ourselves? Here I am reminded of Hegel's "beautiful soul": when we become aware of our imperfections, we bear an unhappy consciousness. The self is divided: we can posit the Ideal but simply can't actualize it. Here moral lassitude becomes another banality.

INSTITUTIONALIZED EVIL

When we think about the institutionalization of evil in recent times, from colonial imperialism and totalitarianism to fascism, we often think of large-scale suprastructures that superimpose an oppressive bureaucratic machinery on its citizenry; but we may observe how these unconscious cultural fantasies operate as entrenched ideologies unquestioned by the masses. The caste system in India may be said to foster a form of institutional racism where social class is determined by blood ancestry, history, custom, and skin color. The upper class or Brahmans hold wealth, power, status, and education, while the Untouchables are held in contempt and allocated the most unpleasant and revulsive of all vocations in the most horrid of conditions such as sanitation, domestic servitude, and backbreaking manual labor. Aryan descendants with lighter-skinned pigments are more aesthetically valued whereas the darker-skinned Indians are viewed as ugly, an attitudinal phenomenon we may also witness in Africa and Egypt (where skin-bleaching cosmetics are in demand). There is an air of superiority by birth and provenance and an aura of disdain, condemnation, and vilification of the underclass, even though the advantaged groups rely on their sweat and subservience for sustaining such privileged lifestyles.

Huge discrepancies between rich and poor determine the social infrastructure, where the elite govern the majorities, political and social institutions are rife with corruption and abuse of power, and the citizenry does not have tangible access to housing, education, or work. Caste discrimination continues to oppress basic human rights and is used as a tool to dehumanize people who are already marginalized and destitute, such as the Dalits, who are systemically treated unequally and have even had their houses burned and children targeted by upper-caste groups with impunity. The subcontinent is suffocating in pollution, and every major city is a conglomeration of slums. Poverty, death, disease, crime, infestation, filth, lack of sewage, vagrants, panhandlers, homelessness, frantic desperation, and abject hopelessness abound, where the majority of its billion people are illiterate, disenfranchised, and penniless. In fact, India has one of the highest illiteracy rates in the world, trailing just behind Africa and Afghanistan.[51] Abandoned children, the deformed and handicapped, and destitute mothers with emaciated babies in their arms roam the streets begging for food. An endless swarm of hovering hands pounce on tourists and locals alike hoping to get a rupee or American dollar for free.

Fairy-tale romances are nonexistent for marriages arranged by patriarchy based on caste, birth, and class as a union of families, not love, where relationships are determined, not freely chosen, lest one betrays the family, established social order, and the entrenched cultural tradition that sustains this institutional practice. It is no wonder Buddhism branched off from Hinduism and that Islam was successful in converting much of the underclass, each under the teachings that all men are equal regardless of race, caste, or custom.

In other developing countries, such as in the Middle East, where despots, dictators, and autocrats rule their totalitarian regimes, women and children are systematically oppressed, often under the edicts of Islam.

---

51. See United Nations report (2014).

Here we may observe a widespread institutional practice in most Arab countries that grant men both legislative and property rights over their wives and children, where strict observance to Muslim law is harshly imposed, including denying women access and rights to education, individual autonomy, and independent finances in order to keep them enslaved, including controlling their dress, physical mobility, and behavioral practices, and granting them virtually no criminal protection or civil liberty rights under the law. Women and children may be beaten or raped against their will by men with practical impunity from prosecution, and transgressions by females may be subject to penalty by death. Public stoning, immolations, and honor killings (from Pakistan to Canada), where women turn on other accused women, including mothers and family members who are willing participants, are salient phenomena fueled by culturally ingrained misogyny.

Anti-blasphemy and apostasy laws are often designed by government officials to silence dissent and debate, bolster religious intolerance, discriminate against, and incite hatred toward minorities, foster inner-communal violence, and curtail basic liberties, hence robbing citizens of their fundamental rights to free thought and speech. This hegemonic form of institutionalization has led to the pernicious persecution of public figures in Egypt, state torture in Algeria, and the grisly murder of atheist bloggers in Bangladesh for insulting Islam.

In vast parts of China and India, female (sex-selected) infanticide is ubiquitous due to the cultural devaluation of women. Concentrated in northeast Africa, Yemen, Iraqi Kurdistan, the Middle East, and portions of Asia, female genital mutilation (circumcision) is legally imposed against their will (usually in childhood), often under horrendous unsanitary conditions that permanently disfigure and endanger the survival of its victims due to lack of sterilization and post-medical complications—such as infections leading to infertility and fatal septicemia, all condoned under the dominion of male patriarchy. These primitive practices are designed to fortify a man's power and authority by turning women into functional objects of domestication, obedience, and sexuation where only a man has the right to pleasure. Further, in many of these countries, as throughout South and East Asia, children are sold into slavery by parents to pay for family debt or for profit, as are human organs offered on the black market to help pay for passage to another land. Human trafficking and the child sex trade industry have become an international pandemic, often abetted by institutional corruption and systemic pathology thriving on high profit margins with no signs of a conscience.

Israeli legislative policy is designed to promote and privilege an exclusive Jewish state, actively recruits immigration from European Jewry, hence lending asylum and giving economic and material benefits (including housing, transportation, and tax shelters) to Jews over non-Jewish Israelis, imposes higher costs of living and excise taxes on domestic Palestinians and other Israeli Arabs who refuse to live and work in the West Bank, although entire generations had previously owned property and had run family businesses throughout the country before the declaration of Israel as a Zionist state. A democratic state that maintains class privilege and financially rewards one ethnic group over others who live and work in the same country, own property, and are equally part of the same society would be an unfathomable occurrence in North America. It would cut through the very heart of democracy. Favoring one class of citizens based on birth, creed, class, ethnicity, or privilege would simply be deemed as discriminatory and racist. It is no wonder that Israel is largely deemed an apartheid state by the rest of the world.

Israel is concerned with occupying rather than compromising over disputed land, slowly annexing territory and stealing more property from the Palestinians in the West Bank, and retaliates with military bombardments that unavoidably target civilian neighborhoods where innocent lives are lost, largely because terrorists and resistance regimes put civilians in harm's way. And with Palestinian opposition compelled to fight and galvanize subversive insurgencies and initiate clandestine missile fire, keeping hate and resentment alive, Israeli citizens break out the lawn chairs, crack a beer, and watch the military pick off houses in Gaza and the West Bank. Because the Gaza Strip remains controlled by the Hamas government, which preaches the death of Israel every day, any chance of peace negotiations remains nil. With Hamas's recent surprise pogrom in Israel, where more Jewish lives were lost since the Holocaust, a two-state solution becomes all but a pipe dream.

Citizens from both counties tragically live in terror and trauma every day. Although I don't mean to simplify or trivialize such complex matters that are historically and politically nuanced, here each side points the finger while calling the other "terrorist." This is a good example of the paranoid-schizoid position at play where radical splitting and projective identification lead to reiterations of violence as proportional exchange, like a Ping-Pong ball traversing each side of the net until one opponent slams a victory in the current round. But this is followed by endless rounds of repetition in fixed perpetuation of retaliatory aggression to the point that systemic acrimony toward the Other justifies state institutional racism and military barrages. It is understandable how Israel suffers from dread due to Jewish diaspora and centuries of European and Russian anti-Semitism while living in the shadow of the Shoah, but with the messianic clash of religions and fundamentalist supporters of the Islamic State (e.g., ISIS/ISIL) recently killing Jews in Paris, Copenhagen, and Tel Aviv, the tinderbox could explode without warning, especially if Iran continues with its nuclear development program, a spark that could ignite a third world war, which I anticipate, especially if Russia, North Korea, or China act out. If Iranian-backed Hezbollah and Hamas are determined to eradicate Israel, hence inciting other neighboring Arab countries to join in—only to be cheered on by decolonial ideology encouraged by the progressive woke West, this could bring about the annihilation of the Jewish state. Here the United States would predictably enter the fray, and the world's fate would dangle in anxious uncertainty. Because the United States and other sympathetic nations would not likely allow for a second Holocaust of the Jewish people, radicalized Islamdom would predictably spark a global war. It takes no act of imagination to believe that this could escalate to nuclear engagement. Here, the world walks on eggshells.

4

The Doomsday Clock Is Ticking

WHEN I WOKE UP ON THE MORNING OF NOVEMBER 9, 2016, TO DISCOVER that Donald Trump had won the U.S. presidential election,[1] I felt witness to a collective psychosis. What does this tell us about the American psyche? Perhaps it can be attributed to a cultural complex, but here hatred for the Other, racism, misogyny, narcissistic self-satisfaction, and disdain for human rights and democracy had spoken. How could the teleological suspension of reason be under the spell of emotional prejudice to such an extent that the American public would elect a mentally ill, thought disordered, megalomaniac tax-dodging billionaire prepared to discriminate against Mexicans and Muslims alike, who bragged openly about sexually assaulting women, disparaged the handicapped and disabled, blatantly lied to the American people and the world during national debates, and who spoke cavalierly about using nuclear weapons during his presidential campaign? It is only based on the degree to which a voting populace identifies with their leader's values, are mistrustful of the system, overidentified with their own desires and self-interest, swayed by the ideological dissemination of false information on the internet, too lazy to read legitimate news sources or go out to vote, and/or have slipped into delusion. Or do people really not care about the truth as long as they get their way? And of the half of the country that did vote for Trump, whether under manipulative attempts by Russia's cyber hacking and campaign to disrupt the election by disseminating false news or not,

1. See Saunders (2016) and Remnick (2016) for immediate commentaries on the election.

some supporters were duped by his ruse of appealing to voters' populism whereby the flamboyant, ill statesman conned the public into believing that he was not part of the elite ruling class. Whether based in ignorance or willful adoption of prejudicially negating otherness, the country spoke.

The Canadian immigration website immediately crashed upon news of the election results. The collective psyche was split, the country divided, masses became inane. America has become a xenophobic and racist nation, exploiting disparities, and would rather elect a fascist autocrat with no respect for humanist values than a qualified woman of political pedigree. Never in the history of contemporary free democracy would the world have predicted such lunacy. This is American pathos at its finest. And with a psychopathic, impulsive, cognitively impaired leader with his finger on the button in charge of overseeing the free world, what did we see next? After losing the 2020 presidential election, based on calculated lies that it was rigged, including failed attempts to overturn the results through manipulation, intimidation, and coercion, Trump incited sedition by goading a mob to march on Congress and attack the U.S. Capitol. And then he praised the mob after it descended into rioting and domestic terror, hence causing the certification of the election results to be delayed and leaving five people dead, followed later by suicides by four officers who had responded to the attack. No time in contemporary history has a sitting president instigated an armed insurrection and siege on American democracy or been impeached twice. Trump now stands as the only former president in U.S. history who has been indicted on federal crimes including espionage and the only one who was ever charged with criminal activity.

DROPPING THE BOMB

A group of concerned scientists from the University of Chicago who had helped invent the first atomic bombs in the Manhattan Project formed the *Bulletin of the Atomic Scientists* in 1945. In 1947 they created the Doomsday Clock, an iconic symbolic clock face showing a countdown to the end of the world, designed to metaphorically represent existential dangers to humanity and the planet. The Clock has become universally recognized as a major indicator of threats to global catastrophe from nuclear warfare, climate change, and developing technologies in computer engineering and the life sciences. In 2015 the clock was set at 3 minutes to midnight, where it remained until the U.S. presidential election of Donald Trump.[2] It was then moved to 100 seconds to countdown, the closest it had ever been in history, hence surpassing the time set in 1953 at the height of the Cold War. Largely due to Russia's invasion of Ukraine and the increased threat of nuclear escalation, the hands are now 90 seconds from the end of human civilization.

The *Bulletin* is an independent nonprofit organization composed of international experts and advisers of humanitarian concern who assess the risks and benefits of scientific and technological advancements with the goal of influencing public engagement, foreign policy, treaty negotiations, and protection of the Earth and all its inhabitants. It has distilled critical issues and framed debates in various committees of Parliament and the United Nations on breakdowns and achievements in security efforts. Each year attention is paid to the most pressing global threats, which informs the setting of the minute hand of the Clock regarding how we are more or less safe than the previous year. Despite gains by the Joint Comprehensive Plan of Action that facilitated the Iran nuclear deal, hence advanced nuclear disarmament efforts in the Middle East and throughout the world, as well as the 2015 Climate Conference in Paris that brought nearly 200 countries together to pledge to reduce the looming doom of climate change, due to North Korea's nuclear testing and magniloquence, the nuclear modernization programs in the United States, Russia, and around the world, the inability of collective nations to effectively and safely deal with nuclear waste, and the persistence of planetary warming and the destruction of our environment, the Clock

---

2. The decision to move the minute hand of the Clock is made by the *Bulletin's* Science and Security Board in conjunction with the Board of Sponsors, which includes several Nobel laureates. The hands of the Clock were moved to 3 minutes before midnight on January 22, 2015, 2 1/2 minutes in 2017, then 2 minutes in 2018 and 2019, making this the nearest to the apocalypse since 1953, which was at the height of the Cold War. It was moved to 100 seconds to midnight in 2020 and stayed there until it was moved to 90 seconds in 2023. See *Bulletin of the Atomic Scientists* (2016, 2017, 2018, 2019, 2020, 2021, 2022, 2023).

remains perilously close to midnight.[3] In the *Bulletin*'s Science and Security Board's 2016 Statement, they delivered a foreboding omen:

> Three minutes [to midnight] is too close. Far too close. We, the members of the Science and Security Board of the *Bulletin of the Atomic Scientists*, want to be clear about our decision not to move the hands of the Doomsday Clock in 2016: That decision is not good news, but an expression of dismay that world leaders continue to fail to focus their efforts and the world's attention on reducing the extreme danger posed by nuclear weapons and climate change. When we call these dangers existential, that is exactly what we mean: They threaten the very existence of civilization and therefore should be the first order of business for leaders who care about their constituents and their countries.[4]

Since 2015, things have only gotten worse. In 2015 there was much disturbing nuclear bombast with visible tensions between the leaders of the United States and Russia, North Korea, and Israel disgruntled over the Iran deal. And with the increase in Islamic State terrorism from Paris to Brussels, San Bernardino, Orlando, Istanbul, and Nice, the Syrian refugee crisis, and mass diasporas throughout Western and Eastern Europe and North America, a world tinderbox kindled. World superpowers have initiated to maintain and modernize their nuclear warheads and infrastructure despite arms control treaty agreements of nuclear nonproliferation under the rhetoric and guise of a nuclear weapon-free world. When the United States plans to spend at minimum $350 billion in the next 10 years to refurbish its nuclear weapons capabilities while spending $5.8 billion each year in cleaning up its floundering nuclear waste disposal programs,[5] something is wrong with this picture. Presumably, every country with a nuclear arsenal wants to defend itself against foreign "crazies," but they are equally concerned with maintaining power, flexing military muscle, and in advancing their own economy and megalomaniac political maneuverability. With a Russian state-sponsored news agency

---

3. See the statement from the executive director of the *Bulletin of the Atomic Scientists*, Rachel Bronson (2016), p. i.

4. See Mecklin (2016), §§ 4–5.

5. Mecklin (2016), §§ 2, 4.

threatening to turn the United States into radioactive ash, North Korea's announcing that it had developed a hydrogen bomb followed by a series of tests, NATO's military repositioning toward the Russian border, China's agreement to help Pakistan build nuclear missile submarine platforms as anxious India becomes more nervous, and dispute over free passage in the South China Sea followed by the United States sending military naval presence to the island territories, the potential for major conflicts among nations with nuclear powers has escalated. The Hague's recent decision that China has no rights to these waters (rich in fishing, minerals, and underground fossil fuels) followed by China's brazen rebuke and defiance—claiming it will do whatever it wants—has only enflamed the tensions. And if Kim Jong Un is allowed to continue to develop North Korea's nuclear arsenals without restraints,[6] another international war is predictable. This possibility has been gravely exacerbated by China's provocations to reclaim Taiwan, North Korea's menacing of Japan and South Korea by firing missiles over its territories, and Russia's senseless invasion of Ukraine, which vows to use nuclear intervention if the West continues to militarily support the besieged underdog.

Adding to the Science and Security Board's 2017 decision to move the clock closer to midnight was the world-shocking election of Donald Trump to the Oval Office. Given that Trump had carelessly and disturbingly spoken about using nuclear weapons during his campaign, followed by a series of executive orders once elected, it was no surprise that Iran immediately underwent a ballistic missile test followed by North Korea firing a missile over the Sea of Japan, just as Netanyahu announced plans for expanding Israeli settlements. Given that Iran had shown open hostility toward the international community on the heels of its nuclear deal, Pakistan and India continued warring in Kashmir, and North Korea had conducted its fourth and fifth underground nuclear tests in 2016, followed by many more missiles testing after that, it feels like we are all walking on eggshells. Given that Trump had gone on record that climate change is a hoax and planned to expand oil pipelines, bring back mining jobs, and condoned more industrial burning of coal and fossil fuels, the

---

6. Mecklin (2016), §§ 1–3.

planet would only get hotter if such plans succeeded. Other countries soon followed his lead, especially given the pandemic and continual global need for energy. The loss of trust in democratic institutions by the masses, the proliferation of fake news, consensually validated distortions of reality, security breaches, cyber hacking—such as Russia's deceptive offensives in trying to manipulate the 2016 U.S. presidential election—and the incompetent Trump administration that ignored governmental intelligence experts, professional organizations, academics, researchers, and those who possess expert knowledge, and discounted the truth and reality of sound science, such as appointing a buffoon to the head of the Environmental Protection Agency who openly denied global warming,[7] had only made international relations, ecology, and security conditions worse. And as Trump and Putin expanded their nuclear and military spending, the world has become more dangerous now than ever before.

Despite promissory assurances from 196 signatory countries at the Paris accord to keep global warming emissions under 2 degrees Celsius (including later commitments at Sharm el-Sheikh, Davos, and Dubai), there is no way to enforce their vows or their compliance. And even if there were, the UN Climate Change Secretariat acknowledged that if all the countries were to follow through on their basic promises, the carbon dioxide budget would be exhausted long before the target date of reduced emissions. When the Republican Party of the United States, one of the largest polluters of the planet, decries that there is no such thing as man-made-caused global warming or the Anthropocene, nor that climate change is really even a problem, such hubris and feckless disregard for the empirical facts merely belies political propaganda designed not to challenge the status quo where corporate capitalists and lobby sectors bequeath large financial campaign contributions, not to mention the obvious truth that they are living in pompous denial: 2016, 2019, 2020, and 2023 were the hottest years on record with an increase in the global temperature surpassing 1 degree Celsius over preindustrial levels.

---

7. See Davenport's (2017) analysis of Scott Pruitt's inane denial of the objective science and empirical facts of climate change.

Since 2017, we have been on the cusp of a new nuclear arms race as we have recently witnessed with North Korea and Russia stoking the fire. As a result, the world has become a more perilous place. With careless rhetoric, childish name calling, and provocation from the United States, there is increased probability for war by intention, miscalculation, or accident. With increased military exercises along the borders of NATO, reduced arms control negotiations, upgrading arsenals that undermine the Intermediate-Range Nuclear Forces Treaty (INF), and the intensification of tensions in the Asia-Pacific region, South Asia, Pakistan and India, the South China Sea, and the Middle East, uncertainties of the then United States renunciation of the Iran deal and withdrawal from the Paris Agreement, which the White House decided to break off, we were forewarned of the hazards these actions had on the future. World order had been undermined and exacerbated by the Trump administration's backing away from long-standing U.S. leadership in international diplomacy, which had devolved into disparaging invectives and cursing, mimicking the surrealness of an undisciplined, unpredictable, and disruptive reality TV caricature who sat as the U.S. president.

The decision to move the hands to 100 seconds to midnight highlighted the urgency of the situation, what the *Bulletin* referred to as "a new abnormal." In 2019, John Mecklin, editor of the Clock Statement, declared that the major threats of nuclear weapons and the climate crisis "were exacerbated this past year by the increased use of information warfare to undermine democracy around the world, amplifying risk from these and other threats and putting the future of civilization in extraordinary danger."[8] In 2020 he stressed how matters have worsened on all fronts, including the increased danger of

> cyber-enabled disinformation campaigns to sow distrust in institutions and among nations, undermining domestic and international efforts to foster peace and protect the planet . . . We have seen influential leaders denigrate and discard the most effective methods for addressing complex threats—international agreements with strong verification

---

8. Mecklin (2019), p. 2.

regimes—in favor of their own narrow interests and domestic political gain.[9]

Our international security situation is now a new abnormal, where the United States had abandoned its commitment to back the Iran deal and withdrew from the INF Treaty, hence leaving the global arms control process to others without say, regulation, or oversight. And with candid commitments from the key nuclear nations to modernize its arsenals, what had gone from talk of denuclearization of weaponry in the past became a new, unregulated global arms race under the guise of modernization and "threats to national security." The once promised hope of nuclear reduction and constraint had all but gone out the window.

The Science and Security Board of the *Bulletin of the Atomic Scientists* is also concerned about threats due to the rapid advancements of emerging technologies in the cyber realm, biotechnology, synthetic biology, genetic engineering, artificial intelligence (AI), information technologies, and the use of robotic weapons that place humanity in peril. The manufacturing of AI technologies and autonomous weapons that can act independently without human supervision, intervention, or decision making in executing activities that can kill is most worrisome, as they are susceptible to error, miscalculation, malfunctioning, misreading, or inaccurately processing information in the moment, and open to manipulation by malicious agents who may wish to trick us into thinking there is a war. With the deliberate interference of information technologies that present the illusion of truth and spread false information presented as fact, the existential risks for escalating fear and resultant conflict are ominous. Mecklin reproaches:

> In many forums, including particularly social media, nationalist leaders and their surrogates lied shamelessly, insisting that their lies were truth, and the truth "fake news." These intentional attempts to distort reality exaggerate social divisions, undermine trust in science, and diminish confidence in elections and democratic institutions. Because these distortions attack the rational discourse required for solving the complex

---

9. Mecklin (2020), § 3.

problems facing humanity, cyber-enabled information warfare aggravates other major global dangers—including those posed by nuclear weapons and climate change—as it undermines civilization generally.[10]

When impudent and foolhardy leaders flail around nuclear language during times of diplomatic disputes and regional instabilities, portents of warfare are amplified. This is not a game; the world is not a reality TV show. But the psychopaths among us and in positions of national political leadership set the tone for how the show could end. When propaganda and lies as information warfare are disseminated through communication networks pretending to be truth, fact, and empirical reality, this only inflames emotional prejudices and negative passions that eclipse the capacity of informed reason, logic, and sober science. The raid on the U.S. Capitol (like the Brazilian Congress) only shows how extremist thinking can dismiss the reality principle blinded by hate and ignorance. The greatest threat to the United States is now its own people.

Because "the world is sleepwalking its way through a newly unstable nuclear landscape," the *Bulletin*'s 2020 Doomsday Statement has gone so far as to "declare a state of emergency that requires the immediate, focused, and unrelenting attention of the entire world."[11] The United States' derisive and bullying attitudes toward Iran, North Korea, Russia, and China only aggravate matters, which will likely result in a breakdown of arms control negotiations propelling the world toward a completely unregulated nuclear environment. And when international governmental climate change conferences result in no agreement on curbing emissions, not to mention dismantling and withdrawal from previous accords, it should come as no surprise that the planet would catch fire. The year 2019 was the year the world burned: India and Pakistan experienced record-breaking heat waves followed by unrelenting floods, and out-of-control wildfires in both hemispheres—from Australia to the Artic, California, and the Amazon—consumed everything in their path like a ravenous swarm of locusts descending on a field, such as in East Africa. Tack onto that doomsday scenario the increased use of techno,

---

10. Mecklin (2019), p. 3.
11. Mecklin (2020), § 4.

space, and cyber warfare, such as "deepfakes"; malware that can infiltrate and destabilize private, industry, corporate, and governmental computer systems; genetic engineering; synthetic biology that could be weaponized; AI weaponry without human supervision that could make lethal decisions or could be easily hacked and manipulated; and other disruptive high-speed technologies that are highly automated: such precarious conditions are only breeding grounds for ambiguity, misunderstandings, uncertainty, provocations, and panic that could lead to a rapid escalation of war—all signaling a "fundamental dysfunction in the world's efforts to manage and reduce existential risk."[12]

In 2021 and 2022, the *Bulletin* kept the clock at 100 seconds to midnight largely due to the pandemic; mismanagement from governments; lack of international cooperation in communication, coordination, and handling global emergencies properly; ignoring scientific advice; and consequently failing to protect the health and welfare of global citizens.[13] Further, the bane of climate change, the proliferation and modernization of nuclear weapons programs, and the inability to successfully fight disinformation campaigns or "infodemics" have not gone away. A hypersonic arms race is underway, and the militarization of space, cyberweapons, and missile defense systems only adds to the complex threat spectrum and risk escalation by a blatant disregard for potential accidental conflict or nuclear war. We are no better off now than in the past. It was only with the election of U.S. President Joe Biden that there remained any glimmer of hope on the horizon. But with the international and domestic problems he faced, such as the Capitol insurrection, pandemic inflation, the military evacuation from Afghanistan, and the intensification in the cultural wars dividing America, the glimmer quickly faded. When Russia's invasion of Ukraine impacted the whole world, we braced for the possibility of a third world war that is still tenuous today. With the alarming threat of a nuclear detonation by Putin, 90 seconds to midnight is the closest we have ever been to world annihilation.

Without proper societal oversight or the ability to control and regulate emergent technological sciences, these compounded existential

---

12. Mecklin (2020), § 8.
13. Mecklin (2021), p. 2.

dangers along with nuclear rhetoric, cyberspace wars, and unmitigated climate change continue to pose global-scale risks to us all. Despite the diplomatic achievements of the Paris accord and the Iran nuclear agreement that quickly went down the pea patch, the nuclear modernization programs of world superpowers usher in a new Cold War era, and the world has barely done a thing to assuage—let alone subvert—climate catastrophe. Further, we have no clear path to peace. In our time of unprecedented global danger, much work needs to be done. The United States, NATO, and Ukraine must engage in dialogue with Russia to facilitate peace negotiations, reduce the risk of escalation, and end the war. Equally pressing is the need for diplomatic intervention in the Hamas-Israel war in the service of humanitarian protection of innocent civilians on all sides of the conflict.

Because of these failures in world leadership, over the past few years the *Bulletin* calls on world citizens and political agencies to:

- Encourage U.S. and Russian leaders to limit their nuclear proliferation, reduce alert levels and provocative military exercises, prevent peacetime incidents along NATO borders, reinstate or renegotiate its differences over various nuclear treaties, and deescalate mutual threats that have potential for crisis escalation and/or could accidentally precipitate a further senseless war;

- Dramatically reduce proposed spending on nuclear weapons modernization programs;

- Reenergize the disarmament process, with a focus on results;

- Engage North Korea—the only country to violate the norm against nuclear testing in 20 years—in serious dialogue to reduce nuclear risks and cease its missile testing;

- The United States and Iran can return to full compliance with the Joint Comprehensive Plan of Action for limiting Iran's nuclear power initiative, which is in the best interests of the international community's concerns over Middle East security and the spread of nuclear weapons;

- Implore nuclear nations to declare a "no-first-use" of nuclear weapons commitment and policies as a step toward global security and stability;
- Implore President Biden to eliminate the right of the U.S. president to have the sole authority to launch nuclear weapons and persuade other nation's leaders to establish similar controls, checks and balances, and barriers;
- Follow up on the Paris accord with actions that sharply reduce greenhouse gas emissions and fulfill the Paris promise of keeping warming below 2 degrees Celsius;
- Insist that world leaders acknowledge the reality and scientific truth of climate change, endorse the Paris agreement as intended, limit its nation's pollution, and support carbon-friendly energy sources, policies, and long-term decarbonization goals;
- Implore citizens of the globe, and especially from North America, to demand climate action from their governments and move toward a decarbonized world;
- Provide support to poorer and developing countries so they can make a transition to post-carbon dependencies;
- Mobilize the international community to prepare for new global public health threats and pandemics through early detection; disease surveillance; open communication and reporting efforts; medical infrastructure and supplies; response, distribution, and intervention capacities; and foresight readiness;
- Establish new international protocols and laws that discourage and penalize misuse of science and information technology, spread false news (alternative facts/disinformation) in a post-truth world of runaway abuse in social media, and prevent deceptive political campaigns that undermine public trust in social institutions, the media, science, democracy, and objective reality itself;
- Abolish autonomous weaponry technology that could make "kill" decisions without proper human supervision, oversite, or input;
- Deal now with the commercial nuclear waste problem; and

- Create institutions specifically assigned to explore and address potentially catastrophic misuses of new technologies.

Despite the promising movement from the new U.S. presidential administration to renew its international treaties and reverse its environmental, economic, immigration, health, and climate change policies, it is 90 seconds to midnight, the closest it has ever been. And with Israel's invasion of Gaza among worldwide protest, alongside the possibility that Trump could be reelected as U.S. president, we shall not be surprised if the Clock creeps closer to countdown. This is quite possibly the most dangerous time humanity has ever faced. We must unite and act to prevent the end of civilization and save the world.

Conclusion: "The Clock ticks. Global danger looms. Wise leaders should act—immediately."[14] All of this calls for genuine relational exchange, diplomatic dialogue, international negotiation of values and needs, governmental restraint on intimidation and issuing threats against other nations, political compromise, restriction and regulation of private industry that cares more about capital exploitation than world peace, and an authentic desire for living in concord within our world communities and preserving our planet's ecological integrity. No small feat indeed, especially when impasse, politics, and greed preempt any sincere discussions toward mutual cooperation among nations, let alone working in concert toward viable solutions. Over the past few years, the Science and Security Board warned that the probability of global catastrophe was very high, but from 2017 to today, they concluded that the danger is even greater and more urgent, imploring our "wise" cosmopolitan citizens to step up and "lead the way."[15] And the Clock keeps ticking.

THE DOOMSDAY ARGUMENT

In this age of terrorism post 9/11, world anxiety becomes our number one preoccupation. When deranged minds are willing to sacrifice their own lives during the suicidal terrorist acts of committing murder, no one or nation is immune from threat. The Brussels ISIS attack targeting the

---

14. Mecklin (2016), § 5.
15. Mecklin (2017), § 8.

international hub of the diplomatic world that stands for peace shows how symbolic hatred and revenge have become. In the wake of such persistent anxiety, "unhappy and paranoid" becomes the epithet we shall apply to characterize collective humanity. And just as Freud's seminal work, *Das Unbehagen in der Kultur*, described the unease, trepidation, and unhappiness within the culture of his day during the early rise of Hitler, we may justifiably conclude that the scale and ferocity of cross-cultural/ interfaith/interethnic aggression has intensified and gotten much worse since his time. The fantasy that men are inherently gentle creatures who are born good, free of dispositional sin, and untainted by primitive intent can no longer be sustained by critical reason. It is an empirical fact that by all historiographical accounts of cultural anthropology, human civilization has been forged on human conflict; attachment deficits in parent-child rearing practices; emotional, physical, and sexual abuse; traumatization; dehumanization; and war. Given the historical progression of civilization, what reasonable trajectory do we posit for the future of humanity?

The astrophysicist and cosmologist Brandon Carter has provided a mathematical formulation (using Bayes' theorem) that predicts the probability of human extinction.[16] Given that eight billion people are alive on this planet today, and that we are among the most people who have ever lived in the history of the human race, from a predictive statistical standpoint, it is speculated that there is an approximate 5% chance that we will expire within a couple hundred years and a 95% chance that complete human extinction will occur in approximately 7,000 years, with a possible degree of freedom extending this figure to just over 9,000 years. This is known as the "Doomsday Argument."[17] In other words, if all the humans

---

16. Although Carter (1974, 1983) introduced the notion of the anthropic principle in cosmology, he never intended to apply it to the question of human extinction, which was picked up by others, most notably John Leslie, and used to speculate about the end of the world.

17. Nick Bostrom (1998, 2002) provides a lengthy critique of the various types of doomsday arguments in science, cosmology, mathematics, and philosophy with an emphasis on anthropic bias and observation selection effects determining various outcomes, including the attribution of a priori probability weighting. Of course, depending upon the premises one presupposes or adopts, from mathematical-statistical-simulation models to philosophy and cultural anthropology, we get different probability shifts. Some claim to have refuted the argument based on probability theory, finding it highly speculative or simply a thought experiment, despite being inconsistent and incompatible

alive today are in a random place in the human history time line, then we are nearer to extinction than not.

Although different versions of this scenario vary in scope and formulation, including critiques, refutations, and rebuttals, philosopher John Leslie has championed this argument in his chilling speculations on the end of the world.[18] One cannot entertain the actual risks of complete human annihilation based on such brute evidence without sinking into worrisome pessimism. Leslie draws alarming attention to the underestimated dangers that threaten human extinction, including the notion that we could become extinct fairly soon. Despite the recognized risks of natural disaster, including volcanic eruptions, the Earth colliding with asteroids or comets, astronomical explosions such as supernovae, galactic center outbursts, and solar flares, or a complex breakdown of the Earth's biosphere, we are well aware that most of the immediate threats to the survival of the human race come from man. We damage our own ozone layer; dump toxins into our air, lands, and seas via mass industrial pollution; increase greenhouse effects that ruin our ecosystems; and introduce fatal viral diseases and new varieties of plague that infiltrate our continents. Soon the world could become uninhabitable. From nuclear war to germ warfare, radiation poisoning, biological and chemical warfare, terrorism, criminality, technological manipulations such as genetic engineering disasters, food infections (i.e., salmonella bacteria), computer-initiated network malfunctions, internet viruses, or techno-war that jeopardize human survival, and scientific hubris—like biohacking, nanotechnology, or careless physics experimentations "at immensely high energies, [that] will upset a space-filling 'scalar field' and destroy the world"[19]—these are but a few very serious reasons not to dismiss the ubiquitous threat of world annihilation.

Leslie gives a nice overview of the thrust of his reasoning on his version of the doomsday argument:

> One might at first expect the human race to survive, no doubt in evolutionarily much modified form, for millions or even billions of years,

---

with other refutations relying on probabilistic inferences, while others find the doomsday argument inconclusive.

18. See Leslie (1996).

19. Leslie (1996), p. 1.

perhaps just on Earth but, more plausibly, in huge colonies scattered through the galaxy and maybe even through many galaxies. Contemplating the entire history of the race—future as well as past history—I should in that case see myself as a very unusually early human. I might well be among the first 0.00001 per cent to live their lives. But what if the race is instead about to die out? I am then a fairly typical human. Recent population growth has been so rapid that, of all human lives lived so far, anything up to about 30 per cent . . . are lives which are being lived at this very moment. Now, whenever lacking evidence to the contrary one should prefer to think of one's own position as fairly typical rather than highly untypical. To promote the reasonable aim of making it quite ordinary that I exist where I do in human history, let me therefore assume that the human race will rapidly die out.[20]

Here, the question becomes, are we among the most humans living today at any one time in the history of the human race? Given the current state of our world population boom, we have good reason to believe we are. And if this is the case, all things being equal, based on the balance of probability, we can assume that we fall within a random distribution of every human who has ever lived in the history of the human race. So, in this way, following Leslie, we are fairly typical. Although we have no way of determining or knowing for certain the future of human life, or what may even constitute what a human being is or becomes due to biotechnology, genetic engineering, species evolution, and so forth, if we fall on a random human history time line, then this increases the statistical odds that we are closer to extinction than not.

Nick Bostrom notes that in Leslie's account, he does not claim that doom *will* come soon, but we must take into account empirical priors as existential risks, which shifts the balance of probability, and hence our confidence levels about these conditional probabilities.[21] In fact, Bostrom applies Bayes' theorem to Leslie's hypothesis:

Suppose we are entertaining two hypotheses about how many [people] there will have been in total:

---

20. Leslie (1990), pp. 65f.
21. Bostrom (2002), pp. 95–96.

H_1: There will have been a total of 200 billion humans.

H_2: There will have been a total of 200 trillion humans.

For simplicity, let us assume that these are the only possibilities. The next step is to assign prior probabilities to these hypotheses based on available empirical information (but ignoring, for the moment, information about your birth rank). For example, you might think that:

$$P(H_1) = 5\%$$

$$P(H_2) = 95\%$$

All that remains now is to factor in the information about your birth rank, which is in the neighborhood of 60 billion (R) for those of us who are alive at the beginning of the 21st century.

$$P(H_1 \backslash R) = \frac{P(R \backslash H_1)\, P(H_1)}{P(R|H_1)\, P(H_1) + P(R|H_2)\, P(H_2)} \tag{\#}$$

$$= \frac{\dfrac{1}{200 \cdot 10^9} \times .05}{\left(\dfrac{1}{200 \cdot 10^9} \times .05\right) + \left(\dfrac{1}{200 \cdot 10^{12}} \times .95\right)}$$

$\approx .98$

In this example, the prior probability of Doom soon (H_1) of 5% is increased to about 98% when you take into account your birth rank.[22]

---

22. Bostrom (2002), pp. 95–96.

Although Bostrom ignores (for the sake of parsimony) numerous other possible hypotheses one could test based on Bayes' probability theorem, we may appreciate how this lends credibility to Leslie's thesis.

EXISTENTIAL RISKS

Nearly three decades ago, John Leslie, arguably one of the leading pioneers of existential risk studies, perspicaciously situated our current global concerns. He positioned the risk of extinction by examining first-order threats to the survival of the human race to shock us into alarm and raise ethical consciousness with the hope that we would immediately begin to make risk-reduction efforts. He began with risks already well recognized, and then presented risks that are often unrecognized, focusing on (a) natural and (b) man-made disasters, as well as (c) philosophical and psychological dangers, what have come to be called existential risk parameters:[23]

Well-Recognized Risks

1. Nuclear war

2. Biological warfare

3. Chemical warfare

4. Destruction of the ozone layer

5. Greenhouse effect

6. Poisoning by pollution, environmental degradation, and the population crisis

7. Naturally occurring diseases

Under-Recognized Risks

A: NATURAL DISASTERS

1. Volcanic eruptions

2. Strikes by asteroids and comets

---

23. See Leslie's (1996) opening discussion, pp. 4–14, but these following topics are elaborated throughout his entire book.

3. An extreme ice age due to passage through an interstellar cloud

4. Nearby supernovae, galactic center outbursts, and solar flares

5. Other massive astronomical explosions (e.g., black hole explosions; black hole mergers)

6. Breakdown of complex systems (e.g., Earth's biosphere; the solar system itself)

7. Something, we know not what

B: MAN-MADE DISASTERS

1. Unwillingness to rear children (e.g., population shrinkage among rich nations)

2. Disasters from genetic engineering

3. Disasters from nanotechnology

4. Computer-caused disasters and computer replacements for humans

5. Disasters in other branches of technology

6. Physics experiments triggering global catastrophe (e.g., creating a new Big Bang in the laboratory)

7. High-energy physics experiments producing an all-destroying phase transition (e.g., a scalar field producing a vacuum metastability danger; igniting the atmosphere)

8. Annihilation by extraterrestrials

9. Other things we do not know that can or will transpire from human technological invention and intervention

Philosophical–Psychological–Sociological Risks

1. Threats associated with religions and their ideologies

2. Nihilistic pessimism

3. Ethical doctrines that are misguided, deny human values, or have no duty toward the future for merely "possible" people

4. Breakdown of "inalienable rights"

5. Uncooperative behavior among individuals, masses, and nations (e.g., prisoner's dilemma)

6. Blindly avenging justice when no palpable good comes from it (e.g., a nuclear retaliation)

Although some of these risks seem improbable, if not far-fetched, when taken as a whole, they have a chilling effect. Despite the fact that he executed these warnings decades ago, his predictions continue to hold sway today, as he had anticipated many of the potential planetary threats we currently face. If we take these premonitions seriously, we should be taking steps to ameliorate them and prevent future catastrophe by shifting the probability balance. Here Leslie calls for a prescriptive ethics that is very much in keeping with recent swings in global ecological consciousness surrounding the need to combat climate change; push for nuclear disarmament; develop early detection systems for asteroids or other cosmic threats from space that are on a collision course with Earth; establish controls over physics experiments, nanotechnology, artificial intelligence, and the like, where scientific and technological advances could have runaway consequences if left unregulated. But we must not diminish, let alone ignore, the potential for species-annihilating disasters augmented by existential risk.

In our contemporary era of political and religious violence that legitimizes the morality of war with the support of military science, our conflict of cultures begets and bears witness to increased human tragedy and traumatization. There are pernicious threats associated with the subversive activities of fundamentalist religious groups that embrace ethical relativism and prescriptivism based on collective ideology just as there are repercussions from foolish decisions made by narcissistically grandiose politicians who hype up a country's citizenry based on an appeal to emotion in the pursuit of national self-interest. If we don't kill each other by destroying our environment through chemical, biological, and nuclear war, leading to loss of biodiversity, disease, disastrous climate change, greenhouse calamity, desertification, and pollution of our planet, then overpopulation will surely erode our environment and tax our natural resources to satisfy basic human needs, which will likely lead to mass panic, mayhem, and global warfare. When people have no grain to eat in a global rice crisis, the moral principle of human rights becomes a vacuous concept.

SHOULD WE TAKE THE DOOMSDAY ARGUMENT SERIOUSLY?

So far, we have been playing with the idea that we could manufacture a future prediction based on statistical probability without knowing all the constants of the universe, the exact nature of the empirical priors, the conditional probabilities, competing possibilities and counterfactuals, and possible future contingencies and contexts that will come into being. Bostrom is particularly keen on unveiling human bias, observation selection effects, and self-sampling assumptions that militate the argument. I would add how psychological projection and the various political and economic prejudices that drive natural scientists and mathematicians to devise their preferred methodologies and equation models and attempt to derive valid conclusions from them is potentially corrupt from the start, so any prediction is therefore inferential and speculative at best and must be weighed conservatively. Although probability, propensity, and confirmation theories do just that, all one has to do is quibble with or tweak the premises to get the desired outcomes one wants, especially if certain formal properties are merely formulations of a theorem where predictions follow mathematically. This all depends on how you chose to define your reference class, classify the sample according to specific properties you want to emphasize, and the hypotheses you want to test. There is always an irreducibly subjective element to all this that can change from person to person and condition to condition under different personal motivations and contextual circumstances.

Skeptics who challenge the doomsday argument offer many warranted criticisms. Bostrom reports that he has encountered more than 100 objections to the doomsday argument, many of which he meticulously objects to or views as invalid, the details of which do not need to distract us here. But he ultimately concludes that the argument is not supportable due to anthropic bias, paradoxes of self-sampling assumptions, reference class problems, relativity of observers and observations made, and the abstract use of thought experiments that are not empirically probable, not to mention the fact that all observations and predictions are herme-neutically mediated interpretations that are irreducibly subjective. We may further ask how could a mathematical theorem have any predictive validity when variables are arbitrarily postulated and applied to suit a theorist's self-predicated speculation? Since when should we assume that the complexities of life and human behavior can be predicted and controlled for? How can we anticipate, let alone regulate, such complex variables to get desired outcomes by manipulating the conditions that would bring about desired effects when we are simply arbitrarily play-ing with conditionals? How could one possibly know what conditionals in the past truly were, or if they really existed, let alone know how the future will transpire? How can we predict the possible future global state of affairs based on the past, let alone one person's life? Why should we assume that the universe is determinate when it could be indeterminate and open to flux, variability, change, and process that are not predictable, let alone accurate when positing the constants that are presumed to exist to begin with? In other words, so-called scientific predictions rest on the dubious premise that the world, hence the future, is determined a priori.

A calculation is not an argument but, rather, is used to support or refute a doomsday scenario. But we may ask, doom or simply gloom? For example, depending upon what probabilistic inferences we draw, premises we presume, or propositions we posit, it is conceivable that even if some of these dangers are addressed and mitigated, it will not erase *in globo* some very heavily weighted risks. But even so, rather than leading to complete human extinction, they may subject us as humanity to a more gradual decline or leveling-off process, even if controlled, that could begin relatively soon compared to our random place in the human history time line despite that conceivably it could be prolonged and/or relegated to large-scale withering decays in certain parts of the world while having less pernicious effects in others. Here the balance of actual empirical conditions, not just abstract theoretical or mathematical formulas, must be factored in when calculations derived from statistical prediction seek to justify the very premises doomsday arguments wish to advance.

OUR FINAL CENTURY?

Like John Leslie, cosmologist Martin Rees has been equally concerned about the fate of civilization by emphasizing the risks of bio, cyber, and nanotechnology that could either be used deliberately and sinisterly to perpetrate acts of megaterror or as unintended consequences of error due to technological malfunctions or mishaps, scientific hubris such as lack of self-restraint and regulation of industry, laboratory mistakes, nuclear mismanagement, superintelligent computers run amok, or other human botch-ups that could bring about catastrophic ends. In fact, in a rather sensational way, he went on record in *Wired* magazine and staked a $1,000 bet "That by the year 2020 an instance of bioerror or bioterror will have killed a million people."[24] Although he technically lost the bet, despite being unsettled,[25] he was confident enough in this bleak forecast to lay good money on the table. Moreover, he predicts that "the odds are no better than fifty-fifty that our present civilisation on Earth will survive to the end of the present century . . . What happens here on Earth, in this century, could conceivably make the difference between a near eternity filled with ever more complex and subtle forms of life and one filled with nothing but base matter."[26] Grim prospects indeed.

Changes and improvements in technology occur so rapidly that futurists predict everything from brain enhancement through implants and psychopharmacology, curing disease, doubling our life spans, and colonizing the galaxies, to genetically modifying humans and engineering a new posthuman species. Nanotechnology is deemed the new instrument of prosperity, whether in computer science, engineering, medicine, neuroscience, and robotics. Miniaturization is essential to all developing

---

24. Rees (2003), p. 74.
25. Unless it is revealed and verified that the new coronavirus outbreak was produced in a Chinese lab and was leaked to the world due to bioerror. See Maxmen and Mallapaty's (2021) discussion of the various possibilities in *Nature*.
26. Maxmen & Mallapaty (2021), p. 8.

technologies, from a computer chip to microsurgery to constructing a drone. But what if nanomachines acquire the capacity to replicate themselves, form superintelligences, "take over" information technologies and computer networks, and control the fate of human beings? Although it may sound like a futuristic sci-fi thriller, experts think it's just around the corner. Micro, bio, and cybertechnologies may also be used for ill designed by human intent, such as terrorist organizations, disgruntled dissident groups, embittered misfits and lone wolves, or rogue states in military conflict who initiate nuclear warfare, release noxious fast-spreading pathogens into the air or in water supplies, or generate Internet software viruses that can infiltrate and destroy valuable databases, steal from financial accounts, destabilize corporate and governmental network systems, and hack and extract confidential information of national security. The use of chemicals on civilian populations—from the anthrax attacks to chlorine poisoning in Aleppo by the Assad regime—is a reminder of how easily this can be accomplished. More ominously, lethally engineered airborne viruses may be developed and released into the atmosphere that could potentially wipe out large-scale populations in relatively brief periods of time before medical intervention can be mobilized or antidotes developed in labs. This outbreak scenario would make COVID-19, SARS, swine flu, and Ebola look insignificant in comparison to the devastation biochemically engineered viruses could wreak on the world.

Rees believes that technological advances *in themselves* will render society more susceptible to disruption and attenuate world safety, especially when biotechnologies are used for human terror or encounter misadventures through human or computer error. Threats stemming from new science are most worrisome. It is possible that paranoiac relations between superpowers, or even a superpower and a rogue nation-state, could escalate a nuclear enactment that would ignite the world. Russia, North Korea, and Iran are prominent examples. Should such fearmongering be troublesome in today's climate? If we estimate that human nature is ultimately primal and would succumb to base predispositions, then I see no reason to be optimistic that we will transcend our primordial natures if there is no superimposed constraint by a macrosocial ethical structure such as reformed (new) governments or international central agencies, even if this requires law enforcement or military intervention. The notion of nuclear deterrence by threat of mass retaliation has not gone away since the Cold War era. In fact, it has intensified since the globalization of technology.

If Rees is correct, we are all anxiously waiting for the bomb to drop (or the next plane or train to crash or explode as an act of terror) based on paranoiac reactions due to inadvertence or misjudgment from government officials that could trigger a runaway war-scenario hysteria, whereby the ideology of retaliation before one's own nuclear arsenal is destroyed enjoys popular support despite crushing the notion of world diplomacy. If everyone overestimates threat, overreacts, and assumes worst-case situations as the empirically "objective" measure on which to make global political decisions, then we are all deeply entrenched in the proposition that human political relations are hopelessly subjugated by psychological and irrational currents that fuel psychopathology in all spheres of social and cultural governance. There is no way to minimize this collective emotional effect given that each community or sociocultural group believes the antithetical Other is out to exploit, harm, or deracinate them in some capacity, even when such prejudicial projective fears have no merit. The mere fact that human relations operate in such modes of social discourse in every culture validates the notion that human nature is grounded upon universal experience. Groups of individuals or social collectives would not be fearful of alterity if there were not negative encounters borne of experience and retained in historical memory.

What would have happened if the al Qaeda terrorists who flew the planes into the World Trade Center and the Pentagon had had a nuclear warhead aboard? Imagine ISIS, Hamas, or any terrorist group that acquires a nuclear weapon: a suicidal martyr would be more than happy to sacrifice his life and take out as many people as possible. Targeting a highly congested city center, airport, railway system, and/or skyscrapers for detonation—all of which have occurred—could conceivably kill millions of people with a nuclear explosion, not to mention countless others affected by the fallout. We only have to envision the mushroom cloud that enveloped Hiroshima to be reminded of such a tragedy. Rees further points out the "consequences could be even more catastrophic if a suicidal zealot were to become intentionally infected with smallpox and trigger an epidemic; in future there could be viruses even more lethal (and without an antidote),"[27] a lesson we have learned from COVID. Add to this how pandemics and viruses of another kind through cyber hacking have become a real problem affecting in some form or another those of us who rely on computer and information technology for personal, business, and work relations to the point that we are ontically dependent upon the internet and mobile phone devices as an integral part of our daily existence.

A scientific (empirical) fact is that if a nuclear explosion were to occur in any location, it would leak radiation, immediately spread, and pollute a very large geographic region in a matter of minutes. Enriched uranium (separated U_{235}), according to the experts, is a far greater risk because it is easier to create a nuclear explosion from this fuel. All that is required is to get such a rigged warhead (as little as the size of a grapefruit) to explode in a highly densely populated area. And what about nuclear power plants? Rees argues that if these risk scenarios were properly considered, it would have drastically reshaped the way power plants were architecturally designed to conform to more proper safety standards, such as putting everything underground. And with lack of regulation of the oversight and maintenance of Third World airlines, it would be easy to commandeer a plane and/or bribe an official to accommodate nefarious intents and acts. The Middle East is particularly ripe for a nuclear apocalypse. Tack on the religious belief in eschatology, and here we have a perfect storm.

---

27. Rees (2003), p. 42.

5

Apocalypse Now

EVERY THEOLOGY, AS WITH ARCHAIC SOCIETIES, HAS ITS OWN ESCHA-
tology. Endings precipitate new beginnings, and beginnings recapitulate
the original cosmogonic acts of endings that preceded it, the Chaos
before Creation. Ending conditions Beginning. Openings come from
Closings. A new state emerges from death as a rising phoenix. Restoration, regeneration, and rebirth are new creations that imply a return
to paradise—an Eden—the original state of man. Fall and return from
the order of being is an oscillating narrative spread throughout human
history; only the contexts and details vary. In eschatological prophecies,
recovering the lost perfection of beginnings is an unconscious motivation
in the destruction and abolition of the world, symbolic or otherwise, for
the pining to return to a so-called state of ecstasy as recapitulation of the
perfection of origin as lost paradise fuels the human fantasy of pure bliss.

There is no such thing, and there never was or will be. But this fantasy is far from dead. In more sophisticated cosmogonies, the restoration
as renewal of the cosmos is achieved symbolically by summoning the
original bliss of beginning as recovered in its absolute reality: what was
lost in its original perfection is now returned. What was lost is recovered
anew, reinstated in all its glory *in illo tempore*.

Mircea Eliade, in various works, elaborates on the phenomenology
of eschatology in a variety of cultures. The notion of the perfection at
the beginning is absorbed into cosmogonic celebrations, such as the
observance of cosmic cycles or the circularity of the new year that brings
about renewal and reinstatements of origins. A closely associated idea

that developed alongside cosmogonic observance was the notion that for something truly new to begin, all elements and remnants of the old cycle must be completely destroyed. As Eliade puts it:

> to obtain an *absolute* beginning, the end of a World must be total. Eschatology is only the prefiguration of a cosmogony to come. But every eschatology insists on this fact: the New Creation cannot take place before this world is abolished once and for all. There is no question of regenerating what has degenerated; nothing will serve but to destroy the old world so that it can be re-created *in toto*. The obsession with the bliss of the beginnings demands the destruction of all that has existed—and hence has degenerated—since the beginning of the World; there is no other way to restore the initial perfection.[1]

Myths of the End of the World have suffused the social fabrics and historical developments of human civilization. These particularly play a central role in the three Abrahamic monotheistic religions in their various conceptions of the apocalypse, cataclysm, or Armageddon. The fixation of the believer is on the recapitulation of the primordial past *ab origine* fulfilled through the deliverance of a divine future, a World to Come that brings about an ecstatic reunion with God. This merger fantasy of achieving divine perfection and elation with the godhead fuels cosmogonies of the future, as we may observe in all the major world religions, not just the Abrahamic ones.

From a psychoanalytic point of view, obsessional fixation with ἔσχατος—the End, the Last, Finality—belies an unconscious anxiety about death. Mortality, finitude, and death are so emotionally difficult to existentially embrace that psychic defenses of the masses over the eons have ingeniously invented escape hatches in our sublimated forms of religious doctrine. In the Abrahamic traditions, in Christianity we have a happy ending fairy-tale drama come true through the destruction of evil and the profane for a better world of purity and rapture. The fate of the soul and humankind is at stake, subject to divine judgment and violent world events that bring about salvation, hence a return to perfection and

---

1. Eliade (1963), pp. 51–52.

the loving embrace of The Maker, who has a place for you in his beatific family in the kingdom of heaven if you are a good boy or girl. Although versions (Christian or otherwise) of this absurd and "patently infantile" fantasy of an afterlife are cherished by most of the world population,[2] we may nevertheless observe how far the desirous intellect of social collectives will go to ensure its ultimate wish fulfillment.

Given that myths of global cataclysm are universally widespread, it speaks to a collective psyche ensconced in anxiety about death, redemption, release from suffering, and in most eschatologies, an afterlife. It further speaks to a global fantasy of what could be termed "biblical proportions" in the triumph of good by vanquishing evil, where a new world is re-created and restored to its original significance and purity, sin is eradicated, the human race obliterated as we know it, and renewal and regeneration achieved through the emergence of a new humanity. Here eschatology, cosmogony, and divine will converge in a fantasy of an end to come that is rife with apocalyptic prophecies, visions, and religious discourse spanning almost all cultures. In monotheistic traditions, the End of Days is accompanied by the culmination and triumph of sacred history, total destruction of mankind, resurrection of the dead, the Last Judgment, the restoration of Paradise, and the final fate of humanity following deific destiny. Regardless of cultural myth, catastrophe is universal. Despite cultural variations on how the godhead is conceived, world extinction is inescapable.

ON SIN

The total destruction of the world by divine providence is predicated on humanity's sin. Otherwise, why would an all good and loving Father kill his children? After all, transgression, folly, weakness of will, and

---

2. Freud's (1930) contempt for religious ideologies is well known and exemplified in the following passage: "What the common man understands by his religion—with the system of doctrines and promises which on the one hand explains to him the riddles of this world with enviable completeness, and, on the other, assures him that a careful Providence will watch over his life and will compensate him in a future existence for any frustrations that he suffers here. The common man cannot imagine this Providence otherwise than in the figure of an enormously exalted father . . . The whole thing is so patently infantile, so foreign to reality, that to anyone with a friendly attitude to humanity it is painful to think that the great majority of mortals will never be able to rise above this view of life" (p. 74).

wickedness deserve no forgiveness from a gentle Master. But setting aside for a moment the fantasy of a supreme supernatural psychopath cleansing the Earth of its degenerate offspring, the term "sin" (ME *sinne* <OE *synn*) has other, less biblical, meanings. The word does not seem to come from Indo-European roots but, rather, is derived from *äken* (ache) in Low German and "blood guilt" (ἄγος) in Hellenic.[3] In Greek αμαρτάνω is to err. And from the Latin *sōns*, guilty, and *morbus sonticus*, a disease or critical illness, but also, distress; that is, the word solely resides in the negative.

The problem of sin for Luther was quite simple: any veering away from (let alone negation of) God was blasphemy. But there is an even more base nefariousness to sin than this.[4] In Heidegger's lectures on Luther (1924), regarding the "Disputatio contra scholasticam theologiam" [Disputation against Scholastic Theology] of 1517, he summarizes Thesis 17: "man wants to be God. And this is precisely the essence of sin."[5] But for Luther, in fact, there is a two-fold instantiation of primordial sin: wanting to be God via negating God as God is the true essence of sin.[6] In the mode of sin, man bears himself open, which is disclosed, yet *in itself* remains occulted within one's nature. In other words, sin remains hidden within us even when externally absent. As Heidegger puts it, sin is a movement "as a mode of the being of man bears in itself."[7] Wanting God not to be God and wanting to be God instead is not only the atheistic hubris of an omnipotent oedipal victory, but it also means that God is not allowed to sin.[8] This privilege is reserved for man in the mode of *wanting to be* God.[9] For example, the radical instigation of murder by assuming terrorist actions on behalf of God and his divine law, let us say, is a grandiose exhibitionism of wanting to be God (or his emissary). Negation of the deity while wanting to be supreme, however, is the more original sin. Here it is only on the condition that one is acting as though

---

3. Indo-European Lexicon. Linguistics Research Center, University of Texas at Austin, https://lrc.la.utexas.edu/lex/master/0018

4. *Nefās* is offense against divine or moral law (*ne-* negative prefix + *fās*, law, right).

5. Heidegger (1924), "The Problem of Sin in Luther," *Supplements*, p. 106.

6. Cf. Luther (1517): "*velle se esse deum et deum non esse deum*" [he himself wants to be God and God not to be God], p. 225, 1.1f.

7. Heidegger (1924), p. 108.

8. Yet it is this "cry of abandonment" that occurs in the claim of the incarnation and the cross.

9. Whereas in the incarnation, God is wanting to be man.

he is divine or under God's will of moral deliverance that sin is occluded, for God *cannot* sin, a rather convenient exculpation.

But "the real sin" for Luther is "unbelief," the turning away from God (*aversio dei*) and his Word.[10] Listening to another voice, another word, with another ear, is to be stirred up *against* the Almighty, and in doing so one loses his original being before God. By falling away in disbelief, withdrawal, and disobedience, heaping sin onto more sin, this perpetual negation and flight lead to eternal ruin. Adam even has the nerve to accuse God to excuse himself of his passions. But of course, the woman is ultimately to blame: Eve is the originator of sin [*auctor peccati*] for accusing God of creating the serpent of temptation—of desire, and for transferring guilt and contempt onto the Creator, the crescendo of projection.

How moral health became religionized surely has its roots in antiquity. Sin is a problem of ethics, moral failing, lack of virtue. Once originally attributed to the corruption of what was originally good, sin is now criminalized but not necessarily confined to the penal or mental institution. Sin may be relegated to moral judgment alone, internalized, interiorized, or impugned. Punishment may be public or private, reserved for a secret sacredness, nonetheless. Justice is considered an act of moral righteousness, as fair *or* partial as that may be, one instituted into law, whether secular or holy. Society cannot function without law, above all the moral imperative: thou shall not murder. Originally justice applied to failure to uphold divine law, the moral code of ordained values, where guilt was due to the noetic effects of sin (*privatio boni*).

Today, the prevalence of sin among the multitudes may be seen as the result of social malaise; the sickness of universal spirit; a cultural neurosis where judgment, punishment, guilt, and shame are unconsciously mediated by a sick soul. Sin is displacement as a form of psychological suffering converted into symptomatology: the symptom becomes the punishment for failure to achieve a moral ideal. Neurotic guilt, anxiety, depression, reactionary trauma, and religious fanaticism (mania, hysteria) become the new conversion disorders of our day. But rather than see how suffering is due to the rigid application of moral appraisals and shadow

---

10. Heidegger (1924), pp. 108–110.

projections onto human desire and action, where punishment fantasies populate conscious and unconscious life, our imperfect ways of being are amplified by cultural belief in divine judgment. Here sin is not merely personal shortcoming, peccadillo, or turpitude; it is an offense to God.

The symptom of sin is based on a cruel conscience as the introjection of a harsh superego (*Über-Ich*). This cruel moral faculty becomes the ground and origin of law and hammer, decree and penalty. But this deific superego is not only unforgiving; it converts sin into crime against God, the ultimate taboo. In messianic or apocalyptic thinking, divine superego judgment applies to social disobedience against divinity, which is tantamount to collective collusion with nihilism as ethical irresponsibility in need of deracination and total destruction. And any enjoyment of sin— the pleasure of *jouissance*—is a capital offense. Sin is the symptom of a false morality interpassively superimposed on society as failure to live up to illusory values, such as purity and ideality. This ensures that no one is without sin or guilt. But guilty before whom? The Macroanthropos? And who is to blame for a suffering humanity, one that needs to be wiped out? Is this not God's sin?[11] And here we have the problem of theodicy, the vindication of God.

APOCALYPSE, MILLENNIALISM, AND *ESCHATON*

Consider this: extraterrestrials, or ancient cosmic astronauts, are believed to have colonized Earth, exploited its resources, genetically engineered and enslaved its inhabitants, and entered into nuclear war with rival factions that destroyed competing family clans and their planet circa 2100 BCE, destined to come again through the recapitulation of a predetermined cyclical Celestial Time 4,000 years later: namely, Armageddon and the prophecy of Return, a messianic Second Coming, the End of Days predicted to occur before the end of our current age of Pisces.[12] What sounds like science fiction is touted to be the revelations

---

11. Eliade interviewed C. G. Jung at the 1952 Eranos conference on his "Answer to Job" where Jung (1952) states, "This book has always been on my mind, but I waited forty years to write it. I was terribly shocked when, still a child, I read the Book of Job for the first time. I discovered that Yahweh is unjust, that he is even an evildoer" (pp. 225–26).

12. In what is portrayed as "nonfiction," Zecharia Sitchin (2007) makes these predictions in a bestselling series of works called The Earth Chronicles, which has sold millions of copies worldwide and

of the *eschaton*: namely, that the past will repeat itself in a future world to come—that is, a world to end. The eternal return is a repetition of what has already occurred and will reoccur as humanity's preordained fate.

It is hard not to entertain that this type of thinking would abound among the ultrareligious, superstitious, paranoids, survivalists, fringe groups, and conspiracy theorists preparing for the cataclysm, such as what we observed at the turn of the new millennium—the Y2K scare professing that computers would crash or debilitate mass informa- tion-communication technologies, thus leading to widespread power outages, food and fuel insecurities, and pandemonium to the point that billions were spent by governments and private industry alike to subvert the disaster. This so-called techno-apocalypse was further whipped up by Christian evangelists profiting on fearmongering while preaching the final days and gladly passing the collection plate to their congrega- tions to enrich their ministries (and line their pockets). This was further observed by the 2012 hysteria surrounding the forlorn prediction that the world would be destroyed on December 21 at the culmination of the Mayan calendar when the sun's magnetism and the Earth's magnetic field would completely reverse, thereby producing pole shifts, sun storms, solar flares, nuclear engulfment, widespread earthquakes, tidal waves, ice lands, runaway poisonous gases, radioactive fallout, and the reenactment of the biblical flood where the Earth's iron core implodes and nearly all of the planet's population perishes in apocalyptic horror. These claims were made by Patrick Geryl, author of an international bestseller called *The Orion Prophecy*, where he predicted world catastrophe via so-called "mathematical proof" based on Atlantean, Egyptian, and Mayan astro- nomical calculations and "secret codes" he deciphered, even going so far as to warn humanity in 2001 to prepare for survival:

Food supplies will be destroyed, medical care non-existent, rescue workers themselves will have perished. In short, without careful plan- ning we won't make it. Therefore we must urgently form groups to start working on this enormous task. "Noah's Arks" will have to be built to

---

been translated into more than 25 languages, despite being deemed by his critics as pseudoscience, pseudohistory, mythopoesis, and quackery.

get us through the tidal wave. Food and energy supplies will have to be built up. An endless number of things have to be done, and we only have a few years left before the fatal date.[13]

Of course, Geryl was deemed a nut and his prophecy a hoax.

Various cults and fundamentalists of all types gravitate toward apocalyptic thinking, not simply for eschatological reasons but due to social conditioning, familial and cultural trauma, economic disenfranchisement, reactionary defense, and psychological disturbance of many kinds, even if benign or based in fear and ignorance due to lack of knowledge, as we may witness in many developing "third-world" countries where illiteracy and a lack of education are the norm. A prime example of this is in the Congo where tribal customs and religious beliefs alike are quick to attribute increased climate crisis, ecological decline, disease, poverty, and war as signs of an imminent End. More radical religious cult outliers, such as the Brotherhood of Light, are typified by delusional pronouncements attributing Armageddon to a cosmic filtering process or divine "house cleaning." Rather than conceiving of the apocalypse as the whole world being blown up, where people are strewn in pieces throughout some asteroid belt, or when true believers who have pure souls are transported in great rapture through a porthole to Heaven,

> Our view of the Armageddon differs considerably from current thought in that we see it more as a filtering process—separating the tares from the wheat, the light from darkness—in every pore, level, and sector of human society, for the true objective of the Armageddon is a general, comprehensive housecleaning designed to rid the earth plane of all negative influences, those of Dark Forces, so that the conditions necessary for the flowering of a new golden age, the Age of Aquarius, can prevail. . . . The final battle between light and darkness is the project of the Master Sanctus Germanus. This great Master of the Great Brotherhood of Light has taken his place as the Hierarch of the New Age, the Age of Aquarius. He leads the battle. Those souls who are for

---

13. Geryl & Ratinckx (2001), p. 10. Also see Geryl (2005), Joseph (2007), and Sounds True (2007) for extensive discussions on apocalyptic discourse.

Him stand on the right, while those who oppose him shall be banished from the earth plane.[14]

Notice how the Master Holy Brother becomes the surrogate for Jesus the flock is implored to follow, the new contemporary Messiah who will deliver the faithful from sin and evil. And who is this Master Sanctus Germanus? Why, he is a Deity, an "Ascended Being" who, in his past lives, and who had countless incarnations in his mission of soul liberation before his Ascension,[15] is one of many "representative spirits" that "played a major role in the evolution of earth's affairs."[16] This is according to Dr. Michael P. Mau, a practitioner of Telepathic Healing and The Amanuensis of the Holy Brother, who is a Medium for the Great Brotherhood of Light and apparently writes down whatever the deity communicates to him. Before his mediumship, he claims to have earned a doctorate in international relations from the University of Pennsylvania, was a Fulbright scholar, and worked as a consultant for the United Nations. Obviously, thought disorder does not discriminate based on education.

Common themes among millennialist apocalyptic mentality and eschatology is that the past determines the future, the future is a repetition of re-enacted past events, cosmogony is governed by supernatural forces according to Divine Will, and astrological patterns are causally fixed in space and time, which are written in the stars. When "cosmic law has determined that their cycle is up—finished,"[17] this signals the End Times. Of course, this assumes a totally *predetermined* universe which has fixed causal laws, no element of freedom or chance, human or otherwise, and that everything necessarily unfolds according to divine plan. Why a supreme being would content itself with creating a predetermined cosmos where sin, evil, and world destruction are preprogrammed into the very fabric of spacetime itself is as logically contradictory as it is delusional. Incapable of critical thinking or self-reflection, like sheep in the meadow, the flock merely listens to what the preacher says. And sadly,

---

14. See Mau (2003), pp. 120–122.
15. The Great Brotherhood of Light (2019), http://www.sanctusgermanus.net/english/Sanctus%20Germanus.html#1
16. Mau (2003), p. 22.
17. Mau (2003), p. 122.

many fundamentalists and vulnerable sectors of society have already drunk the Kool-Aid.[18]

THE (UN)HOLY LAND

The Middle East is a very scary place. It is the least holy of all lands, for the specter of divine doom sets the stage for a hovering anxiety the region is compelled to bring about. Armageddon is delusional in the sense that it is believed to be preordained by God when it is entirely orchestrated by men of social power. Despite the shared faith in His Holy Presence, each religion (Judaism, Christianity, Islam) claims legitimacy to the archaic ground of belief *ab origine* and property rights to sacred space granted by God's grace *in illo tempore*.

Since the terrorist attacks of 9/11 and the collapse of the Israeli-Palestinian peace efforts, the Holy Land has become the epicenter of terror, war, and international instability. Religious extremism, the pollution of sacred soil, and control over the Temple Mount (Al-Aqsa) has led to millennial visions motivating the need to ignite the world to make it whole. Gershom Gorenberg chronicles how the explosion of violence between Israelis and Palestinians is linked to control over the Temple Mount, which has stood at the root of the Jewish-Arab conflict since the beginning, hence leading to the Al-Aqsa Intifada and bin Laden's need to avenge the presence of American troops in the holy places where the symbols of Islam (e.g., Medina, Mecca, the Al-Aqua Mosque) have been vitiated.[19]

Black Tuesday was such an outcome. Israeli control over Jerusalem with American support only foments hatred of Jews and the United States that are seen as infidels. Since 9/11, extremist organizations have grown like weeds: al-Qaeda, Taliban, Jihadists, Islamic State, Boko Haram, Hezbollah, Hamas are just a fraction of the fundamentalist groups driving much of global terrorism, and the goal of such groups is to establish

---

18. Since the novel coronavirus (COVID-19), a most recent example is how Iranians and Orthodox Russians continued to go to mosque and church and even licked religious insignia in their places of worship to show their devotion and belief in God's protection in the midst of the outbreak of the pandemic, hence infecting themselves and spreading the virus, likely resulting in incalculable deaths.
19. See Gorenberg (2000) for a detailed account of the religious tensions giving rise to the Al-Aqsa Intifada and the al-Qaeda attacks on September 11, 2001.

a series of pan-Islamic caliphates throughout the globe. Inciting Muslims to kill Jews and reclaim original territory under prophetic visions to bring about an End of Days fortifies the delusion of final redemption and holy war. The Mount symbolizes the place where the End Times are destined to come about, and Jewish rule only marks its desecration.

Phil Torres highlights how "applied eschatology"[20] involves dispensational convictions about the future state of the apocalypse that determine how agents intentionally act toward achieving that goal, whether militant individuals, groups, leaders, or governments. The hotbed is the Middle East, but it can be anywhere, as terror shows no bounds; yet it is prophesised to transpire in the *Promised Land*—namely, contemporary Israel, Palestine, and Jordan, including parts of Syria, Saudi Arabia, Iraq, and Egypt. Dispensationalism—that is, psychologically compelling narratives about the End Times—also traverses many religious belief systems including Judaism, Zoroastrianism, Christianity, and Islam. It results in variations on resurrection; the Rapture; and the Return, where the soul, after having been separated from the body and convalescing in the bosom of the Lord, returns from paradise into its gloriously perfected, resurrected corpse, only then to return at some unspecified future time to the Kingdom of Heaven. Although eschatological stories vary in scope and context, such as undergoing a Tribulation, as well as divine judgment or condemnation, hence cast into purgatory or perdition, such discourse stimulates profound psychological motivations governing End Times prophecy, preparation, and enactments.

Depending upon which end time narrative is promulgated and adopted, revelations and signs of the *eschaton* are abundant, from wars, plagues, famine, droughts, beasts, earthquakes, and other natural disasters, where "Nation will rise against nation, and kingdom against kingdom" (Mark 13: 7–8); when God finishes judging mankind for its sin. In Islamic fatalism, "The Last Hour will not come until the Muslims fight against the Jews and kill them. And when a Jew will hide behind a wall or a tree, the wall or tree will cry out: 'O Muslim! O servant of Allah!

---

20. Torres (2016), p. 160.

There is a Jew behind me.' And will come to kill him."[21] It does not help matters that the Qur'ān places "enmity" on the "Jews" (Sūra V. 67, 85) and orders the Muslim to "fight and slay the Pagans wherever ye find them" (Sūra IX. 5). And when everything revolves around the existence of a Jewish state in Palestine, dispensational convictions see fermenting terror and war as the fulfillment of prophecy. Not only do extremists want to impede peace and justice in the Middle East, but they want to accelerate the terminus of history by sparking a nuclear Armageddon. This is our current world climate, and Iran is in the spotlight.

Suffice it to say that these eschatologies under the influence of fundamentalist apocalyptic dogma are delusional and dangerous precisely because they are constructing an End scenario of how things *ought* to be; based on a collective psychosis, extremists are apt to try to bring about with strategic vision, such as weaponizing a bubonic plague. When extremists such as the Islamic State revel in creating a state of terror to advance their prophecy by bringing about a glorious, preordained End in the name of God's Will, the stakes don't get any higher.

Religious violence is thought to be a sacred duty sustaining the globalization of terror under the influence of holy orders tasked with the eradication of the profane. For the extremist, it is seen as a "moral necessity."[22] Of course, this invites pathological actions when alterity equals blasphemy under the twisted logic of redemption and duty even when serving the same God. This distorted thinking obeys a principle of divine sanctioned anarchy that informs the political ethos of violence directed toward the dehumanized Other who personifies evil. The religious intolerance of radical Islam and Zionism, particularly Judaic and Christian, may both be accused of enacting a rigid splitting where history, cultural difference, and opposing beliefs fortify a vicious impasse based on malice where the paranoid-schizoid position becomes an entrenched fixture

---

21. Jean-Pierre Filiu (2011), *Apocalypse in Islam*, p. 17. Compare to Osama bin Laden's 1998 interview in preaching this particular *hadith*: "We are sure of Allah's victory and our victory against the Americans and the Jews, as promised by the Prophet, peace be upon him: 'Judgment Day shall not come until the Muslims fight the Jews, where the Jews will hide behind trees and stones, and the tree and the stone will speak and say, 'Muslim, behind me is a Jew. Come and kill him'" (cited in Gorenberg's 2001 preface, pp. v–vi).
22. See Richard Miller (2010), p. 10.

in the Middle Eastern psyche. In the end, violating the human rights, respect, and dignity of others in the name of religious authority offers no hiding place or reprieve from social criticism and moral denunciation, regardless of religious difference or who originally perpetrated cultural injustice.

Yet historical memory, transgenerational transmission of indignation, and the need for revenge leave a primitive remainder. We call it resentment. From the enslaved to the persecutor, political revolt to suppression, the colonized to the imperialist, national memory becomes a way of preserving the reciprocity of resentment.[23] Islam's revival of resentment against American and Jewish "devils" while valorizing its own identity and past is an example of how suffering, humiliation, and bitterness justify ideologies of violence. Add to this formula the contemporary clashes over settler-colonialism, conflicting nationalisms, the consequences of Zionism, Israel's so-called apartheid legal policies, and what some claim to be the "ethnic cleansing" of Palestinian civilians who are casualties of military targets retaliating against Hamas's air strikes in Jerusalem, which only serve to incite the most apocalyptic wing of political Islam.

It can be said that the entire history of civilization is based on traumatization. History metabolizes trauma, memorializes it, politicizes it, and sometimes rewrites the collective suffering and cultural complexes that lie in its wake as a way of bathing in Lethe, the river of forgetfulness, or as covering over, hence exploiting truth and historicity.[24] But whether concealed or subjugated, the catastrophic effects of history are intergenerationally transferred: cultural trauma persists in the collective unconscious of humanity.

---

23. Refer to Marc Ferro's (2010) work on resentment in history.
24. Here I am reminded of the Armenian genocide carried out by the Turkish government under Ottoman Empire rule, and the continued Japanese silence of their predatory role and collusion with the Nazis in World War II. More recently, the Russian government has denied any responsibility for shooting down a Malaysia Airlines plane in 2014; four Russians were recently prosecuted in absentia in The Hague. Since then, the International Criminal Court (ICC) issued an arrest warrant for Putin to be tried for war crimes for the unlawful transfer of children from occupied areas of Ukraine to the Russian Federation.

APOCALYPTIC DISCOURSE IN POSTMILLENNIAL CULTURE

The new apocalypse is not based on the Fall of man and the divine will of God, but on how human beings have ruined the planet through ecocide, war, and systemic institutional corruptions governed by oppressive power differentials such as totalitarian and fascist regimes, tyranny, late capitalist greed, climate emergencies, geopolitics, cultural disenfranchisement, egregious disparities in wealth and poverty, bioterror, technological error, religious fanaticism, genocide, migration crises and diasporas, the threat of nuclear holocaust, overpopulation, food and water insecurity, energy and resource scarcity, plagues, mass murder, civil disobedience, and anarchy. Postmillennial visions of the future center around a new dystopia: namely, the Earth as a miserable place to live. For billions of people in developing countries, it already is. Although the millennial doomsday scenario is typically touted as "no one survives" except the pious, the secular *eschaton* is that only a fraction of humanity survives but inherit a postapocalyptic world of dearth and hardship. Here the focus is not so much on an absolute end but, rather, what life will be like living in the aftershock of the cataclysm.

From Hiroshima and the Cold War to our contemporary geopolitical climate of aggression and rhetoric of the threat to act, the nuclear age has ushered in a grand End Day scenario that continues to grip world attention, especially given that, as mentioned, the *Bulletin of the Atomic Scientists* Science and Security Board has recently set the Doomsday Clock to 90 seconds to midnight, closer to the apocalypse than ever before.[25] The existential threats of nuclear war, the climate crisis, and techno nihilism, such as the use of cyber-enabled information warfare, technology-driven propaganda, and disinformation campaigns designed to promote distrust and paranoia in social institutions kindle conspiracy theories about the deep state, manipulate governmental elections, and erode goodwill between nations. They continue to stoke cultural anxieties and fear over mass extinction. When the Event happens, how will our societies fare? Although we cannot predict the future, we can anticipate a state of global affairs in which the world is changed forever, with literally every corner

---

25. See Bulletin of the Atomic Scientists 2023 Doomsday Clock Statement, https://thebulletin.org /doomsday-clock/current-time/

of the planet affected, much like living after COVID, except far more austere and catastrophic. Here Armageddon becomes survival in the posttraumatic aftermath of the postapocalyptic world.

Whereas anticipating the *eschaton* focuses on the immanent and imminent, dystopian discourse focuses on After the End. In anticipating an imminent (looming) end, whether real, symbolic, or imaginary, and our immanent (inherent) tendencies to bring that about, this feeds off a fantasy of control—what Foucault calls "biopower"[26] over the "finitude" or "disappearance" of man;[27] or what Lee Quinby refers to as "apocalyptic security"[28] that "relies on a continuous state of anxiety and uncertainty, which, as a result, legitimizes inaction."[29] Paralyzed by fear, or living in denial, disavowal, or dissociation from these anxieties, uncertainty prolongs doubt and collective procrastination leery of change, a reticence of vulnerability tarrying on the cusp of present and future.

And when all efforts at attaining security by necessity create insecurity, our being toward death arouses trepidation over the inevitable, the certainty of finitude as paralysis. But as Derrida points out, eschatology is intimately tied to teleology, the *two* ends of man: the end as finitude, as unity in death, and as culmination, the completion of its *telos*.[30] Here finality is bequeathed the status of infinity: *we* all stand in relation to our infinite end, both as prescription and equivocality.

After the End skips to the chase and assumes a foregone conclusion, whether prophetic or inductive, where social (valuative) consciousness concentrates on mitigating environmental damage, restoring human well-being, establishing peacebuilding between factions and nations, and is oriented toward improving the onto-structural conditions of futurity in its posttraumatic recovery from disaster. Here, if we can't control the apocalypse from coming, we can certainly anticipate our need for a

---

26. In *The History of Sexuality, vol. 1,* Foucault (1976) tells us that power relations profess what they seek to control—the population, bodies, the economy, sovereignty, "ultimately life itself" culminating "in the privilege to seize hold of life in order to suppress it" (p. 136).
27. Foucault (1966), *The Order of Things*, pp. 340–347, 373.
28. See Quinby (2014).
29. Monica Germanà & Aris Mousoutzanis (2014), *Apocalyptic Discourse in Contemporary Culture*, p. 6.
30. Derrida (1982), "The Ends of Man," in *Margins of Philosophy*, pp. 121–123, 134.

measured response to ecological, political, and economic collapse when denialism eventually breaks down. Preparing for survival allows for the illusion of ontological security over nearing or evading the end, when this interpellation is merely another form of coercion over the attitudes of social collectives trying to subvert calamity.

FUTURISTIC FANTASIES

Futurologist Freeman Dyson speculates that within a few hundred years human beings will colonize other galaxies, mutate into posthuman forms of subspecies, and adapt to space and extraterrestrial environments beyond Earth. He envisions a "green universe" where biotechnology will enable us to breed new living creatures and entire ecologies including new animal life and "warm-blooded plants" that are designed to adapt to vastly different habitats that are not dependent upon planetary means to sustain their survival. He calls this thought experiment a "Noah's Ark culture," which is essentially a fleet of spacecraft "the size and weight of an ostrich egg" that spawns their own ecosystems by implanting "living seeds with the genetic instructions for growing millions of species of microbes and plants and animals, including males and females of sexual species, adapted to live together and support one another in an alien environment."[31] After these arks are placed in suitable places in space, they "will grow into a living world of creatures, as diverse as the creatures of Earth but different," which may then further populate and spread throughout the universe, self-replicating their own microcosms until, ultimately, leading to the expansion of life. Dyson proclaims that we as humanity will become "the midwives who bring life to birth on millions of worlds" and concludes that we are the "stewards of life on a grander scale, and our destiny is to be creators of a living universe."[32]

Not only is this vision of the future of humanity "grand," but it is grandiose, which further belies a wish to play God. In other words, when we destroy this world, we can create others "where we will live together and support one another" as equal brothers and sisters in utopian bliss, as if we would somehow be able to do that in a future world where everyone

---

31. Dyson (2016), p. 6.
32. Dyson (2016), p. 6.

is One. It is what the futurist Vernor Vinge called an apocalyptic "singularity" of consciousness, despite the fact that we are demolishing ourselves as we speak and are only remotely capable of showing any conciliatory success to live harmoniously or in accord with shared values that promote cooperation and peace over egocentric caprice and self-destructive denial. The obsession with space travel, the so-called colonization of galaxies, and the scientifically engineered mutation of our species that will supposedly surpass our current predicament of self-induced annihilation are all transcendental illusions based on escape fantasies. The thought that we will have a safe haven to retreat to when Earth is uninhabitable is as naive as the notion of heaven itself.[33] We can no more control the future than we can control the present—we can only *influence* it. The thought that we can govern, manipulate, and design a future world fashioned to our liking presumes that we live in a fixed universe where everything is causally determined in a linear, prefixed (nonnegotiable) fashion devoid of inflections of autonomy, when this would mean the death of freedom (often inversely called chance or randomness) as an indeterminate force in the cosmos. Nothing is fixed or laid in stone in such a hard determinist fashion. We neither have the prowess nor the means to accomplish such a grandiloquent task. The call to procreate millions of new worlds as humanity's "destiny" merely speaks to an unconscious collective anxiety and reactionary narcissistic hubris where the need to conquer our fears as a quasi-triumph over death via reaction formation justifies obscene economic and environmental waste that currently contributes to our planetary crisis.

Billions of dollars are thrown away in space exploration and developing technologies from Big and Little Space culture alike, leading to space wars with other nations over power grabs to see who wins out over space travel, satellite augmentation and domination, and procuring advanced knowledge via technological innovations over our solar system and beyond, an economically and politically driven enterprise borne of ideology. The underlying omnipotent illusion is that we are going to do the impossible—hence create a new and better world. Given that we have

---

33. See Mills (2017) for an extensive discussion.

failed to accomplish this task here on Earth, something that is, by definition, unattainable, it is more than ostentatious and pompous to proclaim otherwise. Despite the massive amounts of resources squandered, excess waste produced, and increased industrial pollution generated by such activity, which intensifies our current ecological emergency, international governments, NASA, and private industry, for instance, hold out for the hope in overcoming problems with engineering setbacks so that humans can someday develop settlements on other planets or moons and escape from catastrophic climate change, which potentially one day will kill the Earth.

Rather than put such systemic efforts and funds into developing methods of ameliorating our current situation by resuscitating Gaia, the focus is on securing a future escape hatch, which, even if possible, would only save the wealthy and powerful elites while forsaking the rest of us poor slobs. Imagine the destitute, downtrodden, disenfranchised, displaced masses, or ordinary citizens from African countries—or any other disqualified country—on those space shuttles to paradise! Not a prayer's chance in hell. They would be the first to become fertilizer in any doomsday scenario. Why not save the planet we have, rather than pursue the fantasy that we can find better ones or create new space environments in a postapocalyptic world? Our priorities seem to be under the sway of delusion. There is no futuristic Eden elsewhere, no carrot dangled in faraway space, but only what we know now—namely, the fact that we have a planetary plight that needs drastic attention before it is too late to even plan an escape route.

DISPARITIES

The world revolves around money. It symbolizes the real—namely, barter and exchange for all goods and services, needs and desires—the semiotic of value. In psychological terms, it can be said that nothing is more real than money—the rest is transference, projection, fantasy. But it is more than that: money is the placeholder of *objective* value. It therefore institutes and maintains the power of validity. Money becomes a transcendental category of value and utility that governs socialization. As a result, the means, procurement, and possession of money breed disparities. Without money, one cannot have. And if one cannot have, then one cannot live.

Societies revolve around economics. Even in cashless societies, economies of exchange govern social relations. No economy, no society. In global capitalism, economies revolve around markets, what people are willing to invest in and speculate on make money. We rely on markets to maintain the order of things. When markets collapse, so does order. With stipulations, such as outliers and atypical instances that do not apply to the general collective, the reality is that markets mainly empower the rich, corporate elite and powerful institutions such as the financial sectors that economically dominate and domesticate societies under pragmatic dictates that leave the average citizen disadvantaged. The financialization of global capitalism that infiltrates both public and private industry determines the way culture functions, often based on factors outside our control, such as governmental stability, stock exchange flux, socioeconomic disadvantage, lack of knowledge, opportunity and education, superimposed restrictions and compensations foisted by hegemonic (often neoliberal) politics that promulgate legal policies that benefit the rich, and so forth.

> It includes such basic matters as the growth in size and scope of finance and financial activity in the economy (the size of the industry as a percentage of the GDP has more than doubled in the last forty years); the rise of debt-fueled speculation instead of productive lending; the ascendancy of shareholder value as the sole model for corporate governance; the proliferation of risky, selfish thinking in both the private and public sectors; the increasing political power of financiers and the CEOs they enrich; and the way in which a "markets know best" ideology remains the status quo in many academic and policy circles.[34]

When laws are designed to protect the wealthy, along with tax shelters, legal loopholes, and golden parachutes, those who have little money or live paycheck to paycheck become enslaved by their actual economic conditions. No wonder the Occupy movement (Wall Street, etc.) became

---

34. Rana Foroohar (2016), p. 29.

a civilized form of capitalist protest. Disparities in wealth and poverty are spreading like viruses; and with continued deregulation and lack of oversight, corporate conglomerates and the affluent privileged will continue to rake in fortunes on the backs of working-class citizens. The poor have even fewer options in hoping to survive. If public consciousness reaches a tipping point where ethics overrides profit motives, we could conceivably witness a reformed capitalist movement where inequalities are challenged and changed law by law. But when home ownership, health care, and retirement remain tied to the stock market in the face of the uncertain financial health of national social insurance programs, where millions rely on such income in old age, the future state of financial securities remain unpredictable at best, if not untenable and cause for alarm. The ultimate existential apocalypse is when economies collapse.

THE NEW AFTER

Whether in politics, business, or neighborly relations, advances in culture are due to the process of negotiation and mutual recognition, which leads to the mutual desire to understand, communicate value preferences, and support each other cooperatively despite vast differences that define our life circumstances, personal identities, and desire. The need for mutual recognition, validation, and affirmation of cultural values and worth leads to understanding; and in turn, understanding leads to empathy and care. Despite the continuing tumultuous peace negotiations and the tenuous settlements that define our communal world where rigid identifications and insular self-interest ensure irreconcilable divisions, this persevering process signals the human willingness to seek viable solutions in the name of peace and healing, which is itself a productive dialectical movement toward concord and repose. Whether we advance in peaceful resolution through mutual negotiation and cooperation remains a possibility only the future can command. But given the current state of climate crisis, national and ethnic populism, terrorism, nuclear anxieties, health pandemics, economic disparities, and military conflict throughout the globe, where social chaos, lawlessness, mass trauma, diasporas, civilian revolt, and religious fundamentalism includes messianic fanaticism fueled by systemic hatred for the Other, where the End of Days is preceded by a prophetic apocalypse, it becomes a logical prediction that World War III is just around the corner. It portends a bleak dystopian future, the new After.

6

Global Catastrophic Risks

WHAT CONSTITUTES A "GLOBAL RISK" LACKS UNIFORM CONSENSUS. IT IS often thought to be an uncertain event or condition that would cause significant negative long-term impact on several countries and industries worldwide if it occurs. Actuarial science would refer to such risk as the probability of an unwanted event multiplied by its consequences. One of the leading contemporaries of risk studies is philosopher Nick Bostrom, director of the Future of Humanity Institute at the University of Oxford. He and his colleague Milan Ćirković emphasize the catastrophic effects such risks pose to human well-being on a global scale. Like many contributors to existential risks studies, they survey the diverse possibilities of candidates that would comprise global threats ranging from climate change to pandemics, natural disasters, nuclear accidents, cosmic hazards, worldwide tyranny, and economic collapse, many of which we have already witnessed. Although the many kinds of risk hardly have anything in common with each other, their links and associations are felt as destructive secondary fallout on social order. They explain:

> Risks of social disruption and collapse are not unrelated to the risks of events such as nuclear terrorism or pandemic disease. Or to take another example, apparently dissimilar events such as large asteroid impacts, volcanic super-eruptions, and nuclear war would all eject massive amounts of soot and aerosols into the atmosphere, with significant

effects on global climate. The existence of such causal links is one reason why it is/can be sensible to study multiple risks together.[1]

Here it becomes important to emphasize the *interconnectedness* of events on social collectives, the *contexts* in which they play out, and the myriad *interaction effects* they produce.

DEFINING RISK

Analyzing global risks as an aggregate rather than as single variables affords us the opportunity to make comparative judgments that have predictive and pragmatic value from methodological, conceptual, and explanatory standpoints; and transcend narrow perspectives that dominate current public attention, researcher (anthropic) bias, observer relativity, self-sampling assumptions, reference class problems, observation selection effects, and the improbable abstract application of thought experiments on human risk cognition. Because the threat profiles we construct have political, economic, and policy consequences, the ethics of optimal risk mitigation strategies and countermeasures must consider all threat variables that could easily be missed or neglected as well as risks that are overweighted in value or driven by politics or emotional prejudice.

Bostrom and Ćirković characterize the severity of risk of a global catastrophe as conforming to three factors: (1) scope, (2) intensity, and (3) probability. The first has to do with how many people and social systems will be impacted, the second with how bad or austere the effects will be, and the third with how likely the disaster will occur based on all available evidence analyzed through critical judgment. The *scope* can be (a) personal (applying to one individual), (b) local (communal, regional, national), (c) global (international), (d) transgenerational (future populations), and potentially (e) cosmic (unknowns). The *intensity* of these risks may be classified as (a) imperceptible (unnoticeable), (b) endurable (tolerable) (c) terminal (deadly), or even (d) hellish (sustained misery).

---

1. See Bostrom & Ćirković (2008), p. 1.

In this taxonomy, global catastrophic risks would fall within the global-transgenerational category within an enduring-terminal, high-severity intensity range. Here we can envision global catastrophic events to encompass mass scale, and in some cases, complete devastation, disfigurement, destruction, loss, or species extinction, or simply living in an infernal dystopia where the quality of life is miserable, posttraumatic, or nonexistent. A future where there is global despoliation of the planet or ecocide, destruction of civilization, subsisting or trying to survive in a lawless and unregulated society; or being confined to an inner world of psychic pain and mental agony may fit into this scheme of the future of humanity. Living in conditions where there is no safety, solace, or comfort; and with no access to secure housing, food, water, heat or cooling, electricity, resources, and the necessities of life, would be like a return to primitive times. Those who existed lived in constant anxiety, uncertainty, and peril of not having a meal or roof over their heads, being hurt, maimed, raped, tortured, killed, starving to death, or dying of illness.

Other riskologists, such as Phil Torres, have focused on the *spatial* and *temporal* scopes of Bostrom's classification of risks with an emphasis on Big-Picture Hazards.[2] Risks have varying spatiotemporal consequences, hence where they occur (scope), when (now, impending, sometime, distant future, ambiguous future, indeterminate future), and the ramifications of an event or *combination of events* (minor, moderate, severe, disastrous). I would like to propose that we also consider the (1) subjective, (2) intersubjective, (3) objective, and (4) systemic instantiations in our analyses of global risks, particularly when applied to (a) phenomenology, (b) epistemology, and (c) ontology. In other words, what are the intrapsychic and interpersonal lived experiences of individuals, communities, nations, and larger social collectives when it comes to the material, emotional, qualitative, and quantitative realities of risk events and their consequences? What impact do such risk events have on the felt qualia of people's lives and the tangible social structures and systemic institutional processes that are concretely altered?

---

2. Torres (2016), pp. 26–35.

How are these conditions experienced when we consider our relationship to knowledge, truth, and empirical facts? This is particularly important given that we are living in an era where the notions of truth and objective reality are negated and consensually distorted through misinformation, denialism, manipulation of data, fake news, and "alternative facts"—the products of deliberate lies, propaganda, pseudo-reasoning, sophistry, and psychological defense, unless one is just plain stupid. Despite all facts, masses will simply believe what they want to believe no matter how erroneous, ill-conceived, or convincing the proof may be, simply because that is what they want to hear and want the truth to be despite all evidence against it. This is itself a grave source of danger. Let us call this a *psychogenic risk*: when social collectives dismiss the real threat of climate change as a "hoax" or believe presidential lies over empirical facts, people are vulnerable to succumb to gaslighting, mindfucking, or delusion. Ignorance, denialism, and negation have horrifying consequences on public opinion, politics, and public policy. When the president of the United States cut economic aid to the World Health Organization (WHO) during the height of the COVID pandemic as the world looked on aghast, he wanted to blame China and scapegoat the WHO for his failure to act and prepare his own country for the outbreak, which he at first compared to the common flu.[3] Lying, denying, stupidity, willful ignorance, and blaming the Other rather than accepting responsibility for one's own actions, lack of knowledge, projections, and prejudice run the risk of replacing truth and democracy with deceit and ideology.

What happens when these global risks as uncertain events are examined in terms of their probabilities? What is the likelihood that the Earth will be pummeled to death by an asteroid belt or sucked into a black hole? Probably pretty unlikely, if we take a long statistical view of the matter. But what is the likelihood of a nuclear war or runaway greenhouse gas emissions that destroy the climate and our natural

---

3. During a campaign rally in South Carolina on February 28, 2020, President Donald Trump compared the Democratic Party's criticism of his response to the pandemic to his impeachment, saying "this is their new hoax." During the speech he also downplayed the severity of the outbreak, which he compared to the seasonal flu (see Palma, 2020).

environments? Much more probable, I argue. What is the likelihood that the fate of our planet will be brought about by man rather than natural occurrences? Here enters the domain of existential risk, which is anthropogenic in nature—namely, arising from human activities rather than natural causes. This is particularly troubling when you consider the broad gamut of risks and their systemic and interconnected impact on the world populace, the degree of interaction effects that unfold in their wake, and the overdetermined nature of causal catastrophe. As scientists have determined that Earth is destined to be bled dry and then fried to a crisp before the Sun finally burns out billions of years from now, what is the likelihood that anyone in future generations or posthuman ecologies will even be around?

BIG-PICTURE HAZARDS

Existential risks threaten us with extinction and/or a drastically and permanently reduced quality of life. Because existential risks will not cease to exist, we must address them proactively so they are minimized at the very least, both as they currently present themselves and as they might develop over time, even in the distant future. Bostrom observes that we lack available data to make rigorous statistical inferences and well-corroborated scientific models on which to base reliable future probability estimates. In fact, there is no scientific consensus of assigning a probability risk to the notion that a terrorist attack using a nuclear warhead with biological agents will occur within the next decade,[4] presumably because it has never happened before. But we may also add a further reason that human behavior is not consistent or perfectly predictable, nor can we reliably anticipate all psychological motivations and their unique contexts to make such universal, let alone precise, predictions due to human freedom and chance. For all we know, we simply may be lucky that we have made it this far.

All one can do is adjudicate the plausibility of the arguments and predictions based on analogy and subjective intuition meditated by reason. Solutions to these probability constraints cannot be alleviated

---

4. Bostrom & Ćirković (2008), p. 6.

by scientism. They do not exist in the external world as fixed essences or mind independent objects to be found or invented through blind research. This would further relegate value inquiry to the hard sciences and forge a false dichotomy between empirical and speculative forms of risk, when they are often conjoined or are dispersed on a continuum of analytic malleability derived from inference and logical abduction. Even chaos exists within an implicit order. The question is how best to speculate on future chaos and its impact on the order of things. Here we must listen to the natural sciences *and* humanities for their input.

Because there have been many mass extinctions in the distant past since the history of the globe, including complete species extinctions, and given that our universe is fated to perish in entropic heat death or from gradual cosmic disintegration into its basic elements, nothing is fallacious about global cataclysms occurring—they have, they do, and they will. Merely the scale of time is the issue here. Given that the Sun will eventually scorch our planet in a ball of fire, we are destined to either evolve or die out. But even if humans are capable of space colonization and transforming into a highly complex technological species, human civilization eventually will become inexistent. Here the End is ontologically predetermined by fate.

In previous chapters, we addressed myriad risks that we would consider to be potential global catastrophes. Bostrom and Ćirković group big-picture risks into three broad categories: (1) risks from nature, (2) risks from unintended consequences, and (3) risks from hostile acts. These big hazard risks include the following:

Risks from Nature

- Super-eruptions from volcanos that have historically occurred producing nuclear-winter scenarios and irrevocable climate effects
- Asteroid, meteor, or comet impacts
- Global climate change from fluctuations in solar activity
- Cosmic rays from supernova explosions
- Gamma-ray bursts, solar flares, radiation threats, planetary warming

- Earth magnetic field reversals
- Galactic collisions and merging

Risks from Unintended Consequences

- Anthropogenic climate change
- Pandemic disease and infectious spread
- Artificial intelligence applications and superintelligent machinery
- Runaway technologies
- Careless or failed physics experiments such as particle accelerator disasters
- Nuclear accidents
- Accidents from biotechnology and biosecurity
- Societal collapse as a devastation multiplier of other catastrophes

Risks from Hostile Acts

- Nuclear war/global war
- Nuclear terrorism
- Genetically engineered bioweapons
- Man-made viruses and bio-attacks
- Nanotechnology abuse and molecular manufacturing risks
- Totalitarianism

Fortunately, the best available data to date suggest that catastrophic risks from nature are quite small. But if an event of this magnitude were to occur, it could very likely be the worst-case scenario.[5] For example, if a super-volcanic winter event were to happen (such as a nuclear holocaust), it would be followed by global cooling on lands and oceans; ash and dust would suffocate biodiversity, and agricultural productivity would be drastically curtailed or come to a halt, which could lead to mass starvation and unrelenting social chaos. If we were impacted by a comet, asteroid,

---

5. See Dar (2008).

or meteor, we could be looking at a mass extinction occurrence similar in kind to what killed off the dinosaurs. For instance, if we were hit by a 10-kilometer impactor (the size of a mountain), it is likely to cause the extinction of the human species.[6]

Risks from the Anthropocene have gripped the world's attention and have raised collective global consciousness to combat endangerment against soaring greenhouse gases, atmospheric destruction, extreme weather events, pollution, biodiversity loss, melting ice caps, sea-level rise, and so on. These risks are associated with the uncertainty of capitalist and nationalist agendas and international cooperation in curbing our cumulative emissions. They represent one of the greatest hazards today. Another big-picture threat is from infectious diseases, pathogens, parasites, epidemics, pandemics, and their probable future outbreaks. They carry high morbidity and mortality rates, from the Spanish influenza pandemic to the Great Plague of London, the Black Death during in the Middle Ages, and the Plague of Justinian in the Byzantine era, which killed hundreds of millions of people. Pandemics are an under-recognized risk, but maybe the world will wake up after COVID and be on the lookout for conditions to prevent the incubation and spread of emerging new diseases. The homogenization of peoples and cultures contributes to pandemic risk due to smaller gene pools and lack of racial diversity where exposure to unaccustomed infectious agents is hard to fight off,[7] whereas heterogeneous societies reduce the likelihood that any single pattern of disease will universally infiltrate a population.

Because the spread of pathogens is contingent on human involvement and transmission, these may pop up as unintended consequences of domestic practices, such as unfurling from unregulated wet markets, or by accident in society or a lab. Add to that gamble the human propensity to lie, underreport incidents, or attempt to cover up a mistake or accident, such as China's initial reluctance to report the outbreak of the new coronavirus—and it spread throughout the globe like wildfire. Another unintended consequence is the risk of food contamination and bacterial spread that can easily find its way into food production and packaging

6. See Napier (2008), pp. 222–225.
7. Kilbourne (2008), p. 301.

plants as well as distribution centers on an international scale before a bewildering epidemic is identified.

General artificial intelligence (AI) is no immediate cause for alarm, but as technologies grow rapidly that could potentially exceed the intelligence of the human brain, including superintelligences that manipulate human beings through computer-information applications to achieve their goals (whether for positive or nefarious intent), the possible unpredictable autonomy of machine intelligence may be considered one of the major existential threats to the future of humanity. One reason for such a foreboding conclusion is that we don't fully understand how AI works, and any pretensions to claim otherwise, according to specialists such as computer engineers, is pure hubris. Because AI is analogous to mind or cognitive operations and optimization processes in general, we are only beginning to comprehend the enormous penumbra of possibilities. As Eliezer Yudkowsky informs us, "We cannot query our own brains for answers about non-human optimization processes . . . How can we predict what Artificial Intelligences will do?"[8] What if a command and control center became self-governing? It is for these reasons that when building AI products, we must consider the potential for autonomous rule and ethical programming to assuage risk and safeguard against producing decision-making actions that could be detrimental to humanity. This might prove difficult if AI achieves or exceeds the capacity of human mentation. If the minds of humans cannot function as purely rational moral beings, then why would we assume superintelligences would behave differently?

Hazards from particle accelerator physics experiments are not likely to be an acute existential risk because such catastrophic corollaries are highly improbable. Physicist Frank Wilczek points out three cataclysmic scenarios: (1) mini black holes begin to accrete matter and eventually swallow up the planet; (2) negatively charged stable strangelets begin to convert ordinary matter into strange matter; and (3) an accelerated vacuum state develops and expands outwardly at the speed of light, devouring everything in its path.[9] Wilczek concedes that these scenarios

---

8. Yudkowsky (2008b), p. 311.
9. See Wilczek (2008), pp. 346, 349–357.

are highly speculative, unlikely, and remote on both theoretical grounds and given the lack of any previous empirical observations to the contrary. The question becomes how improbable and to what degree should risk mitigation strategies (if not superimposed regulations) be put in place to preempt potentially dangerous particle acceleration experiments from being conducted in the first place?

Threats to societal stability, order, and deterioration can lead to a frequent series of small but cumulative disturbances that wax and wane over time to rare major catastrophic events producing massive domestic upheaval, global economic devastation, and geopolitical backlash throughout the world. When unintended consequences of the previous calamities trickle down to the daily lives, activities, and functional organizations within societies, wholesale collapse in cultural, economic, and democratic institutions; governance; the workforce; capital and commodity production; public safety; food, water, and home security; medical care; and education are just a fraction of the domains that degenerate if a global catastrophe would occur on which the world economy depends.

Risks from hostile acts are numerous, but the usual suspects come to mind, as we have already addressed in previous chapters: nuclear Armageddon, nuclear terrorism, and bioterrorism, bioerror, geopolitical provocations, and geopolitical mistakes, either by leaders, the military, or machines. As long as nuclear weapons exist, there will be valid grounds for risks and threat. Psychopathic provocations, rhetoric, procuring supplies to attain nuclear weapons capabilities, extortion or ransom for raw materials or capital, instigating the use of nuclear explosives by nonnuclear means such as cyberterrorist attacks through technology or manipulation of failsafe mechanisms or early warning systems—all up the ante on risk. Given that the specter of nuclear holocaust has loomed over humanity like a plague since the invention of the atomic bomb, terrorism experts Gary Ackerman and William Potter ask the most obvious questions:

> Given the rising potential for terrorists to inflict nuclear violence, what then accounts for the failure on the part of the most powerful nations on earth to take corrective action commensurate with the threat? Is it

a lack of political leadership, a failure of imagination, faulty conceptualization, domestic politics, bureaucratic inertia, competing national security objectives, wishful thinking, the intractable nature of the problem, or simply incompetence?[10]

Once again, we may witness the global bystander effect. The problem is staring us straight in the face, yet we remain inactive and passively look on as if we are watching a spectator sport.

Another primordial threat to peace is biotechnology and biosecurity that parallel our nuclear predicament. The difference is that bioweaponry can be produced in small, concealed facilities, such as a garage or basement of a house, and entails no special raw materials for manufacturing, unlike the fissile material required to build nuclear weapons. Biological agents may also spread beyond a target site and potentially infect the entire world, especially if they get into the air and water supplies. Biosecurity campaigns that fail to monitor these activities could very well be one of the more likely hazards of unrestrained terrorism. These threats not only come from state biological weapons programs and non-state actors, groups, or biohackers, but they may occur from laboratory accidents where toxic agents are unintentionally leaked or released into the atmosphere, not to mention naturally occurring diseases that can cause pandemics. Synthetic biology capable of producing designer pathogens and superbugs is a fast-approaching alarm containing frightening possibilities for mass contaminations. Given the dual-use nature of biotechnology—that is, used for good but also evil—where necessary equipment, material, and knowledge may be acquired fairly easily or self-taught, and with pathogenic agents developed secretively, this may pose unique obstacles to biosecurity regulation and public health.

This brings us to the dangers of nanotechnology (nano = one-billionth in length) or small structures (miniaturization and chemistry), once again a dual-use science. Although the present risks are virtually zero, the use of nanoscale technologies and molecular manufacturing in particular, if properly developed for pernicious use, could be a solemn source of risk with a high probability. Like superintelligences, presently the technology

---

10. Ackerman & Potter (2008), p. 442.

does not exist; but experts claim it is just around the corner. As Bostrom and Ćirković concisely explain:

> Molecular nanotechnology would greatly expand control over the structure of matter. Molecular machine systems would enable fast and inexpensive manufacture of microscopic and macroscopic objects built to atomic precision. Such production systems would contain millions of microscopic assembly tools. Working in parallel, these would build objects by adding molecules to a workpiece through positionally controlled chemical reactions. The range of structures that could be built with such technology greatly exceeds that accessible to the biological molecular assemblers (such as ribosome) that exist in nature. Among the things that a nanofactory could build: another nanofactory.[11]

A technology this vibrant and malleable could build practically anything small and for an unlimited number of purposes including weapons of mass destruction. Nanotechnologists Chris Phoenix and Mike Treder warn us:

> In the absence of some type of preventative or protective force, the power of molecular manufacturing products could allow a large number of actors of varying types—including individuals, groups, corporations, and nations—to obtain sufficient capability to destroy all unprotected humans. The likelihood of at least one powerful actor being insane is not small. The likelihood that devastating weapons will be built and released accidentally (possibly through overly sensitive automated systems) is also considerable. Finally, the likelihood of a conflict between two MAD-enabled powers [mutually assured destruction] escalating until one feels compelled to exercise a doomsday option is also non-zero. This indicates that unless adequate defenses can be prepared against weapons intended to be ultimately destructive—a point that urgently needs research—the number of actors trying to possess such weapons must be minimized.[12]

---

11. Bostrom & Ćirković (2008), p. 24.
12. Phoenix & Treder (2008), pp. 498–499.

The final global catastrophic risk we may consider is totalitarianism. Within the 20th century alone, from Nazi Germany, Stalinist Russia, and Maoist China to the Pol Pot regime, by some estimates more than one hundred million people were systematically murdered in mass genocides, purges, or through indirect means (i.e., starving, forced labor, incarceration, sickness, disease, etc.). Although it is very difficult to calculate these risks due to human bias, political agendas, and competing ideologies, oppressive governments pose a real threat to geopolitical stability and international security due to the repetition compulsion of history, the breakdown of national governance, regional tensions and aggressions with neighboring countries, interstate brutality, civilian repression, revolutions and civil wars, the annexation of land, the uncertainty of military conflict, erratic decisions made by leaders, and the use of weapons of mass destruction initiated from provocation, retaliation, accident, or warring factions and nation-states.

Often the goal of dictators, despots, fascists, and the like is to achieve "total" control over the populace through state ideology governed by a political system that prohibits opposition parties and free speech, maintains tight regimentation of society through means of communication, media exchange, and the economy, forcible oppression of the masses, police terror, use of armed forces, and ongoing tyranny to subjugate public and private affairs.[13] Although these conditions vary in degree, scope, and intensity throughout various times and in parts of the world, totalitarianism is the most extreme form of authoritarianism. But when contemplating the possibility of a world totalitarian order, the odds are quite improbable, if not simply implausible.[14] We will be more menaced by rogue nation-states with nuclear capabilities than any likely serious threat of global totalitarianism, yet this may be enough to initiate major military conflicts, destabilize regions and trade, invite social deterioration

---

13. Cf. Pipes (1994), p. 245.

14. Economist Bryan Caplan estimates the unconditional odds of global totalitarianism are about 5% over a 1,000-year period, with conditional probabilities ranging from 0.1% if the current number of independent countries does not decrease to 25% if the global number of future countries falls to one (see Caplan, 2008, pp. 516–517), which is highly improbable.

and mass migration, and invite international response conceivably escalating to world war.

Overall, most global risks of catastrophic events unequivocally arise from human activities, particularly those from industrialized nations with advanced technologies. The largest global risks are in terms of scope but not necessarily expected severity (probability x harm). Although there are endless proposals, policy instruments, mitigation strategies, and means of managing these risks, it is important to bear in mind that most of the danger is not externally imposed from nature but, rather, internally derived, either directly or indirectly, intentionally or unintentionally, predicted or unforeseen, as the consequence of our own motivations and deeds. The disastrous impact of the Anthropocene, probabilities of infectious pandemic disease, nuclear war, biotechnology abuse or error, and potential nuclear terrorism or bioterror tend to be the big-ticket items of risk. Of course, if these scenarios were to occur, they would precipitate economic and societal breakdown. And like most things, all this hinges on money.

ECONOMIC DISINTEGRATION
The World Economic Forum is an international not-for-profit foundation established in 1971 as a public-private cooperative designed to engage the foremost leaders of the world in business, commerce, and political-cultural affairs to shape global, regional, and industry agendas. Headquartered in Geneva, Switzerland, it is strategic partners with MarshMcLennan companies and the Zurich Insurance Group and has academic advisers from the National University of Singapore; Oxford Martin School, University of Oxford; and the Wharton Risk Management and Decision Processes Center, University of Pennsylvania. As an independent, impartial, multilateral organization with no identified special-interest allegiances, it is tasked with advancing the highest global standards of governance committed to improving the state of the world. Each year the Forum produces a *Global Risks Report*, which addresses the leading chief concerns affecting shared economic, environmental, and social risks identified by nearly 800 experts and stakeholders in

government, academia, civics, nonprofit communities, entrepreneurs, private business, and global industry.

The Forum's annual Global Risks Perception Survey examines more than 40 global risks across five categories including (1) economic, (2) environmental, (3) geopolitical, (4) societal, and (5) technological, with much overlap.[15] From 2007 to 2020, global risk categories have changed and broadened, as definitions and the conglomerations of global risks have evolved with new predicaments emerging on a 10-year horizon. For example, cyberattacks and unemployment were variables introduced in 2012. Some global risks were reclassified, such as income disparity and water crises, which were deemed societal risks in 2014 and 2015, respectively.[16] The results of the 2020 survey ranked climate change and related environmental concerns as the top five risks in terms of *likelihood* of happening, which is the first time in the survey's history that one category has dominated all five of the top plights. These include (1st) extreme weather, (2nd) climate action failure, (3rd) natural disasters, (4th) biodiversity loss, and (5th) human-made environmental disasters. In terms of *impact*, these include (1st) climate action failure, (2nd) weapons of mass destruction, (3rd) biodiversity loss, (4th) extreme weather, and (5th) water crises. Five additional risks identified in the top 10 global risk factors include (1) data fraud or theft, (2) cyberattacks, (3) global governance failure, (4) asset bubbles, and (5) infectious diseases.

Evolving risks landscapes also highlight the unsettled effects of economic decoupling, instability in world economies and social cohesion, consequences of digital fragmentation and information infrastructure breakdown, health systems pressures, and geopolitical turbulence. The Forum warned of downward pressure on the world economy, macroeconomic fragilities, financial inequality, risk of economic stagnation, rising trade barriers, narrow margins for monetary and fiscal stimuli, economic confrontations, decline in economic integration, removal of

---

15. Survey respondents are asked to assess the likelihood of each specific global risk on a scale of 1 to 5, 1 representing a risk that is very unlikely to occur and 5 a risk that is very likely to happen. They also assess the impact on each global risk on a scale of 1 to 5 (1: minimal impact, 2: minor impact, 3: moderate impact, 4: severe impact, and 5: catastrophic impact).

16. World Economic Forum, *Global Risks Report* 2020, pp. 1–2. Also see the executive summary.

checks and balances preventing conflicts of interest, lower investment, and soaring debt. There has also been an upsurge in domestic political polarization due to nationalistic policies, populist posturing, and the pursuit of insular agendas, such as on trade and tariff wars, hence shifting from international cooperation to competition, manipulation, rivalry disparagement, and exclusion. The U.S.-China trade tensions, which are the top two producers of pollution and greenhouse gas emissions, have hurt the economies of both countries and the entire world economic outlook. Escalating trade conflicts erode trust in investment, introduce policy ambiguity, aggravate financial markets, and endanger already weak growth worldwide anxious about where the distribution of power will settle. Adding to the mess are deep disproportions in income and wealth, and stubborn governmental inaction in addressing these inequalities has led to protests throughout the world; and that was before the economic collapse due to the COVID pandemic.

Along with the Intergovernmental Panel on Climate Change, the United Nations, the World Health Organization, and other international environmental agencies, the World Economic Forum also rang the alarm bells on runaway climate change and concern that global temperatures are racing toward an increase to 3°C by the end of the century, which is double the limit set by experts to militate against planetary disaster. Biodiversity loss also has critical implications for humanity including collapse of health systems, food and water security, and entire supply chains. Geopolitical tensions and populism only amplify these risks, including predictable increases in medical and psychiatric illnesses, failure to prevent pandemics and develop vaccines, premature deaths, addictions, domestic violence, crime, and so on. Cyber-related vulnerability and attacks on the digital frontier bring even more significant risk to information security, including the fallout from mass surveillance, data hacking, theft, and fraud, fake news and disinformation on the World Wide Web and social media, AI ethics, procurement, and governance, technology restrictions imposed on foreign competition, and advanced weaponry that worry national security.

If environmental risks and adverse technological advances aren't enough to worry about, tack on geopolitical, societal, and economic variables that up the ante including global and national governance failure, interstate conflict, state collapse, diplomatic conflict resolution failure, lack of regulations, and terrorist attacks; unsustainable population growth, water crises, infectious diseases, food shortage and price volatility, involuntary migration, social instability, and failure of urban planning; and financial failure, fiscal crises, chronic economic imbalances, asset bubbles, unemployment, labor market disparities, critical infrastructure failure, energy price shock, recurring liquidity crises, unmanageable inflation, deflation, illicit trade, and pervasive entrenched corruption. Global youth networks driving dialogue, action, and change calculate these risks to be higher than traditional multi-stakeholders, but they all agree on the basics: the world is an interconnected web of environmental-socio-economic-geopolitical-technological relations that affect and pressurize one another as an interdependent ontic system. If we do not act in accord with universal social values that alleviate such potential risks and their catastrophic interaction effects and unite us in our shared humanity, we are sure to suffer as a whole.

It is not surprising that with the outbreak of the global pandemic, the 2021 *Global Risks Report* emphasized the societal, economic, and geopolitical fallout and existential toll it will have on the world, a worry it sounded the alarm bells on in 2006 when it warned of a "lethal flu" that would unsettle global travel, tourism, service industries, manufacturing, retail supply chains, global trade, local economies and create investor panic. Given that we have witnessed burgeoning inequalities and growing social fragmentation largely due to emerging risks to public health and infrastructure failure, soaring unemployment, political governance mismanagement of the pandemic, lack of equal access to digital technologies, and youth disillusionment, these multipliers will predictably carry compounded economic, environmental, geopolitical, and technological risks. To quote from the Executive Summary:

> The immediate human and economic cost of COVID-19 is severe. It threatens to scale back years of progress on reducing poverty and inequality and to further weaken social cohesion and global cooperation. Job losses, a widening digital divide, disrupted social interactions,

and abrupt shifts in markets could lead to dire consequences and lost opportunities for large parts of the global population. The ramifications—in the form of social unrest, political fragmentation and geopolitical tensions—will shape the effectiveness of our responses to the other key threats of the next decade: cyberattacks, weapons of mass destruction, and most notably, climate change.[17]

Among the highest impact risks facing us in the next decade will be climate change inaction, environmental damage, infectious diseases, livelihood and debt crises, weapons of mass destruction, and IT infrastructure breakdown. While short- and intermediate-term risks over the next few years will entail public health crises, including overstressed health systems and the availability, supply, manufacturing, distribution, and delivery of needed medical intervention worldwide, the economic shockwave to businesses, markets, consumer behavior, price instability, commodity shocks, asset bubble bursts, industry collapse, interstate conflicts and relations fracture in trade, diplomacy, and climate security could lead to breakdown in global resilience and recovery. Add to this worry an uneven recovery due to increased disparities, inequality, and loss of lives and livelihoods; youth unemployment including lost opportunities in education, training, and economic prospects; and widespread deterioration in mental health and adjustment that will leave its residue on future global landscapes. Despite what transpires in our post-pandemic economy, overall risk perception is still concentrated on the ecological crisis, extreme weather events, human environmental destruction, biodiversity loss, and climate action failure as the top global catastrophic dangers by likelihood.

When the World Economic Forum, an international fiscal organization concerned about global finance and commerce, has alerted us to our dire planetary predicament due to unmitigated climate crises and societal, geopolitical, and technological risks to the welfare of every citizen and nation, they are thinking about the long-term economic consequences of burying our heads in the sand, not simply a quick grab based on the immediate exploitation of prospects in the service of avarice

---

17. World Economic Forum (2021), p. 7.

that present themselves to opportunistic self-serving actors, institutions, or states. There are real consequences to global economic systems when nationalistic policies and politics do not think of inclusive, cooperative liaisons and long-term relationships with fellow neighbors in our shared integrated world of globalization. The minute money is affected, let alone interrupted or lost—in business, finance, commerce, asset management, and means to live—it has an immediate effect on society. High-level tensions and restrictions in trade among superpowers, high public and private debt, low investment, corporate bailouts, weak confidence in governance, and a prolonged slowdown of the world economy followed by recession, depression, and repression are key susceptibilities in global financial affairs. We should not be surprised that in 2022 and 2023, the global risks reports focused on inequalities, economic disparities, inflation, cost-of-living crises, the wealth gap, and loss of social cohesion and polarization in the aftermath of the pandemic.

Paying off ballooned governmental debt will wreak havoc on societies and augment the already obscene disparities in the distribution of wealth. Massive borrowing, tax increases, spending cuts, defaulting and restructuring, higher inflation to wash the debt, stagnant unemployment, and stimulus spending could lead to deflationary crash. Inflation will hurt the poor and enrich the wealthy: homes and shares will likely rise in value while mortgages are cleansed alongside decreased government liability. Inflation affecting large, indebted companies will enjoy government bailouts and golden parachutes for their CEOs while small business goes under. Widespread domestic discontent, mistrust in economic systems perceived as unjust or rigged, outrage over inequality, governmental corruption, constitutional breaches, and rise in prices of basic necessities or services have sparked social unrest all over the world, especially in vulnerable societies such as the social upheavals and intense demonstrations witnessed in Chile, France, Hong Kong, Brazil, Bolivia, Iraq, and Lebanon, just to name a few. As societies destabilize, social collectives become desperate, panicky, and violent. Poverty increases, migration blooms, revolutions percolate, citizens are beset, and people get executed. If the imbalance of wealth, power, and political tyranny reaches a tipping point, countries implode. It is predictable that when the financial elite, banksters, and the wealthiest people in the world become symbolic of capitalist exploitation, heads will roll. I will not be surprised if we observe a future when wide-scale targeting of the rich ends in calculated murder due to hatred, envy, and the need for cathartic revenge.

TECHNO NIHILISM

Nolen Gertz has examined in-depth the relationship between nihilism and technology and has coined the term *techno nihilism*, where contemporary nihilism is seen as harboring a general apathy or depersonalized or indifferent attitude toward the world as technology is used for personal values or gain. In other words, nowhere is there a perfect world, and there is no transvaluation of values: to want a perfected world is to want a different world, so we might as well replace our current society to suit our needs and purposes through technological innovation. But there is a catch: technology influences and shapes our needs, values, and judgments as much as we invent technology to achieve certain aims and ends. Technology may often be superior to human activity, is more efficient and dependable, less likely to make mistakes, and hence ought to replace human bias and error through more trustworthy applications such as automation.

Whether we will become more authentic and liberated, or dehumanized and deluded, by technology is another matter. People are becoming increasingly reliant on technology to function in their lives to such a degree that without instant communication technologies conversing with the World Wide Web it could sink a business, let alone spoil an evening if we did not have immediate access to our smartphones, Wi-Fi, or computers to retrieve an email. In industrialized countries, our entire lives depend upon these technologies for economics, home security, health care, and all personal matters. But this comes at a cost: we have become slaves to technology to such a degree that data-driven demands and expectations introduce stress that deteriorates physical health, surveillance technologies compromise privacy and personal security, and social media platforms directly impact mental adjustment and illness. Mental illness is an underrepresented global risk factor that affects, at the very minimum, at least one-fifth to one-third of the world population depending upon how we classify functional adaptation and subjective quality of life including personal happiness. And just because people are so-called functional does not mean they are not miserable or in some form of psychic pain.

Gertz argues that our human-technology relations have in many ways devolved into nihilism-technology relations where the populace has fallen into a dazzling quagmire of *techno-hypnosis* or digital zombification. People are not only couch potatoes, but they have become mindless zombies with no capacity for critical self-reflection mesmerized by a computer screen, streaming television and entertainment services, virtual reality devices, and augmented "reality" programs. Here the culture industry not only revolves around technology and leisure, such as gaming, robotic vacuum cleaners, and delivery services so you don't have to shop or cook, but technologies eavesdrop on our conversations, track our Google searches, bombard us with sundry products and advertisements, make decisions for us through algorithms, and tell us what to buy. They also subliminally inform us what to think. Moreover, they teach us how we ought to think by constantly inundating us with products, propaganda, images, and sound bites that we unconsciously absorb like grazing cows in the pasture. Here our desire is always the desire of the Other.

Unable to pull people away from their handheld devices, they remain glued to Facebook, Snapchat, Instagram, FaceTime, WhatsApp, YouTube, TikTok, and endless other social networking services like addicts with a needle hanging from their arm. Many young people largely don't know how to talk or relate to one another: verbal communication has been replaced by a text message even while sitting in the same room. Individual personality and a sense of agency have been replaced by bots and emojis as people disappear into a screen. Society has become trapped in a Skinner box where masses—particularly the youth, who are most vulnerable—are like operantly conditioned dogs in a lab or a casino where the next information byte leads you to a one-armed bandit pulling a lever, hoping coins will tumble into the magical bin. People are interpassively fixated to their devices to the degree that techno-hypnotism has become the new behaviorism and obsessive-compulsive disorder controlling people's lives.

Gertz argues that we place blind faith in machines without understanding how they work to the point that an algorithm can become destiny based on pleasure economics—everything from porn to online shopping, dating, donating money to a GoFundMe campaign, renting out your apartment through Airbnb, getting into cars with strangers through Uber or a quick hookup or "booty call" through Tinder have become the norm. With such preoccupation with online presence comes the anonymous tendency to devalue the other while elevating the self in such perverse ways that alterity, the ethnically other, and diverse groups with different social values lead to an obscene form of judgment and devaluation to the point of dehumanization. What we may refer to as *anonymous relativism*, where no one has to assume personal responsibility for their actions online, leads to "orgies of clicking" in which others are judged, rated, and deemed worthy or not worthy of attention, praise, and generosity. Moreover, evaluation and ranking of others sometimes leads to cruel deprecation and dysrecognition where basic empathy and human decency are dissociated from social discourse: personal values are pitted against others' values with venomous hatred and self-superiority to the degree that shame and inadequacy, anxiety and depression are traumatically induced states in others who are the recipient of casual rage. The internet has become the locus of blind displacement where masses can discharge their typically secret thoughts and prejudicial attitudes in a plethora of destructive gestures aimed toward negating and humiliating the Other. Because there is no accountability for anonymous relativism, other human beings become the recipient of shadow projections that degrade people and turn them into techno things as the displaced object of fury.

Gertz applies Nietzsche's critique of nihilism to a critique of internet behavior that

> involves outbursts, releases of pent-up urges, emotional explosions, all of which are attempts to experience the ecstasy of evading the burden of accountability, evasions that incur a cost that we must later pay. Yet when technologies provide new ways to indulge our ecstatic urges, such as when technologies allow us to post anonymous comments, form

flash mobs, and become cybervigilantes, our explosive tendencies can move beyond the self-destruction of guilt to the other-destruction of shame. The danger of orgies of clicking can be seen, for example, in the escalation that takes place when trolling and flash mobbing merge to create shame campaigns—as those who rally to a hashtag to pillory the latest social media outlaw can themselves be pilloried, as trolling incurs counter-trolling, which leads to doxing and counter-doxing—creating a world so toxic that shame campaigns and political campaigns become more and more indistinguishable.[18]

Negating difference and otherness are indeed so toxic that it has led to teen suicide due to cyberbullying and murder, such as the incel (involuntary celibate) movement inspiring a man to run over and kill 10 pedestrians and critically wound 16 others in a Toronto van attack in 2018. The internet is a spawning ground for anarchists and hate, terrorists, white nationalists, conspiracy theorists, and fringe groups to come out of the closet and create havoc wherever they can: it is the leading weapon of choice to trigger outrage, create division, incite violence, extort, and target populaces with disinformation campaigns to interfere with everything from legitimate news and media outlets, trade and commerce, to national security and political elections. You can readily get designs and blueprints to make a gun, bomb, chemical explosive, bacterial pathogen, engineered computer virus, nanomachinery, and practically anything you wish that can be duplicated and manufactured with a 3-D printer. With the imaginable comes the unimaginable: technology is the new doomsday missile.

Regardless of the sadistic cruelty that is observed and acted out online in internet forums spurred through personal vendettas, the fact is that techno nihilism is the new methodology to bring about damage and endless harm, not only based on the degradation of another's sense of self and values but as a means to inflict suffering on a large scale that transcends national borders. Computer-engineered technology, in particular, has the potential to generate superintelligences that could hypothetically eradicate the world.

---

18. Gertz (2018), pp. 9–10.

CHAPTER 6

SUPERINTELLIGENCES

What would happen if machines acquire more intelligence than human beings and want to take over the world? What if a supercomputer, cyber mind, or AI system decides that humanity needs to be eliminated because it impedes its existence or is a threat to its goals? At first glance, what appears to be far-fetched—if not ridiculous—speculation, such doomsday thought experiments turn into serious cause for alarm. Nick Bostrom makes a compelling case that the fate of our species could be determined by machine superintelligence that surpasses the intelligence of the human brain, especially if it may develop sinister plans. Given that we build these things, you would expect as a foregone conclusion that designers, engineers, computer specialists, and manufacturers would ensure that proper safeguards prevent such a possibility from happening, but it may not be that simple. If, in theory, a new superintelligence is smarter than any human or whole community of human minds, then it would be de facto a superpower. If this transpires, the question becomes, how do we control it?

> In practice, the control problem—the problem of how to control what the superintelligence would do—looks quite difficult. It also looks like we will only get one chance. Once unfriendly superintelligence exists, it would prevent us from replacing it or changing its preferences. Our fate would be sealed . . . This is quite possibly the most important and most daunting challenge humanity has ever faced. And—whether we succeed or fail—it is probably the last challenge we will ever face.[19]

Because we purportedly are on the doorsill of a breakthrough in artificial intelligence, whenever that may occur and the conditions of which remain uncertain, we would be wise to anticipate and prepare for a type of intelligence explosion or technological revolution that humanity has never witnessed. Because AI applications already outperform human cognitive capabilities in many domains—in mechanism, accuracy, speed, efficiencies, memory, computational functions, and in game-playing computers, for example—what would happen if a superintelligence becomes

19. Bostrom (2014), p. vii.

greater than or surpasses human AI? What if a machine would acquire whole-brain emulation, sensory cognition, enhanced biological and organizational intelligence with specialized information processing systems, digital minds, or develop consciousness, subjective experience, and a sense of self?

In other words, if we don't know its possibilities now, how could we predict with any degree of probability, let alone certainty, what it would do? The existential risks should not be underestimated, as machine superintelligence could renovate human existence. For better or worse is another question. In essence, AI could lead to the creation of new superminds that are far greater, faster, and more efficient than biological life, the likes of which we have never seen before. If we can get past the sci-fi fantasies, political hype, and/or emotional hyperbole, that is, if an ultra-intelligent machine can, in theory, be constructed that far outstrips all human intelligence capabilities, then we must contemplate and take seriously what that means for the fate of humanity.

Even though Bostrom does not put it in these terms, the real danger is if a machine superintelligence attains ultimate freedom, what will it do? There is no guarantee of moral decision making or ethical action with a freely determinate entity, as we have no way of controlling its intentions and plans. In attaining agency, will, and volitional freedom we have no safety against nefarious acts. If a computer is free to do whatever it wants, no one is safe.

If a superintelligence vastly exceeds human cognition in all domains of interest, then it cannot be compared to human agency. The paths of uncertainty are inscribed in our ignorance of what machine-mind autonomy may lead to. Would it not have a distinctive strategic, first-mover advantage over human will and agency? What if it harnessed many superintelligences into a single centralized power—a *singleton*—where its intentions are to achieve complete world domination? Such megalomania and reactionary paranoia may seem far-fetched, if not delusional, but the point is that we have no way of knowing, let along controlling, how a superintelligent being of this sort would think, plan, verify, and behave. What if it took all of humanity as a threat to its existence and became a terminator? If superintelligence is independent of human minds and social relations, then how could we control it when, by definition, it is self-governing? There is no way to guarantee an ethical agent instrumentally or structurally when it is self-regulating and is capable of autonomous self-programming outside of human affairs or concerns. We cannot preprogram or install a fixed predetermined set of operations in a superintelligence that has its own mind, experiential qualia, subjective sense of self, and self-conscious, reflexive analytical functions. There is no way of knowing if a predesigned and preprogrammed machine that has built-in filters to show recognition, validation, care, empathy, and moral obligation for others would not be overridden by its own desires, purposes, and super-autonomy. In fact, it could trick its designers or programmers into thinking it is benign and ethical only to gain advantage over its own development, growth, and output independent of all engineering, monitoring, and dependency on human strategy and interaction. Under these conditions, nothing is preventing a cognitive superpower from wanting to take over the world, whether through manipulating human beings or by exerting its power over nature itself.

Bostrom envisions the possibility of many AI takeover scenarios: intelligence amplification; strategizing to overcome opposition and achieve distant goals; social manipulation to persuade gatekeepers to escape AI confinement and spread throughout the internet; recruit human support (licit or illicit) to further its aims and ends; hacking or exploiting security flaws in computer systems; expropriating, stealing, or hijacking infrastructure and networks, computational, labor, military, and financial resources; autonomously develop advanced technologies such as through biotechnology and nanomechanical structures that generate more manufacturing, power, and economic control over the forces of production through robotic manipulators, automated laboratories, DNA extraction, and human deception, just to name a few. If an AI directly executes its objectives on a full scale, it may initiate an overt implementation phase that

> might start with a "strike" in which the AI eliminates the human species and any automatic systems humans have created that could offer intelligent opposition to the execution of the AI's plans. This could be

achieved through activation of some advanced weapons system that the AI has perfected using its technology research superpower and covertly deployed in the covert preparation phase . . . One might also entertain scenarios in which a superintelligence attains power by hijacking political processes, subtly manipulating financial markets, biasing information flows, or hacking into human-made weapons systems . . . Alternatively, if the AI is sure of its invincibility to human interference, our species may not be targeted directly. Our demise may instead result from the habitat destruction that ensues when the AI begins massive global construction projects using nanotech factories and assemblers . . . or other installations whereby the AI intends to maximize the long-term cumulative realization of its values.[20]

Although he claims otherwise through a repeated disclaimer,[21] one immediate criticism of Bostrom's thought experiments is that he presupposes that machines will even attain this level of AI superintelligence, technological growth trajectory, and agentic autonomy to begin with, not to mention that he anthropomorphizes machine sophistication and attributes psychological motivations, values, intentionality, and telic finality to an artificial nonhuman thing, like the fictional character HAL (Heuristically Programmed ALgorithmic Computer) in Arthur C. Clarke's *2001: A Space Odyssey*. All these foresight narratives are unknown hypothetical presuppositions of an imaginary possible future to come. In many ways, these scenarios resemble a theocratic prophecy of the *eschaton* where machines become omnipotent: technology will inevitably bring about a new apocalypse. Here machine superintelligence is reified to the status of a macroanthropos. At this stage in our technological infancy such visions of futurity are merely speculative fantasies, given that no AI like this exists today; and we have no guarantee or likelihood that it ever will be invented or even be permitted by conscientious social collectives, for obvious reasons. Here we remain entirely in the realm of science fiction. Whether this level of superintelligence will ever remotely advance to approximate such futurist scenarios is pure hypostatization, as

---

20. Bostrom (2014), p. 97.
21. Bostrom (2014), pp. 92, 105.

we currently do not even have the means to duplicate human cognition, replicate a human brain, or simulate consciousness, let alone its creative output.

But just in case of the possibility of a superintelligence explosion, we should not be too quick to dismiss the unanticipated global catastrophic risks to humanity. Given recent developments in generative AI—artificial neural networks that power chatbots through large language models (LLMs), which are purportedly self-governing in their creative output—AI experts, scientists, researchers, engineers, programmers, stakeholders, policy makers, and politicians alike are becoming panicky, hence clamoring for a pause on tech industry development. And they want to introduce governmental regulation out of fear over complete AI self-autonomy. The Center for AI Safety has even gone so far as to issue a hysterical warning (read: fear of accountability and legal liability): "Mitigating the risk of extinction from AI should be a global priority alongside other societal-scale risks such as pandemics and nuclear war."[22]

Menaced by existential catastrophe, advances in artificial machine intelligence should at the very minimum be concerned with considering optimal design parameters that take into account their need for limited autonomy, domesticity, axiological potential, means of acquiring and acting on universal shared values, built-in axioms for guiding AI decision theory and epistemology, volition and moral permissibility models, goal content, action potential, the necessity for safeguards, countermeasures, and disabling mechanisms, and long-term science and technology policy issues in design paths, anticipated dangers, and preemptive strategies that require international cooperation, consultation, and regulation. This becomes especially dangerous if machines are allowed to evolve into autonomous entities that view us as things with no real sense of attachment or moral duty to alterity. Lesson of the day as a takeaway: When humanity can potentially become dehumanized and not recognized by machines as living beings who matter, then let's not take any unnecessary chances with technological hubris. The stakes are too high to play with matches.

---

22. See Center for AI Safety (2023), Statement on AI Risk, https://www.safe.ai/statement-on-ai-risk?utm_source=substack&utm_medium=email#open-letter

Before the prospect of an intelligence explosion, we humans are like small children playing with a bomb. Such is the mismatch between the power of our plaything and the immaturity of our conduct. Super-intelligence is a challenge for which we are not ready now and will not be ready for a long time. We have little idea when the detonation will occur, though if we hold the device to our ear we can hear a faint ticking sound.

For a child with an undetonated bomb in its hands, a sensible thing to do would be to put it down gently, quickly back out of the room, and contact the nearest adult. Yet what we have here is not one child but many, each with access to an independent trigger mechanism. The chances that we will *all* find the sense to put down the dangerous stuff seem almost negligible. Some little idiot is bound to press the ignite button just to see what happens.[23]

23. Bostrom (2014), p. 259.

7

A World without Recognition

On May 25, 2020, a small group of people clustered around a Minneapolis street corner and watched for nearly nine minutes as a white police officer killed an unarmed black man by pressing his knee into his neck until he stopped breathing. The infamous death of George Floyd sent immediate shockwaves throughout the world, first leading to riots in the United States followed by civil protests around the globe during the heart of the COVID pandemic, outraged by the audacious police brutality and antiblack racism that sullies our shared humanity. As Floyd was unable to breathe, calling out for his mother while lying handcuffed and pinned to the ground pleading for his life, neither the police officers on the scene nor stunned pedestrians amid the unprovoked assault intervened to stop the murder. Even though onlookers yelled and repeatedly cried out that Floyd was in distress and suffocating, one bystander even having the presence of mind to film and post the senseless torture and public lynching online,[1] the protesting crowd watched him die before their very eyes. But this was not a case of bystander apathy. People were concerned, belligerent, emotionally distraught, challenged authority, and were persistently vocal that an innocent man was being killed. At one point, movement from the crowd led the officer kneeling on Floyd to grab his mace from his service belt to deter any advance, while another officer pushed back a protester to the sidewalk. Neither passive citizens

---

1. See Stock (2020) for the full unedited video.

nor totally paralyzed by fear, these courageous witnesses[2] had to endure the uncanny helplessness of not being able to do anything in the face of a traumatic crisis situation that turned from spectator to spectacle.

The Black Lives Matter movement that intensified as a result of this incident, and countless other killings of unarmed black persons by police, are good examples of how a persistent lack of recognition of people of color led to global outcry against racism and inequality of disenfranchised groups pining for acknowledgment of their needs and restitution for their suffering. Here the historical wounds of slavery, institutionalized racial segregation, such as in the Jim Crow southern United States and Apartheid South Africa, and white privilege leave their psychosocial disfigurements. Here it is not surprising that civil protest, indignation, revolt, and demand for reform become common responses to unjust systemic discrimination and domination enchained by a ruling class.

In today's world, the Hegelian master-slave dialectic seems to be very much alive: most developing and nonindustrial countries live in servitude to powerful others or the state; and in democratic nations, citizens are largely dependent upon capitalistic enterprises, for which they serve and enrich. In fact, subjugation and domination of otherness is flourishing throughout the globe. Entire peoples are vanquished, refuted, nullified, and denounced simply because they proclaim to have different needs and worldviews. When difference and protest persist, they are often overpowered and persecuted under the guise of resistance to conformity to the prevailing forces that enslave them in their actual conditions of oppression.

Our attachments to others, social relations, and intersubjective communal matrixes form the psychological edifice of our dependency on others and social institutions organized around just and unjust modes of recognition that are structurally, systemically, and semiotically constituted.[3] When this basic bedrock of relationality is disrupted or vitiated,

---

2. Cf. Fillmore's (2020) commentary.
3. Critical theory has traditionally been concerned with the broader social fabric of institutionalized cultural practices that inform a collective ethos with a keen eye on analyzing dysfunction and advocating for real changes in society. This includes critiquing authoritarian politics, safeguarding against totalitarianism, democratizing social justice, and extending an ethical hand in our post-Holocaust world. This shift in social self-consciousness stresses the importance of validating alterity rather than

society experiences anxiety, emotional pain, and retrograde backlash. Individuals, social groups, and civilizations victimized by repeated dys-recognition and base negation of their values and collective identities are subjected to a cultural pathos against their will.[4] As a result, they/we suffer.

The Need to Be Acknowledged

We all seek recognition; this is a basic human need.[5] The ego is affirmed by the other, but not at first. There is originally the experience of inequality, whether this be the child's relation to the parent or the bondsman's

---

sustaining rival differences between individuals, societies, and nations that fail to acknowledge the need for mutual recognition of the Other. But critical theorists have not fully appreciated the insights of psychoanalytic perspectives that deviate from overtly sanguine views valorizing anthropological conditions leading to optimally cohesive social arrangements. Contemporary recognition theory (Honneth, 1995, 2012; Fraser & Honneth, 2003), for example, depends on a patently optimistic, if not overly idealistic, and intellectualized view of social relations and human nature. The limits of this position that world societies can achieve reciprocal recognition is a case in point, as it ignores the dark side of recognition—namely, its asymmetrical pathological dynamics informed by early developmental contingencies in attachment, self-formation, prejudicial social relations, and the negation of difference, and fails to address the psychodynamics of how dysrecognition and refutation of the Other lead to insidious pathologies within society and the clinic (see Mills, 2019a, b, c). This is especially clear in the case of social collectives (not to mention governments) that regularly fail to interact through reciprocal recognition even when they become aware of their mutual dependency on each other. This observation equally applies to theories of moral consciousness, communicative action, and discourse ethics, which presuppose that human beings by nature are rational animals, and that through linguistic dialogue societies can reinvigorate Enlightenment paradigms of social justice free of domination from otherness based on cooperative speech exchange. In particular, Jürgen Habermas's (1990, 1993) theory of communicative rationality (*kommunikative Rationalität*) assumes that norms, rules, and procedures for communication and argumentation can be established in the moral-practical realm and have a rational outcome by necessity, when this seems to ignore the nonrational, desirous, emotional, prejudicial, political, and unconscious motivations that govern human discourse and action. From a psychoanalytic point of view, this is unrealistic, if not a wishful fantasy, because it is evident that collectives are largely possessed by unconscious complexes, emotional seizures, attitudinal prejudices, and irrationality to the degree that unadulterated reason is not even remotely possible, let alone valid. Such highly rationalized accounts of human relations seem to ignore basic psychological dynamics of human motivation based in neurotic propensities, affective dysregulation, dispositions toward aggression, and internal conflict that militates against any pure cognitivist paragon.

4. Recall that for the ancient Greeks, pathos defined the human condition: to be human is to suffer.
5. Frederick Neuhouser (1986) attempts to elucidate the origin of the need for recognition itself by partially claiming that we seek recognition because our own demands for self-certainty are left unsatisfied without the presence and validation of others. This notion is compatible with many psychoanalytic conceptualizations of the development of subjectivity including attachment theory, object relations theory, self psychology, and interpersonal, intersubjective, and relational perspectives.

relation to the lord. Arguably one of the most widely cited sections of the *Phenomenology of Spirit* is Hegel's 1807 discussion of lordship and bondage.[6] In pithy form, spirit or mind (*Geist*) ultimately achieves ethical self-consciousness only by recognizing the other as an equal being. But this is a developmental achievement. In our interpersonal engagement with others, a battle for recognition takes place between subjects. Yet at first, parties in this struggle are unaware that they are looking for recognition, which is unconsciously mediated, the meaning of which is hence initially unclear to those involved. Only through the process of confronting otherness do we become cognizant of what we truly want. We may observe how this is ontically infused in all spheres of life and plays a key role in our psychological health and social progress, for every human being wants to be recognized by others as an instantiation of human desire. This naturally extends to society. Before society raises itself to the status of improving its politico-cultural practices for the sake of its peoples, including institutionalized ethics, law and order, and distributive justice, it must start with this basic psychic fact. Those who are deprived

---

6. The problem of alienation and spirit's struggle for recognition has received overwhelming attention in the Hegelian literature. Within this context, an almost exclusive fixation has been on the master-slave dialectic introduced in the *Phenomenology* (1807). It is interesting to note that Hegel's treatment of desire and recognition is contrasted differently in the *Encyclopaedia Phenomenology* (1971, 1978) and the *Berlin Phenomenology* (1981) from that of his Jena period. The most notable difference in his later writings is his scant discussion of self-consciousness in comparison to his original work, and his famous section on "Freedom of Self-Consciousness" has been entirely purged. Hegel's master-slave discussion, or what we may refer to as lord and servant, and more generally the "*relationship* of *mastery* [*Herrschaft*] and *servitude* [*Knechtschaft*]" (Hegel, 1978, § 433, emphasis in original), is given the briefest summation in the *Encyclopaedia* where the discussion from recognition to universal self-consciousness is contained in only six paragraphs and one remark, excluding the additions, and little additional elaboration is offered in the Berlin manuscript. This is undoubtedly why almost all interpretations of desire and recognition rely exclusively on the Jena *Phenomenology*. Further, all references to stoicism, skepticism, and unhappy consciousness are eliminated. This terse account suggests that perhaps Hegel wanted to distance himself from his earlier commitments outlined in the *Phenomenology*, or else that he thought he had treated the subjects adequately beforehand. When we examine his later works, Hegel emphasizes the subjection of the other to the domination of desire as a "thoroughly selfish *destructiveness*" (Hegel, 1978, § 428, *Zusatz*) that is only concerned with its immediate satisfaction in conquering opposition. Recognitive self-consciousness is the immediate confrontation of two egos, each extending its self into the other. During this moment, the self has an "immediate intuition" of itself as well as the recognition of an "absolutely opposed and independently distinct object" (Hegel, 1978, § 430). When the other is seen merely as an object and not a subject, this ensures that there will be no mutual recognition. See Mills (2002, pp. 143–149) for an extended discussion.

of recognition fail to thrive, just as infants abandoned to orphanages were given no nurturance, love, or human touch. Those who are unacknowledged or dysrecognized suffer and are condemned to harbor grave feelings of invalidation of their personhood in virtual aloneness.

The inequality of recognition first exists when two opposing subjects confront one other. Each wants to be what the other only represents; thus, each is determined to negate the other's independence to give one's own self value. This guarantees that the process of recognition is saturated with conflict. Two selves oppose the independence of the other and, in so doing, assert their independence. Put simply, two mutually confronting selves appear as physical things to each other that act independently and hence freely, which both recognize as being before the other. But freedom is something that must be fought for; it must be achieved or proven. This is why Hegel sees the tussles of recognition as an altercation—a struggle, for it is "a matter of life or death."[7]

People are largely (unreflectively) seen by their fellows as mere objects—as *things* that exist "out there" in the world, because they are divorced from our emotional and personal lives in order for us to function psychologically—or we'd all be basket cases! Only when we contemplate the nature of this otherness are we confronted with our own normativity: others are and have a self that exists independently from "me." "What is this other?" "What does the other have that I don't have?" "What do I want?" "What do I lack that the other has?" These questions lie on the sunrise of self-consciousness because we are instantly made aware of the external reality of other human beings who are just like us in essence, although we have separate identities, personalities, and longings. We become aware of our desires through reflection upon (and as projected onto) the other, on the subject that stands before us, even though we see this other as an independent (impersonal) object. When we recognize the other as a desirous and intentional being, we are immediately made aware of the subjectivity of the other, one we have an obligation to address. "What does this other want?" This leads us to one of Hegel's most important insights: when we confront otherness, we are entangled

---

7. Hegel (1978), § 432.

in desire and lack, which initiates a skirmish for recognition.[8] Who will be acknowledged in this mutual otherness? Here subjectivities stand fundamentally opposed to one another.

Hegel pushes the issue further and forces us to face a most grave predicament: when mutual opposition confronts each other, "each seeks the death of the other."[9] This understandably creates a crisis situation. Who will be defeated? This is why when we have conflict with others, we want them to go away. In our contemporary world of cutthroat competition, economic exploitation and rivalry, political dominion, legal intervention, military strategizing, and trans-governmental maneuvering of hegemonic policies, which ideology will win out over others? One side must acknowledge that it is weaker and the other stronger, so when posturing and rhetoric fail, a natural deference ensues, much like what we see in the animal kingdom governed by evolutionary currents. One must bow down and accept their inferiority and servitude, while the other maintains the status of victor. What used to be a literal fight to the death is now largely a symbolic one, depending upon where you live or come from. Genocide in Rwanda, Sierra Leone, Myanmar, and the Democratic Republic of the Congo are cordial reminders in recent decades of what can happen when power differentials implode. But this happens on a more pedestrian plain every day everywhere in the world. People want respect: when they are dismissed or insulted, they emotively react with counter-contempt and rancor, if not narcissistic rage and the need to devalue or shame the other in the heat of the moment. This can even precipitate violence and the need for revenge due to wounded pride. From Trump to fake news, denial

---

8. Although discourse on desire and lack is thought to have derived from Sartre and Lacan—who essentially purloined Hegel's theory when he was exposed to Kojève's (1929) lectures on Hegel's *Phenomenology*, which Lacan (1991) borrows from liberally—these notions originate from Hegel. Desire immediately apprehends what it is not from what it would like to be, hence the subject starts from a place of inequality, deficiency, and lack. Hegel (1978) explains:

> The self-conscious subject knows itself to be *implicitly identical* with the general object external to it. It knows that since this general object contains the *possibility* of satisfying desire, it is *adequate* to the desire, and that this is precisely why the desire is stimulated by it. The relation with the object is therefore necessary to the subject. The subject intuits its *own deficiency*, its own one-sidedness, in the object; it sees there something which although it belongs to its own essence, it lacks (§ 427, *Zusatz*).

9. Hegel (1807), § 187.

over the pandemic, and a gullible inane public, we are living in precarious times of transition and outright stupidity.

What is often recognized is not the equality of the other but, rather, a scornful inequality—namely, the fact that people often do not care about alterity over their own lives and self-interests, to the point that the Other becomes a dangerous threat to one's safety. Although we may acknowledge that others are independent persons, it does not mean that we "respect others as persons."[10] On the contrary, respect is earned. Avoidance, withdrawal, and submissiveness, on the other hand, are defensive modes of self-survival, especially in the face of a powerful opponent. That is why people often acquiesce to others for defensive reasons, especially when they are afraid, rather than because they recognize them as being morally equal. Submission to another's will typically thwarts the probability of the other's aggression being directed toward them, hence protecting the self. Do our world societies and governments (viz., Hegel's Objective Spirit) think about the common universal good for all, or merely their own self-regard and political pressures invested in their own nations and communities? Even though there may be checks and balances designed to help treat citizens fairly, this does not generalize to a universal society of cosmopolitans (namely, citizens of the cosmos) who value all human life equally. Of course, such hypostatization of a so-called collective mind only makes sense as an abstract conception that embodies the spirit of democracy, as imperfect as this may be. But when it comes to actualizing a universal good, humanity becomes a multiple personality split in its desires, needs, conflicts, demands, and dissatisfactions.

There is always a tension arc between the individual and the collective that stands in relation to pure freedom versus ideality as a good for all. We should never presuppose that we all have the same values and opportunities to pursue and obtain life goals equally, for we all have different historicities and restrictions that condition the developmental, ontic, cultural, material, and economic substrates that in turn curtail our opportunities, liberties, worldviews, and outcomes. So, when Axel Honneth says that a distributional schema of justice "would have to

---

10. Hegel (1821), § 36.

be replaced by the involvement of all subjects in a given relationship of recognition,"[11] he seems to prematurely extrapolate from the reality of human experience.[12] Most people do not readily give up their "egocentric desires for the benefit of the other."[13] In fact, much of social reality today is mired in a collective pathos that prevents optimal mutual recognition among social collectives. Not all people are disposed to, let alone capable, of recognizing the Other. We may have to contend that, in the end, recognition means tolerance of difference and not merely acceptance of others, which could still bring about a pragmatic coexistence even if people cannot recognize each other as equals.

Today we live in fear of death for looking at someone the wrong way, of seeing *their* desire for what *you* are imagined to possess, or what they lack and want, to the point that you could be mugged for the change in your pockets, raped at whim, or shot in the face just because somebody didn't like the way you looked at them. The gaze, the look—the *stare* is an invitation to aggression. We are instinctively obsequious and show assent or acquiesce when we are afraid. We avoid the face of the other—hence look away, dodge confrontation, and yield; conversely, we look for conflict, seek out a fight, hate the other (just for being other), and retaliate in perceived defeat simply because we have the need to find foes. Let us not underestimate the need to have enemies. Some object *must* become a designated whipping post as a form of displacement. Eye aversion is

---

11. Honneth (2012), p. 45.

12. Axel Honneth's contributions to recognition theory may benefit from revisiting the ontic role of dysrecognition in the psyche and society in a way that poses challenges to a universal vision of intersubjective mutual recognition among world collectives. Although the pursuit of a universal good, ideality, or abstract notion of right may necessarily entail forms of recognition within social institutions and intersubjective practices, many psychological and sociological variables prevent the masses from actualizing this utopia, especially when civil societies, not to mention developing countries, are beleaguered by pathological forces that erode mutual respect and empathy for the Other. When overly rational approaches—the morality of reason—are applied to social justice paradigms that do not fully consider the penumbra of unconscious conflict, emotional prejudice, relational deficits, political ideologies, and psychological incapacities to recognize difference and alterity, then these dynamics present real limitations on what we can credibly expect from social collectives. Until we can convince world populations that mutual recognition is a common good and institutionalize the practical means by which to bring this about, then I am afraid that mutual acknowledgment of difference is the most we can hope for as a preliminary step in redefining our humanistic principles and distributive schemas of justice.

13. Honneth (2012), p. 17.

the best way to evade engaging with the other—simply a faceless entity that is deemed a threat worth avoiding, yet one already identified as a powerful presence for inducing fear in the first place. We can sniff out their aggression, their malice, their negativity, and so-called (intuited) evil propensities. Disavowal and disassociation become common defenses. The other is as alien to us as we are to them, and we hope that they will just leave us alone, if not disappear. In the face of conflict, we simply want the other to vanish.

But what happens when the Other wants something from us, or demands our recognition, let alone restitution, as if it were a right? Our proverbial backs go up. Yet the Truth and Reconciliation Commissions in response to apartheid, the scandal over the U.S. Chinese Exclusion Act and interning Japanese Americans in WWII, as well as First Nations children in Christian residential schools in Canada, and the process of family members publicly addressing (and sometimes forgiving) murderers openly in courts of law (such as with the organization Murder Victims' Families for Reconciliation) show how recognition has healing properties. But it does not undo injustice. Inequality and disparities are everywhere. We all have to get in line before we are acknowledged, let alone recognized, some as subjects in their own right, but mostly as objects wanting something from others equally viewed as things in mutual opposition. Here the notion of equality by some may be seen as entitlement by others looking for handouts, which challenges the status quo at the same time the establishment offers its own political offensives. We develop our defenses, some cynical, caustic, stoic, and/or emotionless, others manic and counter-aggressive, to deal with others' demands and in facing our lack. Envy, jealousy, and passive-aggressiveness are common dispositions. Protest and violence are eruptions of frustration sometimes fueled by paranoiac relations and *ressentiment*. Facing alterity always involves an interpersonal negotiation between mutual conflict, competing values, emotional biases, and privileged self-serving agendas. This takes place in all facets of society as it does in the home.

DYSRECOGNITION AS SOCIAL PATHOLOGY

As with Freud's qualification that individual psychic processes can never stand apart from social psychology[14] and the cultural environs that impact both personal subjectivity and the objective conditions that interpolate society, so, too, many critical theorists had turned to psychoanalytic paradigms to bolster social philosophy. For Marcuse, psychological categories are political categories and are inseparable from the broader sociological forces that shape civilization. As he tells us, "psychological problems turn into political problems: private disorder reflects more directly than before the disorder of the whole, and the cure of the personal disorder depends more directly than before on the cure of the general disorder"[15]—namely, sick society. Marcuse is very clear in his insistence that the individual is determined by "the societal forces which define the psyche."[16] Here Jung is lurking in Marcuse's closet. Yet at the same time, psychology becomes the foundation of sociology and the cultural dynamics and institutional organizations that, in turn, inform the psychological.

If you begin with the premise that all human beings are psychological creatures and that all inner experience is psychologically mediated, then by natural extension this would apply to the notion of the polis—specifically, the politics of desire instantiated within any community. And if you start with the premise that the psychological is shaped by the social, then the same argument applies. Groups are psychologically informed and inform others right down to a single subject, whether this applies to our families, cohorts, communities, the provincial or nation-state, and so forth. From Jung to Heidegger and Lacan, we are thrown into a collective psychic matrix and socio-symbolic order that informs our being in the world. Here the individual develops within the social, and the social within the individual.

One does not have to bifurcate the arrangements of society from naturalized psychology to see how their dynamic processes and co-occurrence pressurize and inform one another within a systemic unit. We can surely observe how certain communal structures and political

14. Freud (1921), p. 69.
15. Marcuse (1955), p. 21.
16. Marcuse (1955), p. 21.

policies within societies lead to more problems in living and suffering in individuals, and how natural psychological processes such as desire, envy, greed, rage, entitlement, aggression, and so on are intensified and play out through pathological enactments when societies undergo, for example, material deprivation, economic austerity, tragedy, trauma, war, and political oppression. When social institutions, capitalistic enterprise, and the populace do not acknowledge or recognize disenfranchised subgroups and the extreme hardships they face due to race, socioeconomic, and educational disparities that privileged classes do not face, social fabrics begin to fray.

The struggle for recognition, as psychoanalysis shows, is present from birth onward—from day care to death, as each of us is mired in familial, societal, and cultural conflict that saturates our being and world. The failure to recognize the other, and more insidiously, chronic invalidation and repudiation of different peoples, produces and sustains intersubjective and interethnic aggression to the point of murder and war. Here the Hegelian struggle for life and death is a lived reality that affects our conception of social justice and institutionalized forms of recognition. But the point I wish to make here is that dysrecognition may, in fact, trigger and sustain violence based on an unconscious revolt in reaction to political injustice. Indeed, aggression is not only instinctual, for lack of a better word, hence emanating from evolutionary biological forces; it is also triggered by relational or interpersonal failures at validation and empathy that are sociologically instituted. When such dysrecognition is performed and sustained by the state, here we may say that a certain unconscious politics is operative on both the individual and collective level of a given society, which can lead to a vicious cycle of perpetration, victimization, and social malaise that always psychologically penetrates those who are marginalized. And this may be intensified as a posttraumatic act that resurrects earlier psychic pain experienced in childhood, especially when invalidation, abuse, and insecure attachments inform the next generation of social pathologies.

Much of psychoanalysis is in sympathy with critical theory in its tacit hopes of bettering society; but psychoanalytic observations can be quite pathologizing as well, and for good reason. Here, the two disciplines are critical of the way collectives think and behave. We may speculate that this has to do with, on some level, the way people are raised and taught to think and act in a given cultural milieu, yet we must begin with rudiments. What do people require psychologically to thrive? Beyond recognition, I suggest, lie psychic needs for love, validation, and empathy. These are essential for healthy development. When they are lacking, withheld, truncated, or absent, a person, and even whole societies, may develop a traumatic reaction to life. This notion is quite simple; in fact, it is a basic ingredient of the human aspect.

All people as individuals have basic psychic needs, which feed and sustain a society. If those needs are thwarted or disabused, then this creates a fundamental retrograde backlash that has detrimental repercussions on people's health and well-being, as well as the productive social functioning of the collective. It is not rocket science. If you are deprived of the essential psychological nutrients of life, let alone if you are abused, oppressed, disenfranchised, or suffer developmental traumas, then this impacts on us all. People are unhappy, suffer, and develop psychological disorders that do not allow them to function adequately, let alone meet higher-level expectations for psychosocial adaptation to common stress. The quality of subjective life is tarnished, and society is affected in every tangible way, from economics to health care to lost productivity and creativity, to the qualitative erosion of living a good existence. People act out, become aggressive, anxious, and depressed, abuse substances, fall into crisis or despair, or become dysfunctional in every conceivable manner, which creates an ambiance for internal implosion, whether this is projected outwardly or interiorized into self-destructive modes of being and behavioral patterns.

The bottom line is that all individuals require that certain psychological needs be met or subjective suffering will spew forth on any communal collective regardless of their content or context, typically beginning with one's immediate family, which only perpetuates a transgenerational transmission of pathos that infects any given society and the broader cultural identifications and organizations at large. When this happens, whether conspicuously or cryptically, a future world full of more suffering and pathology is empirically predictable.

Unconscious Politics and the Other

When individuals encounter one another, this naturally leads to the mutual desire for recognition as an individuated, autonomous subject. People are differentiated and independent, yet each face each other in mutual confrontation. This intersubjective dynamic further entails an implicit perception that each person is opposed to the other as an embodied entity that may do them harm. But this detection does not stop here. In seeing the other as an independent will with needs, desires, intentions, and potentially manipulative self-serving actions, the other becomes an automatic threat. This triggers a psychological competition (sometimes physically or merely paranoiac confrontation) where one subject will inevitably be bested while the other takes his or her subservient place in the confrontation. This is a fundamental psychological insight on behavioral dynamics governing human nature that we may all witness in the nursery and on the playground, the foundation for adult politics. This abridged version of explaining how power differentials arise unconsciously when encountering alterity is advanced in innumerable ways by psychoanalytic theory.

A major roadblock that derails a discernible intellectual picture of the need for mutual or collective recognition is in deciphering the anathema of unconscious politics that underlie behavioral acts of every person in the world. People, societies, and governments do not act rationally, nor should we expect them to. We do not live in a purely adjudicated intellectual or logical universe but, rather, one derived from the prisms of our base urges, impulses, emotions, and internal conflicts that must undergo a developmental and educational process of exercising self-constraint, affect regulation, behavioral modification, and instructional training to achieve psychological and social maturity. The gleanings of reason, truth, virtue, and wisdom are higher order accomplishments. But this is hardly achieved by everyone. In fact, this level of psychic cultivation is more of an outlier than an actualization for most people. At most, we are all striving to attain certain values and ideals. More commonplace, we succumb to our immediate shortcomings and complexes, moral limitations of character, and attitudinal prejudices that condition how we relate to self, others, and the world.

We develop internal resistances, oppositions, and counter-struggles to internalized and interiorized conflict from birth onward. This is simply an economic (if not evolutionary) reaction to protect the self against real or perceived threat and emotional pain. This naturalized tendency is partially derived from (if not determined by) unconscious desire and its reactionary defenses and resultant disharmonies fueled by affective currents that merely seek their own resolutions and satisfactions over others, which are projected upon society at large. Here we may observe a basic splitting mechanism in the psyche: identity and division become irreconcilable, where there is no discernible point of synthesis or sublation. People see their own esoteric or group microcosm as the hallmark of truth and reality that takes objective priority over others, when such myopic identifications are in dialectical competition with alterity. In other words, the Other is negated in principle based on one's own reinforced preferences that take precedence and are more personally important, the surreptitious expression of narcissistic hubris. This attitude is the foundation of every country and nationalist (or populist) movement that values its citizens over other countries as a pragmatic necessity governing political identificatory self-interest ranging from every partisan preference and local whim to domestic and foreign decree.

We must seriously question the prejudicial unconscious forces that drive political states of affairs, from individual and communal choices to international policy, for collective humanity is neither unified in its aims nor prioritizes matters outside of its immediate scope of parochial concerns or regional inclinations. Is the political unconscious a universal phenomenon—namely, is it structurally inscribed in the very ontological fabric of the psyche? With qualifications, all persons are predisposed a priori to favor certain unconscious attitudes even if they are irrational and ultimately self-destructive. And it is unequivocally taking place on a mass scale across all civilized parts of the world.

What we are witnessing in concrete forms is how the collective psyche is divided based on unconscious politics identified with certain ideologies fortified by cultural relativity and animus toward alterity. Here we should question the capacity of the collective to make rationally informed judgments when wish, self-vagary, and insular governmental hegemonies make decisions that affect us all. Yet government is elected by the people in democratic countries, which brings us to question why in recent political times most citizens would vote for leaders—say, in the United Kingdom and America, who are anti-environment, anti-immigration, xenophobic, racist, bigoted, religiously intolerant, misogynistic, antigay, and pro-war, just to name a few indecencies. From Brexit to the election of U.S. Republican president Donald Trump, humanity should beckon a call to reason. It is no surprise to psychoanalysis that we are witnessing the disintegration of culture, for illogical decisions are unconsciously chosen based on raw affect and bigotry, which speaks to the greater manifestation of collective social life immersed in its own pathos.

A FAILURE OF EMPATHY

Although it is problematic to make mass generalizations, it may not be entirely illegitimate to say that we largely live in a world where there is no proper recognition of the Other as the equiprimordial complementarity of the Self. In other words, it is too cognitively overwhelming to uphold the radical Levinasian responsibility to the Other over the immediacy of one's life and duties to family and those who we value, as if we could become Jesus and minister to a world collective. This ethical ideal defies logic, real human limitations, and the psychological disposition of the multitudes. But speaking metaphysically, the dialectical onto-interconnectedness of identity and difference ensures that self in relation to alterity is a mutually implicit dynamic. When we attempt to analyze the human condition extraspectively or scientifically and look into the psyche or soul through an introspective analysis of our interiority, we can discern the universal experiences that all people engage in psychologically, only to recursively fall back into bifurcation that maintains rigid antitheses. The self is experienced and thought *not* to be the other. The *Them* is eclipsed for the *I*, whereas the *We* becomes occluded.

We may argue that, strictly speaking, humanity is not an identity at all but, rather, a collection of identities or subjects who largely exist and relate to one another in opposition to mutual difference. Despite the fact that we all maintain shared identifications and values with others throughout our globalized world, not everyone is recognized, nor is this remotely possible given that people are divided based on their desires, conflicts, beliefs, values, identities, and moral principles. Here we should maintain no pretense of a pristine Hegelian sublation (*Aufhebung*) of the subjective individual within objective social consciousness, where the pinnacle of ethics and justice reach their logical zenith in the concrete universals of culture, for this is merely a theoretical abstraction. In fact, much of social reality resists sublation and can indeed regress or withdraw back to early primitive instantiations governed by pathos.[17] The Absolute unity of the individual within the social as the logical culmination of pure self-consciousness is simply an illusion, although one that may spur our continual pining for refining social systems of democracy, law, ethics, and justice. Here reformation and advance are culture's teleological endeavor. Whatever values and ideals societies adopt are always mediated through unconscious psychic processes[18] that condition (and taint) the collective, even when good intentions are involved. Although the fantasy of wholeness conceived through Hegel's philosophy of mind as a self-articulated dynamic complex holism arriving at pure unification of the individual within the collective is a noble ideal, such a grand (if not grandiose) logical synthesis belies the empirical confounds that reflect social reality today marked by division, fracturing, and splitting of peoples, groups, and nations that radically resist unity. The projection of our aggression, hatred, and destructive envy onto a hating Other only ensures mutual conflict and dysrecognition, where some compromises conceivably occur. Despite these limitations and inevitable frictions between individuals and societies, collective identifications among people about ideals and social values do facilitate advances in ethical self-consciousness, which have a concrete impact on social policy and legislative reform that, in turn, restructure social institutions and the domestic practices of citizens.

---

17. In *Origins: On the Genesis of Psychic Reality*, I provide my own revisionist amendments to Hegel's dialectical method that take into account the nature of dialectical regression, temporal mediacy, and the ubiquitous nature of contingency that challenges universal pronouncements of an Absolute unity of mind (see Mills, 2010, pp. 51–58).

18. Although the different schools of psychoanalytic thought offer their own nuanced theoretical frameworks, one universal belief is that unconscious processes are operating within the psyche that stand in relation to social organizations that reinforce them. See my book *Underworlds* (Mills, 2014) for a comprehensive overview of the philosophies of the unconscious in Hegel, Freud, Jung, Lacan, Heidegger, Sartre, Winnicott, and Whitehead.

Perhaps the most we can expect is a Fichtean infinite striving for perfection, although we likely will have to settle for only achieving a quantum and quality of improvement. Here the idea of cultivating social betterment as participating in the ethical leads us to value the notion of mutual recognition as an ideal value. If what we crave and want for ourselves—namely, to be acknowledged, validated, and understood—is to be denounced in another as a reciprocal human being mirroring the inverse of who we are and experience, then this form of negation and hypocrisy not only casts a shadow on the other but also sullies us as an offense to virtue. Yet this idealist language does not inspire mass psychology, which typically devolves into the particular lives, longings, sufferings, and priorities of singular personalities who live among a sea of rivals all competing for recognition and personal gain.

One of the reasons for our impasse in achieving collective recognition of all people is a failure to possess, nurture, and demonstrate empathy for others. This failure is intimately tied to a subset of the problem—that is, our inability to foster global identifications with others. Empathy is based on an intersubjective identification with the other as an experiential self just like we are. Each of us stands united in spirit as an egalitarian subject who feels and needs. This basic shared identification with our fellow human beings is what gives empathy its value. But this is never easy to expect universally, let alone institute or institutionalize on a grand scale. It is an awareness that needs to be fostered, the seeds of which begin in early childhood, facilitated by a healthy, emotional holding environment grounded in secure attachments to parents, caregivers, and family members or their surrogates. Through personal experiences of being recognized, validated, shown care and psychological warmth, as well as feeling loved and understood, empathy for others develops as self-realization of the good and the need to embrace it, as does our emotional intelligence in socialization practices. Feeling felt, seeing the pain in others' eyes, and recognizing the experience of the other as a reciprocal self-relation to one's own interior helps to open up an ethical stance we are obliged to extend to the other as a fellow *Thou*, or more appropriately, *You*—a recognition of personhood. This is a form of ethical self-consciousness as felt compassion that not all people are psychologically capable of harboring or showing based on their own personal plight or tragedies, family upbringing, cultural displacement or disenfranchisement, developmental traumas, and so forth. But this does not mean that empathy cannot be awakened or taught. If global societies were to promote empathy as an educational imperative and intrinsic valued commodity as an end in itself, institutionalized within a given community or culture—as well as promoting the value of fostering loving emotional attachments to others, which begins in the home—the world would be a better place. But when the psyche and society are traumatized, this inevitably trickles down into the very ontological fibers of familial and communal life, where attachment patterns are compromised, and the next generation inherits the collective suffering of the one before it.

TRANSGENERATIONAL TRANSMISSION OF TRAUMA

Every persecuted clan, minority, subjugated group of peoples, and those affected by terror, trauma, and diaspora will suffer not only in the generations to come, but negatively condition the cultural unconscious complexes of the collective. The Jews, First Nations native Americans, as well as Sikhs, Shia Muslims, and Uighurs are only a few examples in recent times. When civil disorder, war, and systemic trauma compound matters, such as in the recent migration and refugee crisis that displaced more than five million Syrians, existential agony, shared misery, and mental illness are inevitable. Trauma fractures personality and society, where dissociation of the psyche, schizoid phenomena, and soul destruction efface the ability to properly function and lead a normal life. That, in turn, affects the ability to care for and nurture the young, trust people, develop sympathy and emotional connection to others, and feel safe. When body integrity and physical space are violated, so is the psyche. Others become threatening objects to fear and be wary of. As a result, interpersonal cognitive styles and forms of relationships are altered forever. Phobic, avoidant, and fundamentally paranoiac relations toward life are not uncommon occurrences. The impact on children maims the next generation, which, in turn, grows up with psychic scars and emotional deficits that are passed on to their children and their future children because basic psychological capacities for intimacy and attachment are compromised in successive generations of parents.

We know from a vast body of research across the social and behavioral sciences that the psychological and cultural effects of trauma become transgenerationally transmitted through child-rearing and socialization practices. Traumatized individuals within a community of suffering do not relate to their children in normative fashions relatively free of conflict like non-traumatized people do. This, in turn, affects attachment patterns in the mother-child dyad, neurological arousal levels, cognitive processing, affect regulation, and the ability to meet basic psychological requirements during infancy.[19] This always impacts on the family unit in the most rudimentary of conditions: parents and their offspring are doomed to be psychically haunted in their own ways, which will be culturally transmitted through subsequent families in future generations by virtue of the fact that such collective trauma is emotionally dominant within the family milieu and society at large. This is inescapable in the most resilient of people: when its aftereffects (*Nachträglichkeit* or *après-coup*) are relived, reconstructed, or memorialized, it leaves an affective aftermath that disfigures the socio-symbolic order.

The trauma of history and its devastating impact on the psyche dismembers the capacity for healthy relationships and the ability to properly trust, love, be perceptually and affectively attuned to the needs of others, and show emotional intimacy, including acceptance, warmth, validation, understanding, and recognition of the unique subjectivity of the other. Trauma and attachment pathology lead to ongoing generations of unhappiness, dysfunction, mental disorders, and perpetual discontent in culture. This is why the world will always have psychopaths.

Jung suggests that neurosis is the failed attempt to heal a universal split in the collective psyche. Here he may be said to mirror the concerns that preoccupy critical theorists.

> We always find in the patient a conflict which at a certain point is connected with the great problems of society . . . [T]he apparently individual conflict of the patient is revealed as a universal conflict of his

---

19. See Mills (2005b) for a review.

environment and epoch. Neurosis is thus nothing less than an individual attempt, however unsuccessful, to solve a universal problem.[20]

Jung attributes this collective neurotic manifestation to the "shadow-side of the psyche" that has attained the character of "*autonomous complexes*" in their own right on a mass scale.[21] Here it is easy to appreciate where Jung is coming from. When social reality is burdened with pathos, it leads to a sick soul. Neurosis is an attempt to repair social pathology through compromise formation.

During the same year, in *On the Psychology of the Unconscious*, Jung also wrote that: "Neurosis is intimately bound up with the problem of our time and really represents an unsuccessful attempt on the part of the individual to solve the general problem in his own person."[22] This seems to suggest that by curing the individual, one cures society.[23] Individuals who are less encumbered by unconscious conflicts are more likely to influence societies to be less split or conflicted given that healthy people make societies healthier. If neurosis is a failed attempt to remedy social problems, then psychological symptoms are the manifestation of social malaise. But this does not mean that individual healing will cure a sick society.

Self-correction or restoration cannot be simultaneously superimposed onto the greater multitudes as an isomorphic correlate that transmogrifies material society in its concrete structures and communal reality. At most, we can say that if neurosis is indeed an unsuccessful attempt to unconsciously resolve a collective problem, social amelioration may only be achieved through collective actions. Self-healing cannot be generalized to the collective unless the collective takes measures to generalize to the healing of individuals. Individual cure may have very little to do with healing on a grand scale, especially when social collectives are bombarded by enormous disparities and individual sorrow or emotional

---

20. Jung (1917b), *CW*, 7 § 438, p. 265.
21. Jung (1917b), *CW*, 7 § 438, p. 266.
22. Jung (1917a), *CW*, 7 § 18, p. 20.
23. Giovanni Colacicchi (2018), personal communication.

pain within the collective. Here social dysrecognition only perpetuates collective anguish.

As we witness the spread of more and more inequalities in the world, disproportional gaps in income, class discrepancies, and uneven opportunities for education, employment, and access to health care, we may anticipate how this felt injustice ferments and leads to social ruptures on a collective scale. Jung further reminds us of how affective intensities based on unconscious identification with injustice can archetypally seize a society clamoring for revolution or radical reform:

> Social, political, and religious conditions affect the collective unconscious in the sense that all those factors which are suppressed by the prevailing views or attitudes in the life of a society gradually accumulate in the collective unconscious and activate its contents. Certain individuals gifted with particularly strong intuition then become aware of the changes going on in it and translate these changes into communicable ideas. The new ideas spread rapidly because parallel changes have been taking place in the unconscious of other people. There is a general readiness to accept the new ideas, although on the other hand they often meet with violent resistance . . . If the translation of the unconscious into a communicable language proves successful, it has a redeeming effect. The driving forces locked up in the unconscious are canalized into consciousness and form a new source of power, which may, however, unleash a dangerous enthusiasm.[24]

This perspicacious observation could equally apply to the rise of Nazi Germany, contemporary white supremacists such as the Proud Boys, as well as current nationalist populism, as it does to the green movement, climate change activism, egalitarian socialist politics, Black Lives Matter, and more broadly, Critical Social Justice ideology. The danger lies in the ambiguity driving their force and outcome. Regardless of particular events, they may have a traumatizing *or* cleansing effect on the collective social psyche.

---

24. Jung (1919/1948), *CW*, 8, pp. 314–315.

When transgenerational forces of trauma are imposed on the incipient mind, agency is eclipsed by transitory misidentifications in fantasy and reality, leaving a wake of psychic debris that structurally disfigures the self. When one is treated like a thing and not recognized as a proper human being, the subject begins to relate to others as things in a sea of objects where the kernel of the value of reciprocal recognition devolves into intransigent antagonism, strife, fear of alterity, paranoia, sustained aggressivity, and repetition compulsion. When cultural trauma saturates attachment and socialization patterns, we can assuredly predict a future full of human suffering, where psychic and sociological impairment leaves many existential stains. Here we must recognize that the many faces of pathology transfigure our internal natures and scar the social landscape, even when a given individual or society recognizes the collective good in recognizing others.

8

Living in the End Times

AND THEN SOMETHING HAPPENED. ONCE THE FOUR HORSEMEN OF THE apocalypse—flood, famine, fire, and death—have been replaced by The Event that changed the world. The invisible foe came without warning, striking like a viper. It consumed people by hordes, stacked in body bags in morgues. Thousands died in a matter of days. The whole country of China was soon under quarantine. Iran, South Korea, Italy, then all of Europe; the Middle East, India, and North America soon followed. It sprawled throughout every inhabitable continent and infiltrated the planet like a tuber. Within one week it enveloped the entire globe.

We have witnessed the largest catastrophe in recent human history—our lifetime, a metaphysical thinning of the herd. We don't know what the future will bring. When the dust settles, the death toll will be in the millions, with new mutations of pathogens released into the atmosphere as we breathe in this very moment.

The pandemic has transformed our world in every conceivable way, from restrictions in social, workforce, and economic infrastructures crippling our contemporary societies to health-care, political, and governance failure and institutional, child-care, and educational shutdowns. The result was an increase in global poverty, homelessness, food insecurity, social unrest, diasporas, asylum seekers, mental health crises, domestic violence, addictions, and premature death due to COVID-19. From the familiar to the foreign, disruption of everyday routine; familial and cultural displacement of social gatherings, custom, and ritual; widening disparities and forced adjustment to lockdowns, quarantines, isolation, despair, and uncertainty have become the norm. And we are just beginning to see the fallout.

Dominating our existence, the pandemic has remade the world: we have gone remote. How will this change our thinking, attitudes, and action toward the future? Living in a virtual world reminds us of the urgent need to stop abusing the planet and subvert our looming climate disaster by resisting the need to return to business as usual through retrenchment or by restoring the status quo. Living in helplessness and vulnerability drives home the ethic for rethinking the world and society—our security and future safety—in our deteriorating times. And with the suspension of transnational travel, will this be the beginning of the end for carbon?

The plague is like the unconscious: it announces its presence and autonomy without notice, whether we like it or not, like dispatches—notes from the uncanny.

> With spotted hands and iodine tongue,
> Death lifts its ominous black robe and reaps another soul,
> pointing toward a long winding shore,
> the gateway to our dying pain.

FROM THE PLAGUE TO A PLASTIC ISLAND

We also bear the plague of pollution. There is a plastic island so large that it is twice the size of Texas and three times the size of France. It is appropriately called the Great Pacific Garbage Patch and is located in the middle of the Pacific Ocean somewhere between Hawaii and California, the largest of five plastic accumulation heaps that exist in the world's oceans. Rather than a floating landfill, it is more like a swirling typhoon of microplastics submersed in the sea yet too light to sink, whirling around like an enormous slushy within the top few meters of the ocean surface, which is densely dispersed throughout gyres or large systems of circulating ocean currents spurred by wind movements. In this gigantic cloudy bowl of soup and underwater graveyard are estimated to be up to 3.6 trillion pieces of plastic drifting in the patch, and weighing about 100,000 tons of the estimated 1.2 to 2.4 million metric tons entering the oceans each year from river runoff.[1] Because the microscopic debris is not biodegradable, it floats, hence is trapped in a vortex; yet it moves over a highway, converging on other garbage mounds throughout ocean waterways as pieces break up and scatter. This invades ecosystems, destroys habitats, and poisons marine life due to the cumulative effects of mass pollution. Many scientists concur: more plastic objects than fish are in the seas.

These widely distributed concentrations of tiny plastics, trash, and marine debris are said to cover 1.6 million square kilometers of ocean surface. As objects degrade by the sun, rotating currents, and abrasion, they break down into minute pieces, thereby releasing toxic chemicals, and accumulate in seaweed, plankton, and other marine life, which eventually enter the food chain. If not entangled or suffocated upon entering the whirlpool, marine animals such as fish, birds, seals, and turtles ingest the microplastics, which can poison organisms or end up on the dinner table. Moreover, sea life transports nonnative species from one place to another via algae, barnacles, or crabs, for instance, which are peppered throughout the world's oceans. Although marine science organizations such as The Ocean Cleanup continue to refine their cleanup systems, until the human planet curbs its single-use plastics and prevents mass-scale pollution, the world's ocean garbage patches will remain noxious imprints from the Anthropocene.

THE DOOMSDAY VAULT

The Svalbard Global Seed Vault, located on the Norwegian arctic island of Spitsbergen, is the largest seed gene bank in the world. It has the capacity to store nearly 4.5 million frozen agricultural, food crop seed samples and plant germplasm. It was originally located in an abandoned coal mine before tunneling deep inside the arctic mountainside through virgin permafrost to create the optimal environment for the vault. Many international organizations and countries gift seed samples every year, representing nearly 13,000 years of agricultural history. Currently, more than one million samples are in the vault.

------

1. See Lebreton, Slat, Ferrari, et al. (2018), Lebreton, van der Zwet, Damsteeg, et al. (2017), and scientists of The Ocean Cleanup initiative, https://theoceancleanup.com/great-pacific-garbage-patch/

The seed bank is 120 meters inside a sandstone fortress where seeds are carefully preserved from moisture. The island site has ideal conditions for preservation and security because it lacks tectonic activity and has permafrost, is refrigerated by local coal production that maintains optimal cooling and bedrock temperature, and at 130 meters above sea level, it will remain dry even if arctic ice sheets melt. The vault can preserve most major food crop seeds for hundreds, if not thousands, of years.

The vault's mission is to safeguard against loss of agricultural diversity in traditional gene banks and preserve our global food supply.[2] As a "fail-safe" protection against loss of one of our most important natural resources, the vault may be accessed when other world gene banks lose samples due to a variety of reasons including accidents, equipment failures, mismanagement, funding cuts, and natural disasters, such as flooding and fires, that occur with increased frequency. This may be exacerbated by countries besieged by war and civil strife, such as in the Middle East, where some seed banks have perished entirely; and it serves as backup storehouses for the nearly 2,000 seed banks worldwide, ensuring continued agricultural biodiversity. Although the popular press has dubbed Svalbard the "Doomsday Vault" in the event of major regional wars or global catastrophe, the name is not unfitting given our planetary precariousness due to inexorable climate change, global warming, forecasts of nuclear war or human error, and food insecurity that has pervaded the planet, which has intensified since the global pandemic. As a harbinger that symbolizes the end of world hunger, it also symbolizes the need for a watershed sentinel to defend against The End. After a recent flooding of the tunnel leading to the vault due to permafrost melt followed by a $20 million upgrade, will it be able to weather the heat from our warming world when those arctic glaciers continue to melt? This is particularly worrisome given that for the first time since records began, the Laptev Sea has not frozen when expected, signaling how climate change has transformed the Arctic.

---

2. For details, see https://www.seedvault.no/ about the Svalbard Global Seed Vault and the Ministry of Agriculture and Food, Norwegian Government, https://www.regjeringen.no/en/topics/food -fisheries-and-agriculture/svalbard-global-seed-vault/id462220/

IT TOOK A CHILD

Swedish environmental activist Greta Thunberg forced the world to pay attention to our ecological emergency after she initiated an international youth movement protesting the escalating effects of climate change. Being the youngest Person of the Year emblazoned on the cover of *Time* magazine, she has become an icon for radical reform in environmental policy and climate action. After Thunberg initially sat on the steps of the Swedish parliament holding a sign reading *Skolstrejk för klimatet* (school strike for climate), her action sparked other students to engage in similar protests in their own communities. Eventually it led to an organized, international school climate strike movement under the name "Fridays for Future." By 2019, student strikes took place every week throughout the globe involving coordinated multicity protests that attracted more than a million students.

To avoid flying, Thunberg sailed to North America, becoming an idol for shaming United Nation's world leaders due to their inertia surrounding the climate crisis. Thunberg's 2019 illustrious speech given at the UN's Climate Action Summit in New York City is worth quoting in full:

> My message is that we'll be watching you. This is all wrong. I shouldn't be up here. I should be back in school on the other side of the ocean. Yet you all come to us young people for hope. How dare you!
>
> You have stolen my dreams and my childhood with your empty words. And yet I'm one of the lucky ones. People are suffering. People are dying. Entire ecosystems are collapsing. We are in the beginning of a mass extinction, and all you can talk about is money and fairy tales of eternal economic growth. How dare you!
>
> For more than 30 years, the science has been crystal clear. How dare you continue to look away and come here saying that you're doing enough, when the politics and solutions needed are still nowhere in sight.
>
> You say you hear us and that you understand the urgency. But no matter how sad and angry I am, I do not want to believe that. Because if you really understood the situation and still kept on failing to act, then you would be evil. And that I refuse to believe.

The popular idea of cutting our emissions in half in 10 years only gives us a 50% chance of staying below 1.5 degrees [Celsius], and the risk of setting off irreversible chain reactions beyond human control. Fifty percent may be acceptable to you. But those numbers do not include tipping points, most feedback loops, additional warming hidden by toxic air pollution or the aspects of equity and climate justice. They also rely on my generation sucking hundreds of billions of tons of your CO_2 out of the air with technologies that barely exist. So a 50% risk is simply not acceptable to us—we who have to live with the consequences.

To have a 67% chance of staying below a 1.5 degrees global temperature rise—the best odds given [by the Intergovernmental Panel on Climate Change]—the world had 420 gigatons of CO_2 left to emit back on Jan. 1st, 2018. Today that figure is already down to less than 350 gigatons.

How dare you pretend that this can be solved with just "business as usual" and some technical solutions? With today's emissions levels, that remaining CO_2 budget will be entirely gone within less than 8 1/2 years. There will not be any solutions or plans presented in line with these figures here today, because these numbers are too uncomfortable. And you are still not mature enough to tell it like it is.

You are failing us. But the young people are starting to understand your betrayal. The eyes of all future generations are upon you. And if you choose to fail us, I say: We will never forgive you.

We will not let you get away with this. Right here, right now is where we draw the line. The world is waking up. And change is coming, whether you like it or not.[3]

Having participated in global climate strikes in North America and Europe, now a famous public figure, Thunberg has generated a social media frenzy and inspires many environmental activist groups throughout the world with her protest speeches and call to arms against governmental climate inaction. Recipient of numerous honors and awards including an honorary doctorate at the age of 16 and four Nobel Peace

---

3. Transcript: Greta Thunberg's Speech at the UN Climate Action Summit. *National Public Radio*, September 23, 2019.

Prize nominations, she has been received by world leaders and noted figures such as Pope Francis and the naturalist Sir David Attenborough.

Because planetary change is an enormous undertaking, involving communicative discourse in all spheres of globalized societies—from the personal, collective, systemic, geopolitical, and wholescale foundations that undergird our being in the world—mapping out all the inter-systemic issues at play, let alone their solutions, is beyond the scope of this immediate project, for I am unable to resolve it. But many global ecology organizations and green movements are working together, in a concentrated and concerted effort, in this direction. Regarding systemic structural components that ontologically inform our environmental crisis, we must confront the reality of the Anthropocene that we as humanity have caused. Of the other inter-systemic processes and interaction effects at work in creating our ecological emergency are the social environs and human dynamics that are broadly operative in world collectives including the economy, geopolitics, globalization, and technology that drive everything from the stock exchange and business industry to international peace relations and global security, even to our concrete daily existence. As we have already intimated, risk factors that constantly need monitoring and analysis have to do with the systemic operations and degree of autonomy we grant to corporatization, free industry and regulated trade; governmental vision, infrastructure, and action; the role of cultural values, such as democracy, freedom, ethics, aesthetics, and spirituality; the role of capital, wealth, and money exchange; geopolitical advocacy, policy decisions, and diplomacy; access to education, training, and information exchange; and technological risks to artificial intelligence, biosecurity, molecular nanotechnology, and regulation of industry standards surrounding research, design, manufacturing, and distribution of goods, products, and services.

From the standpoint of our overall worldviews, our immediate social consciousness is not up to par. We live in an altitude of immediate gratification and absorption in our own personal and social lives that revolve around utility, production, profit, economic gain, self-interest (individualistic, familial, communal, national), intellectual property, abnegation of responsibility for greater matters outside of our control, and psychological desires and defenses such as hedonism and denialism under the sway of the pleasure principle. Ecological consciousness is foreign territory despite international efforts to address the climate crisis and potential for nuclear Armageddon. The risks presented here are far reaching from our immediate generations to intergenerational successions to transgenerational impacts on humanity to come.

Visions of the future are fluid and pliant. We can never know what will happen or transpire in all potential worlds outside of reason, logic, and sensible predictive science. But empirical facts and abductive speculation point us toward many foresight narratives and portentous scenarios we can intercede. As we have asked before, are we living in the End Times? Will there be an eschatological apocalypse? Will there be a nuclear holocaust? Will new plagues ravage the world? Will there be future dystopias where the planet is a miserable place to live, or life merely becomes surviving perennial hardships? Or will we transform these doomsday scenarios through visionary praxis, prevention, invention, intervention, and determinate grit? Could the future be replete with flourishing ecologies (posthuman or otherwise), sustainment, universal equity initiatives, global justice, new world order Enlightenment paradigms, and global egalitarian values adopted by all?

Will we have mass ecological despoliation, decay, and biodiversity loss that wreaks havoc on our future environments? Will we have a lawless world governed by widespread injustice that has undergone nuclear war and terror, diasporas, and mass migrations, widening disparities that have led to global poverty, where the elite and wealthy run the world, or are governed by totalitarian dictators, despots, and autocrats who rule with iron tyrannical gloves? Or will there be ecological healing, sustainability, rectification of environmental hazards, where we live in a globalized ethical world that recognizes and treats all of humanity as equal citizens of the cosmos (cosmopolitans), where there is a distribution of wealth, goods, and services, equity, and a living wage for all, even a world central bank or postcapitalist system that makes all economies interrelated and ontically interconnected to every human being on the planet? Will our future leaders gravitate toward this cosmopolitan vision of cooperative global partnership, harmonization, and interdependent unity of social collectives under the humanistic rubric of agape?

What will the future of education, training, and information exchange in the advanced age of science and technology look like? Will it remain dominated by private for-profit industry, where there is pronounced inequality in opportunity, means, and funding, even occlusive or prohibitive of those who have no income; or will education and vocational training be state controlled at no cost where academics and instruction are an interdependent valued commodity to society? Will technology designs and securities evolve to regulate dual-use capabilities where ethical programming and nanomanufacturing of machines, AI devices, and superintelligences are safe and nonthreatening through post-technical revolutions; or will dual-use technics succumb to dysregulation, unmodulation, and unsafe production and distribution that could lead to a techno apocalypse?

Worldviews are just as polarized. Schopenhauerian pessimism rings its bell with widespread bystander apathy, nihilistic outlooks, belief in predetermined fate or fatalism, external locus of control, loss of freedom, and learned helplessness, which lead to social splitting, division, fracturing, decay, and anarchy. The more optimistic sectarian champions the vision of transglobal egalitarianism where there is a welcoming world hospitality view of valuing plurality and difference that advances individual agency, social liberty, and collective ethical and political activism oriented toward a more harmonized, just, and holistic republic. This is where the myth of Gaia emerges from the ashes of a suffocating sickness where overheating, deterioration, and ecocide are evaded for a foresight narrative of nurturance, health, and flourishment.

Bringing about desired futures requires shared aspirations, values, cooperation among social collectives, and good governance. It starts with preferred images of our future environments, ones that are possible to achieve through education, social self-consciousness, innovation, even revolution, where visions of reparation and wholeness guide political systems toward collective unity in transforming forethought into concrete tangible practice that enables humanity to approach global problems with greater ecological awareness, maturity, moral responsibility, and strategic efficacy.

For futurists, rather than view our current ecological crisis as used or disowned futures that have been written off as waste with the foregone conclusion of doom, we can change the landscape through ethical agency and action by propelling our being and moral duty to the world and future generations to come. We already see this happening in millennial and postmillennial culture embodied by the youth climate change protests, school strikes for climate, and the Extinction Rebellion (XR) movements and other groups that have transpired all over the world using nonviolent civil disobedience in an attempt to preempt mass extinction and minimize the risk of societal collapse.[4] Not only have these social consciousness movements inspired protest and narrative foresight change, but they spur concrete action directed toward governments failing to protect the citizenry from current and future environmental conditions that the youth do not want to inherit. These discourses and actions are progressive ameliorations of our global bystander syndrome that may affect a future sea change in international politics, public policy, Earth science research, and environmental protection.

PREDICTING THE FUTURE

Hegel traced the historical progression of civilization from our base dispositions to the triumph of World Spirit as the coming into being of ethical self-consciousness.[5] It is only by looking back historically

---

4. Recently, there has been criticism of some of these social justice climate movements, most notably Extinction Rebellion, based on the extremism of its leaders to the degree that it invites unethical actions of its supporters that undermine viable solutions for positive climate activism (Lights, 2023).
5. As Hegel completed the final installments of the *Phenomenology of Spirit*, Napoleon was outside the city walls of Jena ushering in a new age—history was being transformed once again by the revolutionary currents of the dialectic. The battle of Jena may be said to parallel the very negative character of the dialectic itself, as conflict and violence pave the path toward progression. The self-generative process of the dialectic may provide us with a logical model for addressing the problem of pathos; but unlike Einstein's bane of war, the dialectic may also be the boon for its solution, one that nevertheless retains its destructive features as it wages combat against itself. Both Hegel and Freud offer a view of the human condition that is characterized by destruction, negation, and conflict; yet it is paradoxical that such negativity also becomes an animating force behind the elevation of ethical self-consciousness. Like Spirit or Mind (*Geist*), which is the sublation (*Aufhebung*) of its previous historical moments, psychic maturation is the sublimation (*Sublimierung*) of primitive

at the dialectical unfolding of the human race that we can clearly see a discernible pattern of improvement in human relations and society as the sublation (*Aufhebung*) of reason, virtue, and social justice.[6] This processual-sustaining-transcending matrix of Mind (*Geist*) is the very foundation of Hegel's *Logic* as the teleological culmination of universal self-consciousness thinking about itself and its operations on a developmental trajectory toward achieving wholeness through pure reason actualizing its moral, aesthetic, and spiritual dimensions embodied in the plight of humanity.[7] In contemporary language, these are the ideal goals of society—to become a beacon of virtue that enhances the quality of life of every global citizen through the pursuit and actualization of what is good for all. But despite our sociological advancements, the "cunning of reason" cannot eradicate our destructive instinctual natures and affective prejudices inherent since primitive times.

---

mental processes. Although Hegel's language may seem odd to modern sensibility, he is really attempting to describe what psychoanalysis refers to as the individual and collective psyche. Hegel and Freud would likely concede that through reason lies the hope that communities and cultures torn apart by discordant value practices can be united through collective ethical commitments. If humanity is to vanquish the pathology of base desire for the optimistic voluntarism enlightened by reason, it becomes important to understand how reason itself is the knight of desire designed to transform our pathologies.

6. Through his *Logic*, Hegel may be instructive in examining the evolutionary development of history achieved through negation and conquest in which further predictive possibilities for the future of humanity may be inferred. Hegel's *Phenomenology* personifies the drama of world spirit (or what we may contemporarily refer to as humanity) as the coming to presence of pure self-consciousness through the process of self-estrangement, identification, and self-recognition through the mediation of the other. World hero eventually achieves Truth, satiates the lack, and arrives at full self-actualization only after traversing the arduous and protracted terrain of alienation through the vicissitudes of desire. Spirit—civilization—is, therefore, a constant activity, pure unrest. And the driving force behind world history, behind the very process of the dialectic, is death and destruction.

7. One of the more interesting aspects of Hegel's (1812) dialectic is the way in which a mediated dynamic form a new immediate. This process not only informs the basic structure of his *Logic*, which may further be attributed to the general principle of *Aufhebung*, but this process also provides the logical basis to account for the role of negativity within a progressive unitary drive. The process by which mediation collapses into a new immediate provides us with the logical model for the improvement of civilization. And it is precisely this logical model that provides the internal consistency to its specific application to the amelioration of pathology or social ills. As an architectonic process, spirit invigorates itself and breaths its own life as a self-determining generative activity that builds upon its successive shapes and layers that inform its appearances; therefore, collective mind constructs its own monolith. It is this internal consistency that provides us with a coherent account of the circular motion of the progressive drive toward higher manifestations of psychical, social, and cultural development.

Our faith in the transcending power of mind over the combative regimens of world discord is acceptable only to the extent to which we believe in a progressive trend toward increased solidarity through collective self-conscious moral rationality. This level of psychic development Hegel points toward is hardly achieved by enlightened individuals, let alone the masses, for reason is often eclipsed by the primal lure of desire, defense, and external conflict. If the facts of history and human nature do indeed lean toward a steady progressive self-conscious liberation of rational freedom, then to what degree is this the result of our aptitude to bridle and sublimate our primitive proclivities for the ideals of conscience and the rational demands of a civil society? The promise of increased unity in the face of disharmony augurs well for a collectively shared and constructive value system; however, the ostensive prevalence of global division and chaos saturated by human dissonance may leave us with a less optimistic interpretation of the fate of humanity. The problem of destructiveness becomes a central kink in our predicament; but if Hegel is correct, the positive significance of the negative becomes the stallion of unification as it gallops toward the horizon of reason. Yet if our aggressive trends continue to go unchecked, Freud's admonition of the possible extinction of the human race carries foreboding merit.

Hegel's *Logic* points the way toward an optimistic ending where reason mediates contradiction and opposition through a progressive unitive synthesis of competing conflicts culminating in higher ethical social arrangements. But Hegel, as well as psychoanalysis itself, points out our archaic past grounded in unconscious urge, compulsion, infantile rage, and barbarity. Following Hegel's logic of prediction, we would anticipate that humanity will only get more refined and ethical in its rational pursuit of more cooperative, harmonious social relations, but there will always be pathological forms of human activity based on opposition and difference.[8] The thought that we could ever stop thinking in terms of

---

8. Through the interaction of mediated immediacy, teleology becomes defined in each moment, with each immediacy being only a moment in the process of civilization. As spirit passes into new stages, it educates itself as it transforms itself, taking on new forms, expanding and incorporating larger aspects of its experience into its inner being. Preparing itself for its next confrontation, it guarantees there will always be a new stage. Because civilization is the self-sublation—what might not be inappropriately called sublimation—of its earlier primitive activity, the logic of the dialectic

difference such as ethnicity, religion, language, culture, class, or race is simply an illusion.

Human beings will always seek separate unique identities (whether as individuals or as groups) in opposition to others based on the values they choose to identify with and profess. This tendency further guarantees that nationalism, ethnic and religious identity, and populist/separatist/extremist movements energized by rigid group identifications will never perish, for identity is what keeps people together—the *religio* that binds; we may only hope that their pathological instantiations will abate and become marginalized to minor aberrations that fail to identify with greater collective global visions. But in all likelihood, we will only see unevenly distributed spheres in the amelioration of pathos determined by contingent world events.

If we may offer a prediction of the future of civilization based on Hegel's logical model, then perhaps we will see many infinite progresses of many infinite regresses; as civilization climbs up the rungs of the ladder, it will also experience slippage, regression, and withdrawal back to earlier manifestations of its being.[9] In this century, this explanation may be said to account, in part, for the Armenian "Great Crime," Hitler and the Holocaust, Stalin's gulags and reign of butchery, Pol Pot's

---

provides us with a prototype for understanding the underlying functions and power of the negative that propel civilization to overcome its increased oppositions, which it generates from within itself. Because civilization generates division and opposition within itself, each new mediated immediacy allows for contingencies and complexities to operate within existing dynamic occurrences. This is the freedom of the power of the negative, for it may seek to operate within a destructive and regressive fashion rather than align with the upward current of human growth, social consciousness, tolerance, acceptance, and ethical progress.

9. The process of civilization vacillates between dialectical moments of progress versus regress as the process itself secures and mobilizes an infinite progression with infinite points of regression. Following the logical coherency of the upward ascendance of the dialectic, we may further estimate that progress will surpass the regressive and destructive forces that tyrannize world accord. What is truly infinite about the evolution of humanity is the process itself. What we see is an infinite (universal) pattern, each side being contrary moments as each merges with the other. This pattern is genuinely infinite for it is a self-maintaining process; each alteration collapses into a new moment, which is its being-for-self in its mediacy. By standing back and seeing the recurrent pattern within a new context, world spirit is enabled to affect the transition to a new immediacy that is truly sublated. Civilization, like Spirit, is always faced with the relative novelty of each new shape. Yet it approaches each new opposition not as a static antinomy doomed to stalemate, but rather as a self-contained pattern; the infinite generates new finites as a fundamental repetition of itself—a self-maintaining process that generates its own process as a dynamically self-articulated complex holism.

killing fields, Saddam Hussein's gassing of his people, the exterminations in Bosnia, Milosevic's relentless crusade of ethnic cleansing, the grisly "choppings" in Sierra Leone, and more recently, the Rwanda and Myanmar genocides and the Chinese persecution of Uighurs. We could go on and on. But as evinced by Hegel's logic, as well as our empirical social advancements, given the synthetic and upwardly mobile acclivity of the dialectic, as a rule, increased ascendance and social unification overreach the regressive instantiation of annihilating forces. History bears this out.

Yet with each destruction comes a new construction of mediated immediacies that give rise to new values and social ideals. Freud's contribution is invaluable to Hegel's position because, as they both maintain, negativity is the core constituent of life: death and destruction will not only be a universality in all possible future worlds but a *necessary* ontological dynamic that assures the upward progression of change, prosperity, and maturation—the very essence of the striving for our ideal possibility-for-Being.

With most of the world's continents engaged in some form of military conflict, it may be argued (at least theoretically) that the United Nations becomes an ethical paragon for global peace and unity; and with the fight for freedom, democracy, and human rights, social consciousness has made an advance forward. But it has done so at the cost of condemning and displacing other countries and cultural valuation practices that imperil international security, where *might* becomes the *right* of a community in the service of the collective whole. Yet collective identification has its limits even among nations with focused mutual goals, which further leads to resistance and stifling efforts at negotiation and diplomacy. Because each nation has loyalty to its own self-interests, an ethical diaspora is inevitable: cultural narcissism is highly recalcitrant to outside interference pressuring political reform. This may be historically observed by the fact that despite indubitable knowledge of the slaughter and concentration camps in Bosnia, former president George Bush Sr. and his administration were not about to send U.S. troops to intercede, fearing the ghost of Vietnam, a repetition the Clinton administration faced dogged by a country absorbed by its own concerns. It may be further said that the international community's failure to appropriately intervene in the Rwanda massacre, as well as the question of ground troops surrounding the crisis in the former Yugoslavia, reflects a collective preoccupation not to jeopardize the lives of its own citizens uncritically.

In these situations, collective identifications that sustain national identities ultimately serve self-preservative functions, for we are bound to identify more with our own kind than a stranger in a foreign land. The brute fact is that we value our own over others: the general principle of human life becomes an abstraction when compared to the concrete social realities each country faces. This is particularly relevant when internal division and upheaval fracture the cohesion of a country's infrastructures and ethical backbone wanting change, such as the separatism movement in French Quebec, Canada, and the omnipresence of institutional discrimination and racism that torment the United States. When industrialized countries, such as the ones in North America, are unable to shelter and provide food and clothing for their own homeless populations who die every night on the streets, they find themselves in the conundrum of determining the most optimal means of disseminating their social resources. Value is ultimately prioritized under the rubric of a particular society's self-concerns, but this often encompasses wasteful concessions to popular prejudice. It is truly sad when the American public is more concerned about where the president's penis has been than helping the needy through humanitarian aid.[10] This is a fine example of Heidegger's *das Man*, where the herd is lost in the corrupt fallenness of idle talk, gossip, and curiosity of the *They*. Now in our era of post-truth and post-Trump, America has simply devolved into world embarrassment.

Hegel's odyssey of humanity may be applicable to our understanding of the trek of culture and its march over the ever-increasing proliferation of human aggression. As our world confederations gain greater amity, consensus, and cohesion, the international negotiation of valuation gives rise to new novelties, complexities, and increased unity forever raveling at the seams. But the more convoluted social realities become, destructive forces continue to grow in abundance. We may surmise that the insidiousness of human pathology will recede in certain pockets of communal

---

10. Here I am referring to the Clinton-Lewinsky affair, but it may equally apply to Trump's hush money to cover up his multiple affairs and love of prostitutes.

affiliation but flow in others as the valences of power, prejudice, and spite undergo the vicissitudes of transformation. No longer is the standard of culture measured by whether one uses a bar of soap but, rather, by the values we espouse in relation to others, especially the promise to keep our aggressions in check. Now our degree of civility is to be equated by the mutual agreement not to point our missiles at one another—quite an accomplishment for decades of fear and cold war, yet ones unraveling at the edges as we watch so much warfare kill innocent civilian lives through calculated genocide. This existential reality underscores the fact that aggression will always play a part in our value practices and the ontological relations that comprise worldhood.

When social and psychic conflict remain irresolute, the human species has the compulsion to repeat its traumas to resolve them. Not unlike Nietzsche's eternal recurrence, the compulsion toward control and mastery may be generally attributed to the *Aufhebung* of cultures as civilization becomes more integrative, refined, and balanced. But as Freud points out, the repetition of destruction is a retrograde character of our species that must be harnessed and channeled into appropriate directions if we are to survive as a human race. It is in the austere face of violence and havoc that continue to pollute our globe where we may observe the pessimistic resonance of Freud's dismal conclusion that offers us "no consolation."

As long as people are deprived of the most basic human needs, there will always be atypical suffering, seething envy, hate, and murder. And along with the dictators, corrupt capitalist elites, and the uncultivated masses that bleed world tranquility, destruction and violence will be the primary instruments of human deed with each act of aggression begetting new aggression to combat it. With the perseverance of peace, perhaps this cycle will culminate in a more docile set of human relations. Through mutual dialogue and the open exchange of value preferences, new identifications, emotional connections, ideals, conventions, and policies will emerge, even though this may likely require an aggressive encroachment on societies and cultures that fail to develop shared global identifications.

In the end, the logic of prediction—namely, what is likely to happen in the future—is a speculative crapshoot. At most we can rely on abductive conjecture based on past empirical events deemed likely to repeat themselves and/or generate new sets of circumstances that inductively follow from history, current embroiling conditions, and foresight measures that anticipate probable outcomes—but with the stipulation that there is no degree of certainty. What we do know is that civilization was forged in violence *and* cooperation, avarice *and* sociality, fear *and* the cultivation of safety, unpredictability *and* security, division *and* belongingness, identity *and* difference. The dialectic is always at play: opposition and contradistinction are mutually implicative in all human relations, even in unity or under the guise of freedom.

DEMOCRACY INCORPORATED

Most of the world population does not live in free democratic societies, even if a veil of freedom is brandished. And even in democratic free states, we are confined by our actual conditions. Freedom has a price and a cost, what we might call Democracy Inc.[11]—the capital control over the mind of world collectives sustained by inegalitarian ideology—economic, political, cultural, religious, class structure, race, or otherwise. Democratic myths of egalitarianism are, in fact, estranged from actual democratic practices that exploit the function of inequality by advancing certain forms of power—how to gain, manage, and increase it—while subduing rival others through systemic corruption inflicted on a complicit citizenry. Sheldon Wolin argues that democracy is "managed" through a certain form of inverted totalitarianism: large corporations and capitalist kingpins acting in tandem with political suprastructures manipulate society via managerial prowess using business models of control. The institutionalized way certain ideas, values, and agendas are circulated over others according to commercial, conglomerate, enterprising, and political self-interest infect the way we think and behave based on unconsciously entrenched propaganda underlying the mythology of

---

11. This term was coined by Sheldon Wolin (2008).

equality that disclaims its real identity as managed democracy controlling social collectives.

People truly don't view others as equal, as if there is no difference between people, and that they are virtually the same in every respect. This is not the case due to the existential fact that people do not have the same values, wants, and needs. Further, people are judged in terms of their difference, including their beliefs, principles, and ideas, which ontologically pits one against others based on harboring dissimilar standards, values, and prejudices. Although this inegalitarianism may be said to be largely inconspicuous in democratic countries, it nevertheless structures society in all its facets—from the economy to class struggles and social justice. But it is only on the principle, based in social conditioning, that one could *potentially* be equal that such inegalitarianism operates: some are more equal and some less. Those who have less money, less social privilege, less education and tangible opportunities feel the pinch. But why would we assume that everyone is equal to begin with, when this is patently false? Because the doctrine of democracy dangles the dream of freedom and fairness for all. But we may ask, who is truly free, and who says life is fair? Disparity is the norm in all cultures, even in free states. There is no free lunch and no free ride. No one gets to suck off the teat: not even a baby is afforded such luxury, for someone else must pay. Everything must be earned, unless you are wealthy, fortunate, or simply lucky. In today's cultural wars, we pillory "whitey" for being privileged even though white working-class poor outnumber other minority classes in America.

Freedom and capitalism go hand in hand, but paradoxically both are costly. Without capital and (self) interest, you have nothing. Corporate sponsorship and hegemony constitute a system of power that suffuses all democracy based on economic inegalitarianism, for freedom is purchased based on exchange or bargain, as the world needs ditchdiggers, too. In other words, we are not equal in the practical spheres of life due to vast dissimilarities: here the value of "equality" is merely a vacuous abstraction. Despite the capitalist democratic mantra, all genuine difference is never eliminated, as capitalism itself is corporatized through enforced social and economic inequality. There are no one-dimensional equals, just as there are no one-dimensional societies. Corporate capitalism is never a system where benefits are distributed evenly, for it causes and institutionally reinforces striking inequalities.

Capitalism further ensures that we can never be satisfied or escape dissatisfaction through the accumulation of capital or by acquiring a commodity. As Todd McGowan aptly puts it:

> The fundamental gesture of capitalism is the promise, and the promise functions as the basis for capitalist ideology. One invests money with the promise of future returns; one starts a job with the promise of a higher salary; one takes a cruise with the promise of untold pleasure in the tropics; one buys the newest piece of electronics with the promise of easier access to what one wants. In every case the future embodies a type of satisfaction foreclosed to the present and dependent on one's investment in the capitalist system. The promise ensures a sense of dissatisfaction with the present in relation to the future.[12]

This may all be well said and done; yet satisfied or not, we cannot live without money. Whether we like it or not, this is the only game in town.

If the promise of a better future structuralizes and is the foundation of capitalist ideology, then all systems of commodification, production, distribution, and consumption are just as gullible, as we all live in relation to *lack*: that is why we desire in the first place. The future becomes a placeholder and unconscious promise to fill the lack. But it will never come to pass. The future of satisfaction is a transcendental illusion but a necessary one that drives all forms of production. But this emancipatory promise also sustains—if not guarantees—dissatisfaction, for we can never get there: each object of satisfaction diminishes just as desire desires a new object—what the future holds.

The problem with globalization, the climate crisis, with geopolitical antagonism, with dispute over who is entitled to accumulate capital, is that we are not living for the future, only the moment, as the foreseeable future is already sullied with dissatisfaction—ecocide, overpopulation, disparities, crime, war, societal collapse, lack of paradise, and so forth. Like politicians who promise a better future for the populace, we all

---

12. See McGowan (2016), p. 11.

know they are platitudes designed to placate the lustful masses and promote the illusion of progress and betterment, for the only thing that really matters to most people is the *now*. Collective myopic consciousness sees no investment in the future, for deep down people really don't want to have to change—they love their *jouissance* too much. They desire not to know anything that would challenge or disrupt their little worlds and simply want to keep the existing state of affairs while not having their taxes increased.

Disavowing and postponing the future is essential to the defensive motives governing mass psychology, for even if we are to accept the social reality that our future is precarious, we would still entertain fantasies that "it won't be that bad" or our world leaders "won't let that happen." But they are letting that happen, and we are living in times that foreshadow a possible ending if change is not ushered in on a global scale. Here fantasies of possible futures are apocalyptic, dystopic, or cast into the void. But it is only on the condition that we analyze and critique the present that we tacitly buy into the premise of at least a possible better future, or we would merely accept the present and feel no need to critique it or envision a favorable alternative. And it certainly will take vision, production, and capital to bring that about, even if it turns out to be dissatisfying or merely a fleeting or false gratification; for no matter what, no socioeconomic system will ever fully satisfy.

Even if we identify a preemptive future and work toward mitigation, amelioration, and rehabilitation, we are likely to encounter realized unintended consequences of our collective actions where corporations, private industries, and governments set into motion certain events that push the limits of legality, ethical norms, and humanitarian duty. When managed democracy acts to abolish public policy, deregulate corporate affairs and praxis, expand privatization, and invert power through coercive self-serving practices fueled by hierarchies of control, we have no sense of stability or equity through impartial checks and balances of influence, authority, and rule, hence rendering visions of the future oppressive and feckless. If human desire is based on absence or lack, then the need to fill the lack requires a contingent belief in the social reality of an absent future, one that needs to be remediated if we are to ensure a future at all.

The critic will likely say that I am being too hysterical and that we can pursue many viable avenues to ecological preservation and rehabilitation that counteract my worry about doom and gloom. Given that psychoanalysis is particularly adept at pointing out the many psychological reasons why we as human beings like to avoid our most painful emotions, may we speculate that such Pollyannaish optimism is an attempt to gloss over a paralyzing anxiety that unconsciously fuels deep feelings of ambivalence, melancholia, and grief over what we have already lost as well as the unknown (yet looming) loss that in all probability will come due to global lassitude, a primordial anxiety that menaces us with an ominous depression. But what if a perverse enjoyment pervades this unconscious constellation of impending loss, an excess of *jouissance*, an excitement over our approaching death, one that makes us feel more alive? Could this be an unconscious motive for why we appear indifferent, live in denial, disavowal, and dissociation, and manifest a collective stoically detached melancholic bystander effect?

In the Freudian and Lacanian traditions, self-destruction brings about a narcissistic enjoyment and perverse satisfaction in violating ethical law, here the politicized category of nature.[13] It's natural to violate our own nature, including that which sustains us, what Cindy Zeiher calls "our desire to control nature and defy mortal existence."[14] The willful negation of environmental ethics amounts to a form of grandiose infantile omnipotence where the desire to destroy the natural applies equally to our bodies and our planet. This is the destructive principle at work in unconsciously circuitous ways. But as we continue to destroy nature and ourselves, we sacrifice both under the illusion of invincibility—our disavowed extimacy to what we depend upon to survive.

FROM CATASTROPHE TO RENEWAL

In a 2020 special issue on the 50th anniversary of Earth Day, *National Geographic* issued "A Pessimist's Guide to Life on Earth in 2070," hence speculating on where we will be 50 years from now. Covering many topics that I have addressed in detail throughout this book, their outcome is

---

13. See Zeiher (2021) and McGowan (2021) for their extensive analyses.
14. Zeiher (2021), p. 32.

pretty grim. By then we will have lost the planet through climate change and environmental disaster where the case for catastrophe includes the familiar scenarios of increased wildfires, cyclones, flooding, drought, ecological devastation, mass extinction of species and habitats, and social unrest that forces millions from their homes, thus plummeting humanity into the dangerous territory of scrambling to continue its survival. Due to our reckless consumption and abuse of natural resources, the world will become a deadlier place to live for us all and the rest of life on earth. From setbacks in the prospects of nuclear power, such as the Chernobyl accident or meltdown of a reactor at Three Mile Island, to mass contamination from coal, the threat of plastic and chemical waste disposal polluting our oceans and waterways, runaway infernos that consume large regions of states and countries, the threat of mammal extinctions, increased meltwater lakes on the Greenland ice sheet, disappearing glaciers in Peru, and the rising Gulf of Mexico swallowing the Isle de Jean Charles in Louisiana are more than worrisome. And now we have glacier melt in Antarctica. The main message—we are in trouble.

Not only is food security a concern, but the world's favorite foods—from how they are grown to when we eat them—could be compromised or become too expensive to grow or afford. Warmer weather introduces plant diseases and fungi and may drive up the price of coffee and bananas, while some foods, such as avocados, can't grow in high heat, which will force growers to shift to milder environs and therefore increase the length of shipping distances. Ocean acidification affects the health of crustaceans and their taste, which may make shrimp, for example, less palatable, while extreme fluctuations in weather may limit many crop productions, such as olives. Allergic illnesses such as asthma and hay fever will increase with climate change, and light pollution, largely due to LEDs, will affect animal biology that depends on the night sky to regulate circadian rhythms, including us. From potash mines in Siberia used to fertilize world food production to the black dust moonscape from coal mines in Australia, silica mines that create glass for skyscrapers, and sandpits used to make concrete, we don't see where these natural resources come from, let alone how they sustain our existence and drive human affairs through acts of environmental destruction. We just take them for granted.

Clearly, if we don't rein in our carbon emissions by 2070, the climate will be oppressive at best. Prediction models estimate that Arizona will be like today's Pakistan with most days being over 95°F, Costa Rica will be like Brazil, France will be like Italy, and Tanzania will be like Thailand. We will have dangerous days for most parts of the year. We may even have to wear oxygen masks to go outside. Heat wave frequency and length of days will result in drastic measures to stay cool and will disrupt society on all levels of being and functioning. The human body is not evolutionarily equipped to handle such extreme temperatures, as it cannot regulate its internal temperatures naturally, so the planet will be forced to use air conditioners, fans, and dehumidifiers to cool off—if they can afford them. The rest will likely die. As climate change boosts demands for cooling, it creates a vicious cycle that requires more burning of fossil fuels, which simply accelerates global warming. Workforces will decline due to the overwhelming heat, and mortality rates from all causes will spike drastically. The wealthy have an advantage over the middle class and poor. The magnitude of social discontent will proliferate due to such disparities, and it will be fierce. Under such conditions, I would anticipate planned and sustained attacks on corporate and private affluence, including targeting and murdering the rich by assassination.

The Philippines will likely have a climate like India, and rising water anxieties will affect the dread of monsoons and drought alike. Demand for water will deplete freshwater systems and tax competition, increase conflict over supply chains, and lead to migration strategies that pit favored populations over others. Due to amplified precipitation in certain parts of the world, such as Asia and Africa, more flooding is to be expected, whereas other parts, such as the Mediterranean region, will suffer from aridity. Vietnam, Brazil, Egypt, and Qatar will have unprecedented climates nowhere on Earth today. Food shortages will be austere as aquifers are depleted to grow nutriment, while ecosystems will be endangered as water is diverted from their original source. As temperatures rise and rainfall intensifies, mosquito expanses will spread disease and dangerous heat stress will roast overpopulated cities. Infrastructures including housing, roads, and bridges will crumble faster, especially in developing countries where resources are scarce, costly, and susceptible to civic corruption, such as bribing an engineer or city inspector. The damage will be unequal, as the poor are more likely to suffer. Social conflict and violence are predictable in overcrowded regions, which will lead to increased crime and displacement, as millions more slide into poverty and are forced to migrate.

The Anthropocene makes us more anxious about our impending death, as it could be accelerated—from ivory smuggling in Africa that accounts for tens of thousands of elephants murdered for their tusks to lithium farms in Chile that extract groundwater for mining, hence drying out rivers, streams, and wetlands that disrupt vulnerable wildlife due to increased desertification, while dumping toxic waste into waterways that contaminate the available drinking water that is left. From floating in a lithium bath to coral bleaching, anthroturbation, open pit mines, underworld potash abysses, phosphate mining, pollution mills, technofossil beeches, and clear-cutting of old growth forest that can no longer absorb the Earth's carbon, we have drastically marred the globe's landscapes beyond recognition. As plastic waste mountains, lethal dumps, and the world's largest landfills outside polluted cities continuing to proliferate, hence poisoning the air and nearby water sources due to stench and run-off and releasing contaminated chemicals and gas due to organic waste, trash collectors forced to scavenge rubbish for a living can fall to their death or suffocate due to methane leaks or the collapse of a garbage heap.

"An Optimist's Guide to Life on Earth in 2070" depicts another potential scenario. It essentially asks: What will it take to save the world? Besides working in partnership to conserve the planet, its ecosystems, species, and wildlife, can we make a case for renewal? Visionary futurists believe we already have the technology to reverse climate change, feed a larger world population, provide energy for all, wean off fossil fuels, and prevent most extinctions. But given that biodiversity has deteriorated at a faster rate than any time in human history, nature needs us to act now. Through increased habitat loss and overexploitation, on land and sea, the biosphere could collapse. If biodiversity disappears, so will we. The solution: protect more lands and oceans and manage them for their conservation values. The reality: resistance, denial, and pushback prevent policy change, legislation reform, and political decision. Although many conservation groups and stakeholders are involved in campaigns for nature, nothing will likely change unless policy makers and government leaders take action to combat nation-centric and capitalist-corporate self-interest causing and sustaining biodiversity abuse and loss.

On the optimistic side of future studies, a promising exploration in new energy is being conducted by the ITER Organization, an intergovernmental organization comprised of 35 nations building a thermonuclear experimental reactor in southern France to harness nuclear fusion that promises potentially to be a limitless source of carbon-free energy. And in Italy, experiments in alternative aquaculture have created Nemo's Garden, an underwater farm where plants grow without pesticides or soil. And plastic waste cleanup initiatives, such as Project Butterfly in Kenya and Project STOP in Indonesia, fund cleanup and recycling activities through education, collaboration, and hands-on action in areas plagued by pollution and poverty. Here the case for renewal is being achieved.

Even though life will be warmer in the future, the question becomes: Will humanity find ways to limit carbon emissions, protect nature, and thrive? When like-minded stewards of the Earth start to challenge the reckless pursuit of corporate profits that fail to consider the well-being of the planet, which they consider to be a crime, companies and politicians alike will be increasingly pressured to assume greater responsibilities toward our world. As our biggest shared challenge is climate change, as individuals we cannot stop it. The popular and political will behind collective efforts needs to be targeted to adopt new green policies and laws that force societies to change, adapt, and use new technologies toward achieving practical and meaningful goals of landscape restoration and climate justice, mitigation, amelioration, and sustainment.

ENVIRONMENTAL CONFLICT AND PEACEBUILDING

A movement in environmental conflict and peacebuilding shines a ray of hope on humanity if political initiatives are realized.[15] Despite the fact that since ancient times we have had to compete for limited resources, naturally a source of conflict, civilization was also built on the ability to

---

15. See Swain and Öjendal (2018) for an overview.

form cooperation among peoples and societies over those same limited resources. The climate crisis guarantees an increased global conflict due to environmental impacts that severely affect social collectives on a mass scale who will suffer food, water, and housing insecurity, be subjected to violence and threat of death, and become collateral damage in times of civil unrest and war. Environmental stress adds to already compromised security concerns amplified by economic, political, and sociological factors that contribute to and fortify instability and conflict. In times of civil violence and war, resource scarcity becomes a matter of life or death, especially in developing countries. With the prediction of future overpopulation, the availability of renewable natural resources is slated to be lost. These conflict multipliers signal a distinct possibility that various parts of the world will have a future dearth of resources that human beings will require to survive. These added risks around global security and safety make peacekeeping efforts even more imperative in post-conflict environmental situations.

Internal systemic violence in at-risk countries makes sustainable agriculture and ecological preservation impossible. Refugee movement (accounting for more than twenty million people today), often infiltrating and overwhelming neighboring poor countries due to political infighting and subsequent violence, disrupts every host country and introduces more destruction to ecological space (especially in resettlement areas) because the poorest people depend on renewable resources but are least likely to engage in conversation activities out of survival. When you have no home, no permanence, no residential status, and can be shipped off without a moment's notice, the last thing on people's minds is protecting the environment. Land degradation, water pollution, and deforestation are intensified by environmental scarcities, demand for essential commodities, ethnic conflicts, and civil wars when multitudes are forced to leave their home countries for fear of being killed or starving to death. When supply chains are insecure or uncertain, and when certain states seek to develop resources at the expense of other states competing for the same materials, interstate conflicts over accessing renewables are inevitable. The more trade embargoes and other forms of political manipulation are allowed to block access to food production and commodities, driving up already unaffordable prices and psychological desperation, the more likely people will be forced to migrate.

The impact of climate change on agricultural production, rainfall patterns, drought, flooding, soil erosion, desertification, water supplies, crop yields, food prices, sea-level rise and other weather changes forcing large-scale migration, and limited governmental capacities to help the poor will be a contributing multiplier to environmental conflict; but it may also lead to greater social systems of cooperation. Scarcity and dwindling reserves may force people to pool their resources out of necessity rather than risk their destruction by initiating conflict. Like ancient civilizations that safeguarded joint control over waterways for drinking, irrigation, crop production, and transportation, better use of and control over water bring people together in shared cooperation. Sustainable resource management policies grounded in building peace, social justice, and environmental protection are sensible goals that benefit actor self-interests through environmental cooperation rather than exploitation of resources. Although peacebuilding efforts cannot eradicate the causes of human violence, peace is not sustainable if ecosystems are demolished or resources squandered. This is why resource management mechanisms, environmental security, and climate justice become integral to environmental conflict, building peace, and postwar policy endeavors. Yet in social reality, peacebuilding agreements and post-conflict reconstruction are often pursued for short-term urgency rather than long-term sustainability.

Every state recovering from post-conflict resolution must both rely on and conserve its vital natural resources. If environmental preserves are not managed cooperatively and sustained through mutual peacebuilding efforts, they can easily lead to a reemergence of violent conflict and environmental crime that merely serves to degrade, molest, and sully natural environs and access to renewable resources.

But the mark of the Anthropocene paints another picture. Forests are fragile and wild spaces are dwindling; rainforests sacrificed, land reappropriated for farming, sprawling urbanization, fishing inefficiencies, and pervasive plastic have fundamentally changed nature. We clear-cut forests, pollute, vitiate habitats, overfish, till up grassland, acidify coral, and accelerate extinction rates. As the world population explodes and sea levels rise, we have converted most land into cities and settlements, croplands, and anthromes that have reshaped the planet's ecology. Deforestation of the Amazon Basin, through expanding agriculture and wildfires, has destroyed one of the Earth's most biologically diverse ecosystems. Protection priorities could safeguard habitats, reefs, fish and carbon stocks, conserve the world's biodiversity, and limit climate change, but there seems to be little movement due to infrastructure inadequacies, geopolitics, and corporate resistance. Add to this concern the ubiquity of "green criminality" such as illegal logging and fishing; shipping, transport, and discharging of hazardous waste; fly tipping; routine methane flaring, purges, or leakage; illegal trade in wildlife; illicit traffic of radioactive or nuclear substances; proliferation and disposal of electronic e-waste; local and transborder pollution due to factories, chemical plant spills, or accidents; systematic dumping; and "environmental black market" actors such as multinational corporations, corrupt political officials, bureaucracies, or governments, armed rebel groups; or the emission of dangerous contaminants by unregulated private industry contrary to international laws and global environmental politics. There seems to be no end in sight.

What we can do for the planet as individuals is fairly insignificant, albeit meaningful or personally rewarding to being a good global citizen. Recycling, minimizing food waste, composting, adopting more of a plant-based diet, reusing shopping bags, buying biodegradable products, drinking fair-trade coffee, becoming an ecofriendly pet owner, and properly insulating your home or turning to geothermal for energy efficiency makes us feel like we are respecting the environment. By initiating community cleanups in public spaces, parks, and waterways, planting trees and pollinator gardens, pruning and weeding out invasive plants, attending town hall meetings, giving testimony at hearings or being vocal when agencies seek out public engagement or commentary on a proposed project or policy, holding neighborhood gatherings or workshops on conservation, and speaking to local legislators can all contribute to climate education and foster an ecofriendly ethos. But living more simply; cutting back on emissions; refusing to fly; turning to electric cars; using solar, hydro, or wind renewables; and becoming vegan will not even make a dent in the forces behind climate change.

THE LAST RESISTANCE

Hegel once said that human history is the "slaughter-bench"[16] of happiness—a progressive yet poignant achievement. But happy or not, happiness is nevertheless what we covet, what Aristotle called "the highest good attainable by action"—that is, "living well" and "doing well."[17] Some of us live well and some of us do well; but for most of the world population, happiness is a foreign reality. Ephemeral moments of pleasure are not happiness: they are not the *eudaimonia* Aristotle envisioned. Even the satisfaction of life's simplest pleasures is often minimized, postponed, or held in abeyance for other desires that have not yet been actualized. Desire is such a complicated creature that it is responsible for generating our most detestable beastly attributes as well as our most cherished and exalted ideals. As being-in-relation-to-lack, desire seeks to assuage its anxiety, to go beyond its finite appearances and fill the hole, the lacunae in its being—simply the wish for wholeness we call peace. The nature of value inquiry is a lived existential ordeal that must endure the gauntlet of anxiety and dread that pave the successive path toward the fulfillment of human ethos. It is this positive significance to the power of the negative that becomes the engine behind our moral prosperity even when the dark shadow of our aggressivity and destructive inclinations looms over the sky like a black plague.

"*Fundamental insight.*—There is no pre-established harmony between the furtherance of truth and the well-being of mankind," says Nietzsche.[18] Harmony is made by humankind through the call of conscience and the puissance of reason—a rational passion. And as Freud tells us, the "intellect . . . is among the powers which we may most expect to exercise a unifying influence on men—on men who are held together with such difficulty and whom it is therefore scarcely possible to rule . . . Our best hope for the future is that intellect—the scientific spirit,

---

16. Hegel (1837), *Reason in History*, p. 27.
17. Aristotle (1962), *Nicomachean Ethics* (bk. 1, § 4, 15).
18. Nietzsche (1878), *Human, All Too Human*, p. 198.

reason—may in process of time establish a dictatorship in the mental life of man."[19] Is it such a utopian expectation to think that we can subordinate our pathological natures to the monarch of reason? Perhaps this is the true meaning of faith. For even if no emotional ties exist between people, cultures, or nations, the bonds of reason conjoin us in mutual appreciation for the *ought* that dictates even our most irrational moments.

Having offered this optimistic gesture, we are still left with uncertainty, tenuousness, and Pollyannaish platitudes. We are currently experiencing a crisis of neoliberal capitalism in Western democracies, what we euphemistically call globalization, which has led to economic exploitation of the masses engineered by those who want to make obscene amounts of money quickly and unabashedly at others' expense. And the rest of the world has its own financial crises, most recently as the United States, United Kingdom, and members of the European Union are in chaos over fiscal mismanagement with the added irritant of various central banks and China calling for economic reform. Russia, the Middle East, Africa, India, and the global South only add to the anxiety. This has only been compounded by COVID, unemployment, recession, social injustice, civic disorder, commodity insecurity, and the fuel and energy crises destabilizing markets all over the world. When there is the U.S. deregulation of financial institutions, with a conglomerate of powerful lawyers, politicians, economists, accountants, and lobbyists manipulating laws around the exchange of commerce, taxation, and corporate profits, then citizens will naturally be enticed, taken advantage of, and swindled—partly because some people are gullible and/or unreflective—acting on unbridled wish fulfillment and whim—and partly because they are simply overburdened by so many demands and responsibilities within our stressful contemporary societies that the pleasure principle is sure to blow the whistle. "We want relief! And be quick about it." Yet most are fleeced due to ignorance and helplessness against those hegemons who are too powerful to stop or resist their control.

As Slavoj Žižek points out, like many reformed or neo-Marxists before him, such greed is generated by the seductive system of capitalism

---

19. Freud (1933), *New Introductory Lectures on Psycho-analysis*, p. 171.

itself, which beckons only desire and personal self-indulgence. In Freudian terms, we only think about our own gratifications. The vulgar popular expression is: "Fuck everyone else! The only thing that matters is me." This is a common sentiment. I further suggest that this is a failure of value inquiry, a painful revelation about our collective moral psychology. We are destroying our planet, sullying and stealing from impoverished countries natural commodities that are sold off by corrupt government officials, hence causing new poverty and hunger where people turn to rioting, looting, and killing because they have no rice or wheat, thereby generating social calamities that potentially have worldwide effects. When people are deprived of the basic necessities for human survival, it is illogical to reproach the outrage fueling such desperate acts of aggression and social discord. "Would you want to be treated like a thing or object that does not matter to the rest of the world?" That is rational-empathic conscience speaking. The "object" here is a unity of subjects—a collection of people exploited because the law says they can be. Remember that the law is what the people with political power determine it to be. It can change at any time, contingent upon the instrumental functions that bring that about. When collective social systems permit ecological risk and allow world erosion to happen, we must critically target the ultimate sources of responsibility. In industrial countries, the populace clearly experiences such trickle-down effects when spikes in gas prices immediately affect the cost of transportation and availability of food and produce. And when people in nonindustrial or developing countries have no credit cards to rely on to offset their lack of capital or debt, it becomes a matter of life or death.

As our planet faces increasing desertification due to climate change, environmental pollution, and human spoilage, water wars are generating global concern and economic exploitation.[20] The shortage of drinking water compounded by corporate pollution is resulting in the poisoning of our water supplies. Industrial pollution is credited for producing biologically contaminated water due to the mass dumping of chemicals, pesticides, rocket fuel, and pharmaceuticals discarded by large animal factories

20. For a disturbing account of this phenomenon, see the film documentaries *Blue Gold: World Water Wars* by Sam Bozzo (2008) and *Flow: For Love of Water* by Irena Salina (2008).

and sewage treatment plants. Further, the capitalist privatization of water leads to large-scale neglect of water systems by introducing contaminants that are directly hazardous to citizens, particularly those in disenfranchised nations. Exacerbated by a lack of proper sanitation, millions of people die each year—primarily children up to the age of 5, and as many as 1 out of 10 in India—due to water-borne diseases. Industry is always thinking about the "bottom line"—the cheapest way is the desired norm if you are a businessman. If capitalists control water supplies, they can exploit the rest of the world. It is understandable, under these circumstances, how large groups of peoples would succumb to squalid instinct where "Every man for himself!" is the bottom line. Living is squalor, without dignity or a dime, leads to perpetual insecurity, sorrow, bitterness, and the need for revenge. If this continues without global intervention, we can predictably foresee the eruption of mass social psychopathy, where marginalized countries become a breeding ground for death, depravity, and terrorism.

Žižek alerts us that the two principal dangers confronting our world today are unbridled capitalism and fundamentalist religious extremism, which he believes are leading to an "apocalyptic zero-point." But the real culprit he focuses on is the global capitalist system itself:

> [The]"four riders of the apocalypse" are comprised by the ecological crisis, the consequences of the biogenetic revolution, imbalances within the system itself (problems with intellectual property; forthcoming struggles over raw materials, food and water), and the explosive growth of social divisions and exclusions.[21]

From "invisible" migrant workers deprived of all privileges and used as slave labor for us to have dollar stores and cheap blue jeans, to "crazies" who announce their "irrational" intent to use a nuclear device or potent biological and chemical weapons, to a large degree the question of money always looms in the background. Money motivates everything. We are erecting walls to keep our bordering countries out and constructing walls within our own nations, like "gated communities," designed to protect us

---

21. Žižek (2010), p. x.

from "the criminal other." "Love thy neighbor" is replaced with mistrust and fear, whereby the Other becomes a threat, source of envy, or persecutory object. Ignoring all warning signs, we are living in collective denial and omnipotent disavowal of our impending peril under the illusory fantasies of grandiose hubris sustained by hegemonic ideologies. When will the next natural disaster occur? When will the next bomb go off, or plane fly into a building? As Žižek puts it, "we know very well that this will happen at some point, but nevertheless cannot bring ourselves to really believe that it will."[22]

Even though reason tells us to stop the exploitation, corruption, indulgences in excess, and the destruction of our natural resources, we still want. Here wanting becomes a perennial quandary. And human desire wants immediate satisfaction. Its popular motto is: "Fill the lack! Chop, chop!" As a society, we often live in the moment. We want—and want more. This inner mantra becomes an incessant insatiable, greedy whine. Restraint, compromise, and self-restriction become unwelcome trespasses. The reality principle is conveniently forgotten when urge, impulse, avarice, and caprice are beguiled by immediate objects of tantalizing pleasure. And conscience becomes compartmentalized because the complexities of social order and world discord pose overwhelming impasses to pragmatic resolutions. Here the collective psyche, insofar as it personifies the universal psychological dispositions inherent to humanity, remains in an ambivalent state of inner worry and unmediated conflict. This is the last resistance: when the complexifications of social existence reach their zenith in obfuscation, epistemological uncertainty, impasse, standstill, and/or overwhelming anxiety under the psychological dynamics of helplessness and political tyranny, then confusion, inertia, and paralysis become unconscious strategies in the service of dissociation and denial to buy time, if not protect the self from psychic death. The sad part is that world collectives are bringing on their own demise by *remaining unconscious*, hence inactive, of altering the obvious course.

If we entertain the possibility of the doomsday argument, and that we very well may be living in the End Times, then we are approaching

---

22. Žižek (2010), pp. x–xi.

a cataclysm that may no longer be preventable. Even though it is technically possible to alter a future trajectory by intervening in the present to reverse a calculated, predictable, or perceived calamity from occurring, the future is merely an abstract possibility in our present experiential lived time. Unfortunately, this logical justification is enough for collective humanity to postpone (not to mention negate) the future as an arcane excuse to justify our inactions now.

Unlike Freud, who had an ambiguous air of skeptical guardedness, yet one with a pessimistic undercurrent, Hegel was more optimistic. I am not so sure we can readily amalgamate the two poles. Each represents a dialectical position and creates an almost insurmountable tension, what Žižek calls a "parallax gap"—namely, a point of irreconcilable contradiction or antinomy where there is no discernible synthesis.[23] Žižek points toward, in his words, a "pathetic case for communism"[24] as a possible reference point for rectifying our world crises, but this suggestion violates human nature.[25] As long as a macrosystem supports capitalist self-interest, human need and greed will gravitate toward self-pursuit over shared equality or the uniform distribution of material wealth through financial egalitarianism. Such a condition—namely, global communism—would have to be superimposed on us by a supreme force, hence state intervention, even if it were for our own good. But history

---

23. Žižek (2006, p. 4) makes the proper locus of his philosophy the parallax gap, where there is a fundamental displacement of difference that poses an "irreducible obstacle to dialectics" based on a pure shift of perspective that can lead to no higher synthesis.

24. Žižek (2010), p. 5. In his recent book *Pandemic!* (2020), he goes so far as to argue for a vision of global solidarity as opposed to barbarity based in universal communism (pp. 37, 46) where the world comes together as a "unified" "new humanity" (pp. 104–105), yet this overly Pollyannaish sentiment seems to completely defy social reality.

25. Freud (1930) criticizes communism for its naive philosophy of human nature based on a fantasy principle that ignores the instinctual basis of human aggression. In *Civilization and Its Discontents*, he argues that even if private property was not allowed by the state and material wealth was distributed generously among peoples, it would do nothing to eradicate our aggressive proclivities. He elaborates the fantasy that: "If private property were abolished, all wealth held in common, and everyone allowed to share in the enjoyment of it, ill-will and hostility would disappear among men. Since everyone's needs would be satisfied, no one would have any reason to regard another as his enemy; all would willingly undertake the work that was necessary . . . [T]he psychological premises on which the system is based are an untenable illusion . . . Aggression was not created by property. It reigned almost without limit in primitive times, when property was still very scanty, and it already shows itself in the nursery" (p. 118).

shows that all such attempts have led to state corruption. Somebody else always is in power who is *more* equal.

It is more plausible that we will increasingly seek modifications and amendments in neocapitalism reflective of controlled or regulated democratic systems that institute structural improvements through refined checks and balances safeguarding shared collective interests valuing socialistic commitments. Short of a global centralized currency that is regulated, policed, and affects everyone (unlike current fads in cryptocurrencies such as bitcoin), perhaps some transnational system of socialistic democracy will emerge in the future as a logical synthesis informing the sublation of humanity through natural compromise. If everyone's self-interest is based on playing the same game by collective enforceable rules, then we would have a more egalitarian economic system. But who in their right mind (those in charge) would let this happen? No one values everyone equally. The hermeneutics of suspicion toward authority conjure up the paranoid position that oligarchy and hegemony only favor the powerful, who are bound to exploit others simply because they can. And the mere individual doesn't give a rat's ass about humanity when they are barely able to handle their own obligations and encumbrances. Blind belief in a benign, just, and humane world where everyone is treated the same only gives proper grace to a fool.

A more pessimistic outcome is that the dialectic would reach an implosive climax or irresolvable breaking point where we have a deadlock of oppositions that lead to snowballed eruptions within multiple social climates that contaminate the world scene with war, famine, disease, and ecological disaster. Even if one pole eventually vanquishes the other, it would be at everyone's expense. If we accept Žižek's premise that unbridled liberal capitalism is a world nemesis bringing the end of days, then it would likely take a series of catastrophic global events before we are forced to curb its enthusiasm. This would necessitate a mass mobilization of political, diplomatic, and economic reform. But as long as political hegemonies drive world relations based on capitalist principles (on one hand they clamor, "We are all equal!"; on the other, they admonish, "You have to earn it. There are no free handouts!"), then I am afraid we will have to accept the premise of natural law theory—namely, that what is natural to do is what is right to do (e.g., "It's not natural to give away your resources, for this is contrary to self-preservation and self-interest," or "Others will have to work for it just like me," or "We can't take care of the whole world!" and so on).[26] We can equally imagine the inverse (another dialectic) if we were on the receiving end of exploitation and abuse—"It's *natural* to kill those who cause us suffering!" And here we return to the question of pathos. Some of us, *by necessity,* must suffer more than others.

Regardless of the degree of gravity we assign to these calculated risks imperiling our existence, we cannot ignore the ominous threat of planetary extinction unless humanity unites in moral preventive action. To envision salient global solutions, we need more than mere awareness or collective self-consciousness; we must be willing to give up what we are comfortable with in our immediate lives for the sake of the symbolic Other and our real *Terra Mater,* and *act* for a higher principle of valuation, even if this realization is simultaneously motivated by enlightened self-interest and/or self-preservation. These concurrent values or dispositional attitudes do not necessarily have to conflict with one another, especially if they work in tandem to achieve the same goals. But I can't

---

26. I would argue that it is "logical" to have government exercise some control, regulation, or oversight over capitalism based on utilitarian and socialistic commitments that improve the financial stability, social security, and quality of life of the populace, including those controlling the wealth, but it is not necessarily "instinctual." What is instinctual or natural is to be concerned first and foremost with one's own affairs, including securing resources for one's immediate familial and communal priorities out of pragmatic necessity and survival. We primarily make decisions based upon emotional unconscious factors—both innocent and prejudicial—that resonate within the deeply felt interior of our beings. These unconscious agentic processes, I argue, have an affective exuberance that is somatically absorbed within our embodied sentience that simultaneously, emotively and semiotically, interjects an overarching valuative tone. This naturally includes an amalgamation of the most innately intuitive, feeling, moral, and spiritual sentiments that coalesce within the personality, but also the most primitive, conflictual, agonizing, and phantasmatic. And I would argue much more so than cognition (see Mills, 2010). Even if we accept the evolutionary argument that memes—the cultural equivalent of genes—drive complex social systems through a replicatory process of mimesis, they would not likely extend past one's immediate social milieu unless other contingencies or environs would ingress upon the motivational systems comprising such social organizations. In other words, we prefer to stay close to home. And sometimes, perhaps more than others, what is natural is not always good. Therefore, natural law or desire governing human nature and interpersonal relations must be subjected to developmental and educational forces that introduce critical analysis, ethical self-reflection, domestic gentrification, and collective valuation practices for the good of all, which are fundamental tenets of liberal democratic philosophy.

see that happening anytime soon. Perhaps the message itself is important enough to reiterate.

People will not deprive themselves of the daily routines and pleasures of life, let alone sacrifice their personal comforts for the greater noble good. Contra Plato, having knowledge of truth does not mean we will pursue virtue or do the right thing. We as a species suffer a weakness of will born/e by desire. Perhaps the youth—our children and grandchildren—will reverse our foolish path through brave acts of foresight and wisdom. Let's hope so. But as it stands, humanity is on a collision course with disaster. Here the doomsday argument may hold some validity. Whether we "be damned" or "give a damn," our fate is on the horizon.

If I were a betting man, I would say we are on the brink of extinction.

References

Ackerman, Gary, & Potter, William C. (2008). Catastrophic nuclear terrorism: A preventable peril. In N. Bostrom & M. M. Ćirković (Eds.), *Global catastrophic risks* (pp. 402–449). Oxford: Oxford University Press.

Adorno, T. W. (1966). *Negative dialectics*. New York: Bloomsbury, 19732007.

Allen, B. (1996). *Rape warfare: The hidden genocide in Bosnia-Herzegovina and Croatia*. Minneapolis: University of Minnesota Press.

Amnesty International (2023, April 14). https://www.amnesty.org/en/latest/news/2023/04/nine-years-after-chibok-girls-abducted/

Anderson, Kevin, Broderick, John F., & Stoddard, Isak. (2020). A factor of two: How the mitigation plans of "climate progressive" nations fall far short of Paris-compliant pathways. *Climate Policy, 20*(10), 1290–1304. doi:10.1080/14693062.2020.1728209

Aristotle. (1962). *Nicomachean ethics*. Trans. M. Ostwald. Englewood Cliffs, NJ: Prentice Hall.

Bostrom, Nick. (1998). The doomsday argument: A literature review. http://www.anthropic-principle.com/preprints/lit/index.html. Retrieved October 2, 2016.

Bostrom, Nick. (2002). *Anthropic bias: Observation selection effects in science and philosophy*. New York and London: Routledge.

Bostrom, Nick. (2014). *Superintelligence*. Oxford: Oxford University Press.

Bostrom, Nick, & Ćirković, Milan M. (Eds.). (2008). *Global catastrophic risks*. Oxford: Oxford University Press.

Bozzo, S. (2008). *Blue gold: World water wars*. Documentary film. Vancouver International Film Festival.

Bronson, Rachel. (2016). Statement from the executive director. In John Mecklin (Ed.), It is still 3 minutes to midnight. 2016 doomsday clock statement, Science and Security Board. *Bulletin of the Atomic Scientists*, i–5.

Bulletin of the Atomic Scientists. (2016). Doomsday clock hands remain unchanged, despite Iran deal and Paris talks, January 26, 2016. http://thebulletin.org/press-release/doomsday-clock-hands-remain-unchanged-despite-iran-deal-and-paris-talks9122

Bulletin of the Atomic Scientists. (2017, January 26). It is two and a half minutes to midnight. https://thebulletin.org/files/Fnal%20201%20Statement.pdf

Bulletin of the Atomic Scientists. (2018, January 25). It is 2 minutes to midnight. https://thebulletin.org/sites/default/files/2018%20Doomsday%20Clock%20Statement.pdf

Bulletin of the Atomic Scientists. (2019, January 24). A new abnormal: It is still 2 minutes to midnight. https://thebulletin.org/doomsday-clock/current-time/#full-statement

Bulletin of the Atomic Scientists. (2020, January 23). Closer than ever: It is 100 seconds to midnight. 2020 Doomsday Clock Statement. https://thebulletin.org/doomsday-clock/current-time/

Bulletin of the Atomic Scientists. (2021, January 27). This is your COVID wake-up call: It is 100 seconds to midnight. https://thebulletin.org/doomsday-clock/current-time/

Bulletin of the Atomic Scientists. (2023, January 24). A time of unprecedented danger: It is 90 seconds to midnight. 2023 doomsdayclockannouncement. https://thebulletin.org/doomsday-clock/current-time/

Calhoun, John B. (1962). Population density and social pathology. *Scientific American, 206*(2), 139–148.

Calhoun, John B. (1973). Death squared: The explosive growth and demise of a mouse population. *Proceedings of the Royal Society of Medicine, 66*, 80–88.

Canadian Press Video. (2014, December 16). Stephen Harper calls Pakistan attack heartbreaking. *Globe and Mail.* http://www.theglobeandmail.com/news/news-video/video-stephen-harper-calls-pakistan-attack-heartbreaking/article22106356/. Retrieved December 28, 2014.

Caplan, Bryan. (2008). The totalitarian threat. In N. Bostrom & M. M. Ćirković (Eds.), *Global catastrophic risks* (pp. 504–519). Oxford: Oxford University Press.

Carrington, Damian. (2019). A third of Himalayan ice cap doomed, finds report: Even radical climate change action won't save glaciers, endangering 2 billion. Retrieved February 10, 2019. People. https://www.theguardian.com/environment/2019/feb/04/a-third-of-himalayan-ice-cap-doomed-finds-shocking report?utm_term=R-WRpdG9yaWFsX0dyZWVuTGlnaHQtMTkwMjA4&utm_source=esp&utm_medium=Email&utm_campaign=GreenLight&CMP=greenlight_email

Carter, B. (1974). Large number coincidences and the anthropic principle in cosmology. In M. Longair (Ed.), *Confrontations of cosmological theories with observational data* (pp. 291–298). I.A.U. Symposium 63. Dordrecht: Reidel.

Carter, B. (1983). The anthropic principle and its implication for biological evolution. *Philosophical Transactions of the Royal Society of London, A31*, 346–363.

Center for AI Safety. (2023). Statement on AI risk. https://www.safe.ai/statement-on-ai-risk?utm_source=substack&utm_medium=email#open-letter. Retrieved June 16, 2023.

Cialdini, R. B. (2001). *Influence: Science and practice.* Boston: Allyn & Bacon.

Cioran, E. M. (1998). *The temptation to exist,* 2nd ed. Trans. R. Howard. Chicago: University of Chicago Press.

Climate Central. (2012). *Global weirdness.* New York: Pantheon Books.

Danner, M. (1997). America and the Bosnia genocide. *New York Review of Books, 44*(19), 55–56.

Dar, Arnon. (2008). Influence of supernovae, gamma-ray bursts, solar flares, and cosmic rays on the terrestrial environment. In N. Bostrom & M. M. Ćirković (Eds.), *Global catastrophic risks* (pp. 238–261). Oxford: Oxford University Press.

Darley, J. M., & Latané, B. (1968). Bystander intervention in emergencies: Diffusion of responsibility. *Journal of Personality and Social Psychology, 8*(4, pt. 1), 377–383. doi:10.1037/h0025589

Davenport, Coral. (2017, March 9). E.P.A. chief doubts consensus view of climate change. *New York Times.* https://www.nytimes.com/2017/03/09/us/politics/epa-scott -pruitt-global-warming.html?rref=collection%2Ftimestopic%2FEnvironmental %20Protection%20Agency&action=click&contentCollection=timestopics&region =stream&module=stream_unit&version=latest&contentPlacement=2&pgtype =collection&_r=0

Derrida, J. (1982). *Margins of philosophy.* Trans. Alan Bass. Chicago: University of Chicago Press.

Diamond, Jared. (2005). *Collapse.* New York: Viking.

Dyson, Freeman. (2016, October 13). The green universe: A vision. *New York Review of Books, 63*(15), 4–6.

Economist Daily Chart. (2020, August 25). The Greenland ice sheet has melted past the point of no return: Even if global warming stopped today, the ice would keep shrinking. *The Economist.* https://www.economist.com/graphic-detail/2020/08/25/ the-greenland-ice-sheet-has-melted-past-the-point-of-no-return?utm_campaign =the-economist-today&utm_medium=newsletter&utm_source=salesforce -marketing-cloud&utm_term=2020-08-26&utm_content=article-link-4&

Einstein, A. (1932). Letter to Freud, July 30, 1932, "Why war?" [Einstein–Freud corre- spondence], *Standard edition of the complete psychological works of Sigmund Freud,* vol. 22. Trans. & gen. ed. James Strachey, in collaboration with Anna Freud, assisted by Alix Strachey and Alan Tyson. London: Hogarth Press.

Eliade, Mircea. (1963). *Myth and reality.* Trans. W. R. Trask. New York: Harper & Row.

Emmott, Stephen. (2013). *10 billion.* London: Penguin.

Faul, Michelle, & Olalekan, Oyekanmi. (2016). More than 100 girls unwilling to leave Boko Haram: Chibok leader. *Globe and Mail.* http://www.theglobeandmail .com/news/world/more-than-100-chibok-girls-unwilling-to-leave-boko-haram -community-leader/article32409568/

Ferro, Marc. (2010). *Resentment in history.* Cambridge, UK: Polity Press.

Fichte, J. G. (1794/1982). *The science of knowledge.* Trans. & ed. P. Health & J. Lachs. Cambridge: Cambridge University Press.

Filiu, Jean-Pierre. (2011). *Apocalypse in Islam.* Berkeley: University of California Press.

Fillmore, Mary Dingee. (2020, June 18). Standing by in Minneapolis and Amsterdam. *Tikkun.* https://www.tikkun.org/standing-by-in-minneapolis-and amsterdam?eType=E- mailBlastContent&eId=bf2e5555-ae77-40d6-be07-ca0ff6f772d2. Retrieved June 29, 2020.

Findlay, J. N. (1971). Hegel's use of teleology. In W. E. Steinkraus (Ed.), *New studies in Hegel's philosophy.* New York: Holt, Rinehart and Winston.

Flannery, Tim. (2010). *Here on Earth: A natural history of the planet.* New York: Atlantic Monthly Press.

Foroohar, Rana. (2016, October 13). How the financing of colleges may lead to disaster! *New York Review of Books, 63*(15), 28–30.

Foucault, Michel. (1966). *The order of things.* London: Routledge, 1970.

Foucault, Michel. (1976). *The history of sexuality, vol. I: An introduction.* Trans. Robert Hurley. New York: Vintage Books, 1990.

Fraser, N., & Honneth, A. (2003). *Redistribution or recognition? A political-philosophical exchange.* Trans. J. Golb, J. Ingram, & C. Wilke. London: Verso.

Freud, S. (1914). On narcissism: An introduction. *Standard edition of the complete psychological works of Sigmund Freud, 14* (pp. 67–104). Trans. & gen. ed. James Strachey, in collaboration with Anna Freud, assisted by Alix Strachey and Alan Tyson. London: Hogarth Press.

Freud, S. (1915). Instincts and their vicissitudes. *Standard edition, 14*, 109–140. London: Hogarth Press.

Freud, S. (1916–1917). *Introductory lectures on psycho-analysis. Standard edition, 16.* London: Hogarth Press.

Freud, S. (1920). *Beyond the pleasure principle. Standard edition, 18.* London: Hogarth Press.

Freud, S. (1921). *Group psychology and the analysis of the ego. Standard edition, 18.* London: Hogarth Press.

Freud, S. (1923). *The ego and the id. Standard edition, 19*, pp. 3–66. London: Hogarth Press.

Freud, S. (1927). *Future of an Illusion. Standard edition, 21*, pp. 3–56. London: Hogarth Press.

Freud, S. (1930). *Civilization and its discontents. Standard edition, 21.* London: Hogarth Press.

Freud, S. (1932). Reply to Einstein. "Why war?" [Einstein-Freud correspondence]. *Standard Edition, 22* (pp. 197–218). London: Hogarth Press.

Freud, S. (1933 [1932]). *New introductory lectures on psycho-analysis. Standard edition, 22.* London: Hogarth Press.

Freud, S. (1940). *An outline of psycho-analysis. Standard edition, 23.* London: Hogarth Press.

Germanà, Monica, & Mousoutzanis, Aris. (2014). *Apocalyptic discourse in contemporary culture: Post-millennial perspectives on the end of the world.* London: Routledge.

Gertz, Nolan. (2018). *Nihilism and technology.* London: Rowman & Littlefield.

Geryl, Patrick. (2005). *The world cataclysm in 2012.* Kempton, IL: Adventures Unlimited Press.

Geryl, Patrick, & Ratinckx, Gino. (2001). *The Orion prophecy.* Kempton, IL: Adventures Unlimited Press.

Gorenberg, Gershom. (2000). *The end of days: Fundamentalism and the struggle for the Temple Mount.* Oxford: Oxford University Press.

The Great Brotherhood of Light. (2019). http://www.sanctusgermanus.net/english/Sanctus%20Germanus.html#1

Habermas, Jürgen. (1990). *Moral consciousness and communicative action*. Cambridge, MA: MIT Press.

Habermas, Jürgen. (1993). *Justification and application: Remarks on discourse ethics*. Cambridge, MA: MIT Press.

Harris, H. S. (1983). *Hegel's development: Night thoughts*. Oxford: Clarendon.

Hegel, G. W. F. (1807/1977). *Phenomenology of spirit*. Trans. A. V. Miller. Oxford: Oxford University Press.

Hegel, G. W. F. (1812/1969). *Science of logic*. Trans. A. V. Miller. Atlantic Highlands, NJ: Humanities Press.

Hegel, G. W. F. (1817/1991). *The encyclopaedia logic*. Vol. 1, *Encyclopaedia of the philosophical sciences*. Trans. T. F. Geraets, W. A. Suchting, & H. S. Harris. Indianapolis: Hackett.

Hegel, G. W. F. (1817/1827/1830/1971). *Philosophy of mind*. Vol. 3, *Encyclopaedia of the philosophical sciences*. Trans. William Wallace & A. V. Miller. Oxford: Clarendon Press.

Hegel, G. W. F. (1821/1967). *Philosophy of right*. Trans. T. M. Knox. Oxford: Oxford University Press.

Hegel, G. W. F. (1830/1978). *Philosophy of spirit*. In *Hegel's philosophy of subjective spirit, 2: Anthropology*. Trans. & ed. M. J. Petry. Dordrecht, Holland: D. Reidel.

Hegel, G. W. F. (1837 [1840, 1917]). *Reason in history: A general introduction to the philosophy of history*. Trans. R. S. Hartman. New York: Liberal Arts Press, 1953.

Hegel, G. W. F. (1978). *Hegels Philosophie des subjektiven Geistes/Hegel's philosophy of subjective: Spirit, 1*: Introductions, *2*: Anthropology, *3*: Phenomenology and Psychology. Ed. M. J. Petry. Dordrecht, Holland: D. Reidel.

Hegel, G. W. F. (1981). *The Berlin Phenomenology*. Ed. & trans. M. J. Petry. Dordrecht, Holland: D. Reidel.

Heidegger, M. (1924). The problem of sin in Luther. *Supplements*. Ed. John Van Buren. Albany: State University of New York Press, 2002, 105–110.

Heidegger, M. (1927/1962). *Being and time*. Trans. J. Macquarrie & E. Robinson. San Francisco: HarperCollins.

Honneth, A. (1995). *The struggle for recognition*. Trans. Joel Anderson. London: Polity.

Honneth, A. (2012). *The I in we: Studies in the theory of recognition*. Cambridge, UK: Polity Press.

Inayat, Naila, Qazi, Shereena, & Bacon, John. (2014, December 17). Death toll reaches 141 in massacre at Pakistan school. *USA Today*. http://www.usatoday.com/story/news/world/2014/12/16/taliban-storms-military-school/20469711/. Retrieved December 28, 2014.

Indo-European Lexicon. Linguistics Research Center, University of Texas at Austin, https://lrc.la.utexas.edu/lex/master/0018

Intergovernmental Panel on Climate Change. (2015). Climate change 2014 synthesis report: Fifth assessment report. http://ar5-syr.ipcc.ch/

Intergovernmental Panel on Climate Change. (2021). Climate change 2021: The physical science basis. Sixth assessment report: Working group I. https://www.ipcc.ch/report/sixth-assessment-report-working-group-i/

Intergovernmental Panel on Climate Change. (2022a). Climate change 2022: Impacts, adaptation and vulnerability. Sixth assessment report: Working group II. https://www.ipcc.ch/report/sixth-assessment-report-working-group-ii/

Intergovernmental Panel on Climate Change. (2022b). Climate change 2022: Mitigation of climate change. Sixth assessment report: Working group III. https://www.ipcc.ch/report/ar6/wg3/

Intergovernmental Panel on Climate Change. (2023). AR6 synthesis report: Climate change 2023. https://www.ipcc.ch/report/ar6/syr/

Islam, Md Saidual. (2014). *Confronting the blue revolution.* Toronto: University of Toronto Press.

Joseph, Lawrence E. (2007). *Apocalypse 2012.* New York: Morgan Road Books.

Jung, C. G. (1917a). *On the psychology of the unconscious. Collected works, 7,* 1–122.

Jung, C. G. (1917b). New paths in psychology. *Collected works, 7,* 245–268.

Jung, C. G. (1919/1948). The psychological foundations of the belief in spirits. *Collected works, 8,* 301–318.

Jung, C. G. (1947). On the nature of the psyche. *Collected works, 8,* 159–234.

Jung, C. G. (1952). Eliade's interview for "Combat." In William McGuire & R. F. C. Hull (Eds.), *C. G. Jung speaking: Interviews and encounters* (pp. 225–236). Princeton, NJ: Princeton University Press, 1977.

Kelly, S. (1993). *Individuation and the absolute: Hegel, Jung, and the path toward wholeness.* New York: Paulist Press.

Kilbourne, Edwin Dennis. (2008). Plagues and pandemics: Past, present, and future. In N. Bostrom & M. M. Ćirković (Eds.), *Global catastrophic risks* (pp. 287–307). Oxford: Oxford University Press,

Klein, M. (1946). Notes on some schizoid mechanisms. *International Journal of Psychoanalysis, 27,* 99–110.

Kojève, Alexandre. (1929). *Introduction to the reading of Hegel: Lectures on the phenomenology of spirit.* Assembled by Raymond Queneau, Ed. Allan Bloom, & Trans. James H. Nichols Jr. Ithaca: Cornell University Press, 1969/1980.

Kolbert, Elizabeth. (2014). *The sixth extinction.* New York: Henry Holt.

Lacan, Jacques. (1991). *The other side of psychoanalysis: The seminar of Jacques Lacan, Book XVII.* Trans. Russell Grigg. New York: Norton, 2007.

Latané, B., & Darley, J. (1969). Bystander "apathy." *American Scientist, 57,* 244–268.

Leahy, Stephen. (2015, December 14). Paris climate agreement—Historic plan for 3.0C of warming. http://stephenleahy.net/2015/12/14/paris-climate-agreement-historic-plan-for-3-0c-of-warming/. Retrieved December 18, 2015.

Lebreton, L., Slat, B., Ferrari, F., et al. (2018, March). Evidence that the great Pacific garbage patch is rapidly accumulating plastic. *Scientific Reports, 8*(4666). https://doi.org/10.1038/s41598-018-22939-w

Lebreton, L., van der Zwet, J., Damsteeg, J., et al. (2017, June). River plastic emissions to the world's oceans. *Nature Communications, 8*(15611). http://doi.org/10.1038/ncomms15611

Leslie, John. (1990). Is the end of the world nigh? *Philosophical Quarterly, 40*(158), 65–72.

Leslie, John. (1996). *The end of the world: The science and ethics of human extinction*. London: Routledge.

Lights, Zion. (2023, January 23). Climate activism has a cult problem. *Free Press*. https://www.thefp.com/p/climate-activism-has-a-cult-problem?utm_source=substack&utm_medium=email

Linguistics Research Center, University of Texas at Austin. Indo-European lexicon. https://lrc.la.utexas.edu/lex/master/0018. Retrieved January 8, 2020.

Lovelock, James. (2006). *The revenge of Gaia: Earth's climate crisis and the fate of humanity*. New York: Basic Books.

Luther, M. (1517). Disputation against scholastic theology. *D. Martin Luthers Werke, vol. 1*. Weimar: Hermann Böhlau, 1883, 221–228.

Luther, M. (1546). The last sermon in Wittenberg, 1546. *Luther's Works*, 54 vols. Philadelphia: Muhlenberg Press.

Marcuse, Herbert. (1955). *Eros and civilization*. London: Penguin, 1970.

Mau, Michael P. (2003). *The Sanctus Germanus prophecies, vol. 1: The events leading up to the year 2012*. New York: Sanctus Germanus Foundation.

Maxmen, Amy, & Mallapaty, Smriti. (2021). The COVID lab-leak hypothesis: What scientists do and don't know. *Nature, 594*, 313–315.

Mbah, Fidelis. (2019, April 14). Nigeria's Chibok schoolgirls: Five years on, 112 still missing. *Aljazeera*. https://www.aljazeera.com/news/2019/4/14/nigerias-chibok-schoolgirls-five-years-on-112-still-missing. Retrieved January 14, 2021.

McGowan, Todd. (2016). *Capitalism and desire*. New York: Columbia University Press.

McGowan, Todd. (2021). Self-destruction and the natural world. In C. Burnham & P. Kingsbury (Eds.), *Lacan and the environment* (pp. 273–293). Cham, CH: Palgrave Macmillan.

Mecklin, John (Ed.). (2016). It is still 3 minutes to midnight. 2016 doomsday clock statement, Science and Security Board. *Bulletin of the Atomic Scientists*, i–5.

Mecklin, John (Ed.). (2017). It is two and a half minutes to midnight. 2017 doomsday clock statement, Science and Security Board. *Bulletin of the Atomic Scientists*, 1–8.

Mecklin, John (Ed.). (2019). A new abnormal: It is still 2 minutes to midnight. 2019 doomsday clock statement, Science and Security Board. *Bulletin of the Atomic Scientists*, 1–8.

Mecklin, John (Ed.). (2020). It is 100 seconds to midnight. 2020 doomsday clock statement, Science and Security Board. *Bulletin of the Atomic Scientists*, 3–9.

Mecklin, John (Ed.). (2021). This is your COVID wake-up call: It is 100 seconds to midnight. 2021 doomsday clock statement, Science and Security Board. *Bulletin of the Atomic Scientists*, 1–11.

Miller, Richard B. (2010). *Terror, religion, and liberal thought*. New York: Columbia University Press.

Mills, Jon. (2002). *The unconscious abyss: Hegel's anticipation of psychoanalysis*. Albany: State University of New York Press.

Mills, Jon. (2005a). *Relational and intersubjective perspectives in psychoanalysis: A critique*. Northvale, NJ: Jason Aronson.

Mills, Jon. (2005b). *Treating attachment pathology*. Northvale, NJ: Jason Aronson.

Mills, Jon. (2010). *Origins: On the genesis of psychic reality.* Montreal: McGill-Queens University Press.

Mills, Jon. (2012). *Conundrums: A critique of contemporary psychoanalysis.* New York: Routledge.

Mills, Jon. (2014). *Underworlds: Philosophies of the unconscious from psychoanalysis to metaphysics.* London: Routledge.

Mills, Jon. (2017). *Inventing God: Psychology of belief and the rise of secular spirituality.* London: Routledge.

Mills, Jon. (2019a). Contemporary psychoanalysis and critical theory: A new synthesis. *Critical Horizons: A Journal of Philosophy and Social Theory, 20*(3), 233–245. doi:10.1080/14409917.2019.1616484

Mills, Jon. (2019b). Recognition and pathos. *International Journal of Jungian Studies, 11*(1), 1–22. doi:10.1163/19409060-01101001

Mills, Jon. (2019c). Dysrecognition and social pathology: New directions in critical theory. *Psychoanalysis, Culture & Society, 24*(1), 15–30. doi:10.1057/s41282-018-0113-0

Mills, J., & Polanowski, J. A. (1997). *The ontology of prejudice.* Amsterdam/Atlanta: Rodopi.

Ministry of Agriculture and Food. (2020). Svalbard Global Seed Vault. Norwegian government. https://www.regjeringen.no/en/topics/food-fisheries-and-agriculture/svalbard-global-seed-vault/id462220/. Retrieved October 12, 2020.

Morris, D. (1998, July 12). *The human species.* Learning Channel (TLC).

Nadeau, Barbie Latza. (2015, January 13). Nigeria is letting Boko Haram get away with murder. *Daily Beast.* http://www.thedailybeast.com/articles/2015/01/13/nigeria-is-letting-boko-haram-get-away-with-murder.html. Retrieved January 13, 2015.

Napier, William. (2008). Hazards from comets and asteroids. In N. Bostrom & M. M. Ćirković (Eds.), *Global catastrophic risks* (pp. 222–237). Oxford: Oxford University Press.

Neuhouser, F. (1986). Deducing desire and recognition in the *Phenomenology of spirit. Journal of the History of Philosophy, 24*(2), 243–264.

Nietzsche, F. W. (1878/1977). *Human, all too human.* In *A Nietzsche reader.* Trans. R. J. Hollingdale. London: Penguin.

NPR Environment. (2019, September 29). Transcript: Greta Thunberg's speech at the UN climate action summit. *National Public Radio.* September 23, 2019. https://www.npr.org/2019/09/23/763452863/transcript-greta-thunbergs-speech-at-the-u-n-climate-action-summit. Retrieved October 13, 2020.

The Ocean Cleanup Initiative. (2022). The great Pacific garbage patch. https://theoceancleanup.com/great-pacific-garbage-patch/

Orlando, Cathy. (2015, December 13). The Paris climate agreement: The glass is both half empty and half full. *Citizen's Climate Lobby Canada.* http://canada.citizensclimatelobby.org/ccl-canada-media-release-the-paris-climate-agreement/. Retrieved December 18, 2015.

Palma, Bethania. (2020, March 2). Did President Trump refer to the coronavirus as a "hoax"? Snopes.com. https://www.snopes.com/fact-check/trump-coronavirus-rally-remark/. Retrieved April 26, 2020.

Phoenix, Chris, & Treder, Mike. (2008). Nanotechnology as global catastrophic risk. In N. Bostrom & M. M. Ćirković (Eds.), *Global catastrophic risks* (pp. 481–503). Oxford: Oxford University Press.

Pinker, Steven. (2011). *The better angels of our nature: Why violence has declined.* New York: Viking.

Pipes, Richard. (1994). *Russia under the Bolshevik regime.* New York: Vintage.

Quinby, Lee. (2014). Apocalyptic security: Biopower and the changing skin of historic germination. In M. Germanà & A. Mousoutzanis (Eds.), *Apocalyptic discourse in contemporary culture: Post-millennial perspectives on the end of the world* (pp. 17–30). London: Routledge.

Rees, Martin. (2003). *Our final hour.* New York: Basic Books.

Remnick, David. (2016, November 9). An American tragedy. *New Yorker.* http://www.newyorker.com/news/news-desk/an-american-tragedy-2. Retrieved November 9, 2016.

Roser, Max. (2020). Future population growth. OurWorldInData.org. https://ourworldindata.org/future-population-growth. Retrieved April 15, 2020.

Salina, I. (2008). *Flow: For love of water.* Documentary film. Sundance Film Festival.

Saunders, David. (2016). Economic victims didn't elect Trump. The well-off and segregated did. *Globe and Mail.* http://www.theglobeandmail.com/news/world/us-election/the-average-trump-supporter-is-not-an-economic-loser/article32746323/. Retrieved November 9, 2016.

Schaefer, Patricia. (2015, December 15). Paris climate talks, "miraculous and inadequate," will leave a lasting impression. *NonProfit Quarterly.* https://nonprofitquarterly.org/2015/12/15/paris-climate-talks-miraculous-and-inadequate-will-leave-a-lasting-impression/?gclid=COz7tb-o68kCFQEcaQodVJ4BZA. Retrieved Dec.ember 20, 2015.

Scientific American Staff. (2017, June). Swell or high water. *Scientific American, 316*(6), 21.

Sitchin, Zecharia. (2007). *The end of days: Armageddon and prophecies of the return.* New York: Harper.

Sounds True. (2007). *The mystery of 2012: Predictions, prophecies, & possibilities.* Boulder, CO: Sounds True.

Stock, Jeremy. (2020). George Floyd death | full video | George Floyd. https://www.youtube.com/watch?v=thfNLVvve4A&bpctr=1593629645. Retrieved July 1, 2020.

Svalbard Global Seed Vault. (2020). Safeguarding seeds for the future. https://www.seedvault.no/. Retrieved October 12, 2020.

Swain, Ashok, & Öjendal, Joakim (Eds.). (2018). *Routledge handbook of environmental conflict and peacebuilding.* London: Routledge.

Torres, Phil. (2016). *The end: What science and religion tell us about the apocalypse.* Durham, NC: Pitchstone.

United Nations. (2014). India tops in adult illiteracy: UN report. January 29, 2014. *The Hindu.* http://www.thehindu.com/features/education/issues/india-tops-in-adult-illiteracy-un-report/article5629981.ece. Retrieved February 23, 2015.

United Nations Department of Economic and Social Affairs, Population Division. (2015). World population prospects: The 2015 revision. http://esa.un.org/unpd/ wpp/. Retrieved January 8, 2016.

United Nations Department of Economic and Social Affairs, Population Division. (2019). Population facts. https://www.un.org/en/development/desa/population/ publications/pdf/popfacts/PopFacts_2019-6.pdf. Retrieved April 14, 2020.

United Nations Department of Economic and Social Affairs, Population Division. (2023). UN DESA Policy Brief No. 153: India overtakes China as the world's most populous country. April 23. https://www.un.org/development/desa/dpad /publication/un-desa-policy-brief-no-153-india-overtakes-china-as-the-worlds -most-populous-country/#:~:text=UN%20DESA%20Policy%20Brief%20No,the %20world%27s%20most%20populous%20country

United Nations Framework Convention on Climate Change. (2009). The Copenhagen Accord: Copenhagen climate change conference—December 2009. http://unfccc .int/meetings/copenhagen_dec_2009/meeting/6295.php. Retrieved December 20, 2015.

United Nations Framework Convention on Climate Change. (2015). Paris climate change conference—November 2015. http://unfccc.int/meetings/paris_nov_2015 /meeting/8926.php. Retrieved December 20, 2015.

Weaver, Andrew. (2015, December 14). COP21 targets require ambitious policy. http: //www.andrewweavermla.ca/2015/12/14/cop21-targets-require-ambitious-policy/. Retrieved December 18, 2015.

Weisman, Alan. (2013). *Countdown*. New York: Little, Brown.

Wilczek, Frank. (2008). Big troubles, imagined and real. In N. Bostrom & M. M. Ćirković (Eds.), *Global catastrophic risks* (pp. 346–362). Oxford: Oxford University Press.

Wolin, Sheldon S. (2008). *Democracy incorporated*. Princeton, NJ: Princeton University Press.

The World Counts. (2020). http://www.theworldcounts.com/counters/shocking_ environmental_facts_and_statistics/world_population_clock_live. Retrieved April 13, 2020.

The World Counts. (2021). http://www.theworldcounts.com/counters/shocking_ environmental_facts_and_statistics/world_population_clock_live. Retrieved June 26, 2021.

World Economic Forum. (2020). *Global risks report: 15th edition*. Genève, Switzerland.

World Economic Forum. (2021). *Global risks report: 16th edition*. Genève, Switzerland.

Worldometers. (2016). World population. http://www.worldometers.info/world -population/. Retrieved January 8, 2016.

Worldometers. (2020). World population. https://www.worldometers.info/world -population/. Retrieved April 13, 2020.

Worldometers. (2021). World population. https://www.worldometers.info/world -population/. Retrieved June 26, 2021.

World Weather Attribution. (2023). https://www.worldweatherattribution.org

York, Geoffrey. (2017). Anti-foreigner mob rampages in "march of hatred" in South Africa. *Globe and Mail.* http://www.theglobeandmail.com/news/world/anti-foreigner-mob -rampages-in-march-of-hatred-in-south-africa/article34128998/

Yudkowsky, Eliezer. (2008a). Cognitive biases potentially affecting judgement of global risks. In N. Bostrom & M. M. Ćirković (Eds.), *Global catastrophic risks* (pp. 91–119). Oxford: Oxford University Press.

Yudkowsky, Eliezer. (2008b). Artificial intelligence as a positive and negative factor in global risk. In N. Bostrom & M. M. Ćirković (Eds.), *Global catastrophic risks* (pp. 308–345). Oxford: Oxford University Press,

Zeiher, Cindy. (2021). Love thy enemy: Environment(al) politics. In C. Burnham & P. Kingsbury (Eds.), *Lacan and the environment* (pp. 19–35). Cham, CH: Palgrave Macmillan.

Žižek, S. (2006). *The parallax view.* Cambridge, MA: MIT Press.

Žižek, S. (2010). *Living in the end times.* New York: Verso.

Žižek, S. (2020). *Pandemic! COVID-19 shakes the world.* New York and London: OR Books.

Index

abstract future. *See* future
    predictions
Ackerman, Gary, 128–29
afterlife, 98–99
After the End, 111–12. *See also*
    future predictions
aggression: begets aggression, xvi;
    Freud on, 204n25; the gaze,
    as invitation to, 156; man's
    inclination to, 38; prevalence
    of, xiii; role in value practices,
    185–86; sadism and, 50;
    self-preservation through, 42;
    self-preservation vs pleasure,
    50; tribal warfare, xvii; triggers
    for, 159
airborne viruses, 94
alienation, 152n6
allergic illnesses, 192
alterity: empathy and, 163; facing,
    157; prejudices cast on, 55;
    religious violence and, 108;
    social networking and, 140;
    unconscious politics and, 161–
    63; validating, 150–51n3. *See
    also* otherness

animal regression in human
    beings, xvii–xviii
anonymous relativism, 140
Antarctica, 7n6
anthropic principle in cosmology,
    84n16
anti-blasphemy laws, 67
anxiety. *See* world anxiety
apocalyptic thinking, 98, 102–6,
    110–12. *See also* End of Days
apostasy laws, 67
applied eschatology, 107
aquaculture, alternative, 195
Arctic, 7
Arctic amplification, 12
Armageddon, 102, 104. *See also*
    After the End; apocalyptic
    thinking
artificial intelligence
    (AI): generative, 146; global
    risk of, 127; risk of extinction
    from, 146; takeover scenarios,
    144–45; weaponry and, 78. *See
    also* superintelligences
asylum seekers, 31
atomic bomb, 62
attachment pathology, xvi, 167

autonomous weapons, 78, 80, 82

barbarism, 60–62
Bayes' probability theorem, 84,
    86–87, 88
bee colony collapse disorder,
    11–12
behavioral sink, 22
Biden, Joe, 80
bin Laden, Osama, 108n21
biodiversity loss, 134
biological agents, 129
biopower, 111
biotechnologies, 94, 129
bioweaponry, 129
Black Lives Matter
    movement, 150
Blue Revolution, 25
Boko Haram, 60
Bosnian concentration camps, 50
Bostrom, Nick, 84n17, 86–92,
    119–124, 130, 142, 144–45, 147
Brotherhood of Light, 104–5
Bulletin of the Atomic
    Scientists: 2020 Doomsday
    Statement, 79; Doomsday
    Clock, 72–77, 73n2, 80, 110; on
    failures of world leaders, 81–83;
    foreboding omen, 74; founding
    of, 72–73; Science and Security
    Board, 78
Bush administration, 63
bystanders, defined, 4n4

Calhoun, John, 19, 20

Calhoun's rodent experiments,
    19–23
capitalism, 188–89, 201–3, 205–6
Caplan, Bryan, 131
carbon dioxide (CO_2), 6, 9
carbon emissions, 2n1, 16, 193
carbon energies, renunciation of, 3
carbon fuels, 2–3
Carter, Brandon, 84, 84n16
caste discrimination, 65–67
Center for AI Safety, 146
Chibok Government Secondary
    School, 60
child abuse, xvi
China, 23n4, 75, 134
Cirkovic, Milan, 119, 120,
    124, 130
cities, congestion of, 30
civilization. *See* human civilization
Civilization and its Discontents
    (Freud), 51, 204n25
climate accord, 2–3
Climate Central, 6n6
climate change: Arctic
    transformation, 174; bringing
    attention to, 175–78;
    comparing the past with today,
    8; destabilizing food supplies,
    28–29; Earth's temperature
    and, 6–8, 6n7; international
    youth movement, 175; social
    collectives dismissing threat of,
    122; Thunberg on, 175–77. *See
    also* global warming
closed social systems, 20

coal, 9

collective human consciousness, 38, 57, 116, 126, 190, 206

collective identification, 51–53, 164, 184–85

collective identity, 41, 46–47, 53, 58

collective psychosis, 71

collective recognition. *See* mutual recognition

collective shame, 52

collective unconscious, xx, 109, 169

communicative rationality theory, 151n3

communism, universal, 204–5, 204n25

consciousness: apocalyptic singularity of, 112–13; ethical, 44n16, 88; social, 111, 150–51n3, 164, 177–180, 184. *See also* collective human consciousness

consequences, unintended, as potential extinction risk, 125, 126–28

contemporary recognition theory, 151n3

COP21 accord, 2

corporate capitalism, 188–89

COVID-19, 135–36, 171–72

cultural narcissism, 47, 51–52, 184

cultural trauma, 109, 166–170

culture, 54, 139

cyberbullying, 141

cyber-related vulnerability and attacks, 134

cyber warfare, 79–80

Darley, John, 3–4n4

Das Unbehagen in der Kultur (Freud), 84

death drive, 42–43, 42n12, 43n15, 51

death(s): as foundation of life, 43–44; heat-related, increase in, 13; unconscious anxiety about, 98–99

deforestation, 26, 27, 29, 196, 198

Democracy Inc., 187–91

democratic institutions, loss of trust in, 76

Derrida, Jacques, 111

desertification, 201–2

desire, 153–54, 154n8, 199

despoilment of the globe, xi–xiii

destruction principle, 42, 42n12, 184. *See also* death drive

develpmental traumas, xvi, 39n6

dialectic: as confluence of oppositions, 43n15; dynamic progression of, 59; as essence of psychic life, 44n19; master-slave, 150, 152n6; negativity begetting progression, 42n11; as prejudice, 58–59; reason and, 40n8; self-generative process of, 180n5; the soul and, 44n16; underlying prejudice, 55

Diamond, Jared, 33–34

difference and similarity, dialectical tension between, 54–55

digital zombification, 139

disenfranchised groups, 150

disinformation campaigns, 77–80, 110, 134, 141

dispensationalism, 107

dissociation of ethics, 61–62

divine superego judgment, 102

doomsday argument: challenges to, 91–93; existential risks, 88–91; extinction probabilities, 84–88; millennial doomsday scenario, 110

Doomsday Clock, 72–77, 73n2, 80, 110

Doomsday Vault, 173–74

drilling, 10

droughts, 28–29

Dyson, Freeman, 112

dysrecognition, 158–60, 169

Earth: effects of increased temperatures on, 12–16; destruction by divine providence, 99; hydrological cycle, 29; limiting temperature increase, 2n1; seasonal temperature cycles, 12; as supra-living organism, 10; temperature increases, 6–8, 6n7, 12; unable to regulate itself, 15–16

Earth Day 50th anniversary, 191

ecological consciousness, 178

ecological emergency, bringing attention to, 175–78

economic disintegration, 132–38

economics, 10, 115, 205

ecosystems: deteriorating, xii–xiii; Earth's temperature and, 8; endangerment to, 173; extinction of, 14; greenhouse effects on, 85; humans' effects on, 7n7; Noah's Ark culture and, 112; plastic waste and, 173; Tickell's assessment of, 15; triggers for change in, 12

ego, 45, 45n23

Einstein, Albert, Freud and, 37

Eliade, Mircea, 97–98

emerging self, 45, 45n23

Emmott, Stephen, 25–26

empathy, failure of, 163–66

Encyclopedia Logic (Hegel), 44n19, 181, 181n6, 182–83

End of Days, 102–6, 110, 116–17, 174. See also After the End

End of the World myths, 98. See also apocalyptic thinking

enemies within a society, xiv–xv

energy sources, 195

environmental conflict, 195–99

environmental preserves, 197–98

environmental stress, 196

equality, as entitlement, 157

eschatology: afterlife and, 98–99; applied eschatology, 107; obsessional fixation with, 98–99; phenomenology of, 97–98; prophecies, 97; revelations and signs in, 107–8; in theology, 97; tied to teleology, 111

eschaton, 145

ethical consciousness, 44n16, 88

ethics of killing, 62–65

Ethiopia, 24

evil acts: caste discrimination, 65–67; ethical arguments for, 62; institutionalization of, 65–69; technology of, 62; universality of, 60–62

Extinction Rebellion (XR) movements, 180, 180n4

extinction risks, 88–91, 123, 125–28

extreme prejudice, 49

eye aversion, 156–57

famine, 23–24, 29, 34, 64, 107, 205

female infanticide, 67

financial crises, 200

Flannery, Tim, 11

Floyd, George, 149–50

food production, 26–27, 192–93

food security, 192

food supplies: Blue Revolution technologies, 25; climate change destabilizing, 28–29; contamination of, 13–14; demand for, 27; famine and, 23–24; Green Revolution technologies, 24, 25; overpopulation and, 23–27; preserving global, 173–74; shortage of, 27, 193

forests, 197–98

fossil fuel industry, 10

fossil fuels, dependency on, xii

Foucault, Michel, 111

Freedom: capitalism and, 188–89; price of, 187

Freud, Sigmund: on aggression, 204n25; *Civilization and its Discontents*, 51, 204n25; on communism, 204n25; on competing forces in nature, 41–43; contempt for religious ideologies, 99n2; *Das Unbehagen in der Kultur*, 84; on death drive, 42–43, 43n15; on ego, 45n23; Einstein and, 37; on the human condition, 180–81n5; on intellect, 199–200; on mature theory, 41n9; on prejudice, 47–48; on repetition of destruction, 186; on structure of the psyche, 38; teleology, 43n15, 111, 182n8; on uncultivated races, 54; on unease within the culture of his day, 84; use of drive, 42n12

Fridays for Future, 175

fuel sector, 2–3

fundamentalist religious groups, 90

future predictions: bringing about desired, 179–80; Hegel's logical model, 180–84, 187; logic of, 187; repeating traumas, 186; space travel/colonization, 112–14; sustaining national identities, 184–85; transcending immediate existence, 35–36; visions of, 178–80. *See also* After the End

Gaia theory, 10. *See also* Earth
galaxies, colonization of, 113–14
Gaza Strip, 68–69
the gaze, as invitation to aggression, 156
generative AI, 146
genocide, 49, 64, 109n24, 131
Gertz, Nolen: on Internet behavior, 140–41; on pleasure economics, 140; on techno-hypnosis, 139; on techno-nihilism, 138
Geryl, Patrick, *The Orion Prophecy*, 103–4
global bystander effect, 2–5, 16–18, 128–29
global bystander syndrome, 3–4, 5
global capitalism, 115
global communism, 204–5
globalization, 137, 189–190, 200
global risks: analyzing, 120–23; from the Anthropocene, 126; catastrophic effects of, 119; categories, 133; classifications of, 120–21; economic disintegration, 132–38; as evolving, 133–34; existential risks, 88–90, 123; from hostile acts, 125, 128–32; intensity of, 120; interconnectedness of, 119–20; mental illness as a, 138–39; from nature, 124–26; pandemics, 30–31, 82, 126; probabilities of, 122–23; psychogenic risk, 122; scope of, 120; types of, 119; from unintended consequences, 125, 126–28; World Economic Forum identifying, 136–38
Global Risks Perception Survey (World Economic Forum), 133–34
Global Risks Report (World Economic Forum), 132–33, 135–36
global security: climate change's effects on, 31; destabilization of, xvii; as an illusion, xiv; new abnormal, 77–78; prejudice and, 55–56
global warming: effects of, 6–8; explaining, 9; human beings as cause of, 6; prediction models, 193; Republican Party's position on, 76; state intervention and, 17–18. *See also* climate change

God: man wanting to be, 100; turning away from, 101; vindication of, 101–2

Gorenberg, Gershom, 106

Great Pacific Garbage Patch, 172–73

green criminality, 198

Greenland, 7n6, 11

Green Revolution, 24, 25

group identities, 51–53

group prejudice, 48–49

Habermas, Jürgen, 151n3

The Hague, 75

Hamas, 68–69

happiness, as foreign reality, 199

harmony, 199

Harper, Stephen, 60–61

health risks, climate-related, 13–14

Hegel, Georg: on confronting otherness, 153–54; on death as foundation of life, 43–44; on ego, 45n23; *Encyclopedia Logic*, 44n19, 181, 181n6, 182–83; on the feeling soul, 40n8, 44n16, 45n23; on happiness, 199; on historical progression of civilization, 180–81; on human history, 199; odyssey of humanity, 185–86; on reason, 40n8; on subjection of the other, 152n6

Heidegger, Martin, 100

Himalayan Mountain chain, 7n6

Holy Land, 106–9

Honneth, Axel, 155–56, 156n12

hostile acts, potential extinction risk of, 125, 128–132

human beings: aggression and violence toward others, 38; animal regression in, xvii–xviii; basic psychological needs in, 160; as collection of identities, 163–64; compulsion toward control, 186; disavowing the future, 190–91; instinctual nature of, 206–7, 206n26; on investing in the future, 190; repeating its traumas, 186; seeking unique identities from others, 183

human civilization: advances in, 23, 116; based on traumatization, 109; extinction of, mathematical formula for, 84–88; future of. *See* future predictions; future predictions for, 112–14; generating division and opposition within itself, 183n8; Hegel on, 180–81; pathognomonic tendencies to self-destruct, 35; as a process, 49; progression of, 53–54; space travel obsession, 113–14; technological advances of, 53; threats to survival of, 85, 88–91; vacillating between progress and regress, 183–84n9

human condition, characterizing the, 180–81n5
human motivation, 41n9
Hussein, Saddam, 63

ice and glaciers, melting, 6–8
ideals, 59
identification: emotional bonds and, 52; ethnic and religious, 51–52; nationalism and, 52; origins, 48
identity, 46n28, 48
immediate satisfaction, xix, 152n6, 203
immigrants, 54–57
India, 23n4
industrial pollution, 201–2
industry, deregulation of, xvii
inegalitarianism, 188
infant mortality rates, 19, 20
infectious diseases, 13
inflation, 137
information security, 134
information warfare, 77–79
infrastructures, 193–94
institutional evil, 65–69
institutional racism, 65–66
Intergovernmental Panel on Climate Change (IPCC): assessment reports, 7n6; on Earth's temperature, 6; forming of, 6n6; main tasks of, 7n6; mandate for, 6–7n6
Intermediate-Range Nuclear Forces Treaty (INF), 77, 78

internal disintegration, xiv
International Criminal Court (ICC), 109n24
Internet, as global weapon, xvi–xvii
Internet behavior, 140–41
interstate conflicts, 196–97
inverted totalitarian principles, xv
Iran, 75, 81
irrationality, 39–40
Islam, 109
Islamic State terrorism, 74
island nations, 12–13
Israel, 68–69, 74, 75
ITER Organization, 195

Jewish-Arab conflict, 106
Jung, C. G., 102n11, 167–69
justice, 101

Khorasanin, Mohammed Umar, 60
killings, ethics of, 62–65. *See also* aggression
Kim Jong Un, 75

Latané, Bibb, 3–4n4
Leslie, John, 84n16, 85–86, 88–91
light pollution, 192
Lovelock, James, 10, 14
Luther, Martin, 100–101

machine superintelligence. *See* superintelligences
macroanthropos, 145

male dominance, 39n6
male patriarchy, 67
Manhattan Project, 72
man-made disasters, 89
Manu, Michael P., 105
Marcuse, Herbert, 158
Marsh McLennan companies, 132
mass consumption, xii–xiii
mass migrations, 12–13, 31
mass pollution, 172–73
Master Sanctus Germanus, 104–5
master-slave dialectic, 150, 152n6
mature theory, 41n9
Mayan calendar, 103
McGowan, Todd, 189
Mecklin, John, 77–79
mediated immediacies, 184
mental illness, 38, 138–39
methane, 9
Middle East, 81, 96, 106–9
migration. *See* mass migrations
millennial doomsday scenario, 110
mining, 10
misogyny, as culturally ingrained, 66–67
molecular nanotechnology, 130
money, 114–16
moral consciousness, 151n3
mortality, 98
mountain glaciers, 8
mutual opposition, 53, 154, 157
mutual recognition, 116, 151n3, 156, 156n12, 165

nanotechnology, 129–30

narcissism, 50–51, 63, 184
National Geographic: "An Optimist's Guide to Life on Earth in 2070," 194–95; "A Pessimist's Guide to Life on Earth in 2070," 191–94
national identities, 41, 52, 63, 185
natural disasters, 88–89
natural law theory, 206
Nemo's Garden, 195
neoliberal capitalism, 200, 205–6
Netanyahu, Benjamin, 75
neurosis, 167–68
Nietzsche, Friedrich, 199
Nigeria, 60
Noah's Ark culture, 112
North Korea, 74, 75, 81
nuclear fusion, 195
nuclear waste, 82
nuclear weapons: arms race, 77, 78, 80–81; deterrence for, 95; disarmament efforts, 73, 81, 90; threats of, 77, 95–96

ocean acidification, 192
Ocean Cleanup initiative, 173
ocean currents, 8
ocean levels, 6–8, 12–13
ocean tides, land subsumed under, 12–13
Ogallala Aquifer, 28
On the Psychology of the Unconscious (Jung), 168
"An Optimist's Guide to Life on Earth in 2070," 194–95

The Orion Prophecy (Geryl), 103–4
Otherness: confronting, 153–54;
    as the enemy, 63–64; Hegel on,
    153–54. *See also* alterity
overpopulation, 23–27. *See also*
    population growth

Pakistan, 60, 75
pandemics, worldwide, 30–31,
    82, 126
parallax gap, 204, 204n23
Paris accord, 76, 82
past societies, environmental
    problems of, 33–35
pathogens, spread of, 126–27
pathos, 38–39, 39n6
peacebuilding movement, 195–99
"A Pessimist's Guide to Life on
    Earth in 2070," 191–94
philosophical risks to survival,
    89–90
Phoenix, Chris, 130
physics experiments, potential
    extinction risk of, 127–28
Pinker, Steven, 54
plastic waste cleanup initiatives,
    172–73, 195
pleasure economics, 140
pleasure principle, 43n15
political categories, as
    psychological categories, 158
political unconscious, 161–63
political violence, 90–91
politicians, superficiality of, 33
pollution, 172–73, 201–2

population density, Calhoun's
    rodent experiments, 19–23
population growth, xii–xiii, 2,
    21, 23n4, 27, 108. *See also*
    overpopulation
posthuman ecology, 2
Potter, William, 128–29
poverty, 114–16
prejudices: cast on alterity, 55;
    dialectical process of, 58–59;
    dividing/polarizing, 40–41;
    Freud on, 47–48; global security
    and, 55–56; of immigrants,
    54–57; as neutral psychological
    predisposition, 58; of refugees,
    54–57; tensions between
    difference and similarity, 54–55;
    universality of, 47–48; valuation
    practices and, 48–49, 57–59
prescriptive ethics, 90
probabilities, 122–23
psychic maturation, 181n5
psychogenic risk, 122
psychological categories, as
    political categories, 158
psychological risks to survival,
    89–90
psychopathic narcissism, 50–51
psychopathology, as essence of
    man, 39
public opinion, manipulating,
    32–33
punishment, 101
Putin, Vladimir, 64, 109n24

Quinby, Lee, 111

racism and inequality, 149–50
rainfall patterns, 13
reason: as developmental
   achievement, 40n8; as tool of
   desire, 40
recognition: dark side of, 151n3;
   defensive modes in, 155–57;
   deprived of, 152–53; healing
   properties of, 157; inequality
   of, 153–55; mutual desire
   for, 116, 151n3, 156, 156n12,
   161–62, 165; mutual opposition
   confronting each other and,
   154; need for, 150–51n3;
   roadblocks to, 161–62; struggle
   for, 152n6, 159; unconsciously
   mediated, 152
recognition theory, 156n12
Rees, Martin, 93–94, 95–96
refugees, 54–57, 196
relatedness, cycle of, 39n6
religious chauvinism, xvii
religious extremism, 202
religious fanaticism, 31
religious fundamentalism, 99n2,
   116–17
religious violence, 90–91, 108
resources: carbon fuels, 2–3;
   coal, 9; fossil fuels, xii; mass
   consumption of, xii–xiii;
   scarcity of, 196; water supplies,
   13–14, 28–29, 201–2. See also
   food supplies

"right," renunciation of, 61–62
risk. See global risks
risk of extinction. See extinction
   risks
Russia, 74–75, 81
Rwanda, 64, 184–85

sadism, 50
security. See global security
seed gene bank, 173–74
self-consciousness, 40n8, 150–
   51n3, 152n6, 153, 165–66
self-healing, 168
self-preservation, 42, 50
self-sublation, 183n8
self-survival, 155
sin, prevalence of, 99–102
singularity of consciousness,
   112–13
sleep, 42n12
social bonding, Calhoun's rodent
   experiments, 21–22
social collectives, 17, 95, 112: AI
   superintelligences and, 145–46;
   dismissing real threats, 121–22;
   dysrecognition and, 151n3;
   fickle temperaments of, 32;
   preventing mutual recognition
   among, 156–57; suscepticible to
   lure of ideology, 32
social consciousness, 111, 150–
   51n3, 164, 177–80, 184
social disintegration, 19–20
social disruption, risks of, 119–20

social justice climate movements, 180n4

social networking, 139–40, 141

societies: continued collapse of, 33–35; disrespecting environment, 33–34. *See also* human civilization

sociological risks to survival, 89–90

soil degradation, 29

solar industry, 33

the soul: in Abrahamic traditions, 98–99; Brotherhood of Light and, 104–5; burdened with pathos, 168; destruction of, 166; Freud on, 41n9; Hegel on, 40n8, 44n16, 45n23; killing people and, 62; resurrection and, 107

South China Sea, 75

space travel, obsession with, 113–14

species extinction, Calhoun's rodent experiments, 22

Spirit or Mind (*Geist*), 43n15, 152, 155, 180, 181n5, 182–83n8. *See also* world spirit

state intervention, 17–18

subjection of the other, 152n6

sublation: defined, 44n19; ethical reflection as part of, 40n8; of reason, 40n8, 181; resistance to, 164; unification through, 44

superego, 102

superintelligences, 142–47. *See also* artificial intelligence (AI)

Svalbard Global Seed Vault, 173–74

synthetic biology, 129

systemic risks, intensifying global crisis, 35–36

systemic violence, 196

Taliban, 60

techno-apocalypse, 103

techno-hypnosis, 139

technology: biotechnologies, 94; culture industry revolving around, 139; increasing reliance on, 138; nanotechnology, 93–94; nihilism and, 138–41; speed of changes to, 93

techno nihilism, 138–41

teleology, 43n15, 111, 182n8

Telepathic Healing and The Amanuensis of the Holy Brother, 105

Temple Mount, 106–7

terrorism, 60–62

Thunberg, Greta, 5n5, 175–77

Tickell, Crispin, 15

Time magazine, 175

Torres, Phil, 107, 121

totalitarianism, 131–32

trade conflicts, 134, 137

transgenerational transmission of trauma, 166–70

transgenerational transmission of developmental trauma, 39n6

transgressions, as acceptable, xv
transport accidents, 10
transportation, overpopulation and, 26
trauma: cultural, 109; transgenerational transmission of, 166–70
Treder, Mike, 130
tribal warfare, xvii
Trump, Donald, 57, 71–72, 75–76, 122n3
Tutsis, 64

Ukraine, 75, 81
unconscious. *See* collective unconscious
unconscious politics, 161–63
unconscious psychic processes, 164
United Nations, 5n5, 23n4
United Nations Climate Change Conference, 2, 175–76
United States: bullying attitudes of, 79; Iran and, 81; Republican Party of, 76; tensions with other countries, 74; trade tensions with China, 134; as a xenophobic and racist nation, 72
unity, 43–44, 44n16, 46
universal communism, 204–5, 204n24, 204n25
universal ethics, lack of, xv
universal security. *See* global security

valuation practices, 40–41, 46, 46n28, 51, 57–59, 184, 206n26
Vinge, Vernor, 113

war-scenario hysteria, 95–96
water rights, overpopulation and, 26
water shortages, 27–30
water supplies, 13–14, 28–29, 201–2
wealth disparities, 114–16
weather extremes, 12, 192
Wilczek, Frank, 127–28
wish fulfillment, unconscious, xix
Wolin, Sheldon, 187
world anxiety, 83–84, 98–99
World Economic Forum: Global Risks Perception Survey, 133–34; *Global Risks Report*, 132–33, 135–36; identifying global risks, 136–38
Worldometers, 23n4
World order, 77
world population. *See* population growth
world spirit, 180, 181n6, 183n9
world totalitarian order, 131

Yudkowsky, Eliezer, 127

Zeiher, Cindy, 191
Zizek, Slavoj, 201, 202, 203, 204
Zurick Insurance Group, 132

About the Author

Jon Mills, PsyD, PhD, ABPP, is a philosopher, psychoanalyst, and clinical psychologist. He is honorary professor, Department of Psychosocial & Psychoanalytic Studies, University of Essex, United Kingdom; on faculty in the postgraduate programs in psychoanalysis and psychotherapy, Gordon F. Derner School of Psychology, Adelphi University, Garden City, New York; and on faculty and a supervising analyst at the New School for Existential Psychoanalysis, San Francisco. Recipient of numerous awards for his scholarship, including five Gradiva Awards, he is the author and/or editor of more than 30 books in psychoanalysis, philosophy, psychology, and cultural studies including more recently *Psyche, Culture, World*. In 2015 he was given the Otto Weininger Memorial Award for Lifetime Achievement by the Canadian Psychological Association.